Soil Fertility & Human and Animal Health

The Albrecht Papers, Volume VIII

by William A. Albrecht, Ph.D.
Edited by Charles Walters
Foreword by John Ikerd

Soil Fertility
& Human
and Animal Health

The Albrecht Papers, Volume VIII

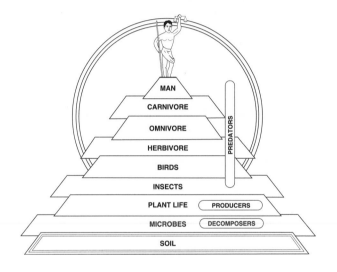

by William A. Albrecht, Ph.D.
Edited by Charles Walters
Foreword by John Ikerd

Acres U.S.A.
Austin, Texas

Soil Fertility & Human and Animal Health

Acres U.S.A.
P.O. Box 301209
Austin, Texas 78703 U.S.A.
(512) 892-4400 • fax (512) 892-4448
info@acresusa.com • www.acresusa.com

Printed in the United States of America

Publisher's Cataloging-in-Publication

Albrecht, William A., 1888-1974; and Charles Walters, editor
Soil fertility & human and animal health / William A. Albrecht., Austin, TX,
ACRES U.S.A., 2013
    xxvi, 293 pp., 23 cm.
    Includes Index
    Includes Bibliography
    ISBN 978-1-60173-036-7 (trade)

    1. Agriculture — crops & soils. 2. Soil management.
    3. Soil — plant relationship. 4. Soil fertility 5. Plants — nutrition.
    I. Albrecht, William A., 1888-1974 and Charles Walters, 1926-2009
    II. Title.

    SF95.A43 2013   631.4

**Dedicated to the
Memory of Joe D. Nichols, M.D.,**

the long-time president
of Natural Foods Associates,
a holistic medical practitioner
who lived and did the Albrecht word.

Table of Contents

Soil Fertility and Human Health

Soil Fertility & Human and Animal Health

About the Author

Dr. William A. Albrecht, the author of these papers, was chairman of the Department of Soils at the University of Missouri College of Agriculture, where he had been a member of the staff for 43 years. He held four degrees, A.B., B.S. in Agriculture, M.S. and Ph.D., from the University of Illinois. During a vivid and crowded career, he traveled widely and studied soils in the United States, Great Britain, on the European continent, and in Australia.

Born on a farm in central Illinois in an area of highly fertile soil typical of the Cornbelt and educated in his native state, Dr. Albrecht grew up with an intense interest in the soil and all things agricultural. These were approached, however, through the avenues of the basic sciences and liberal arts and not primarily through applied practices and their economics.

Teaching experience after completing the liberal arts course, with some thought of the medical profession, as well as an assistantship in botany, gave an early vision of the interrelationships that enrich the facts acquired in various fields when viewed as part of a master design.

These experiences led him into additional undergraduate and graduate work, encouraged by scholarships and fellowships, until he received his doctor's degree in 1919. In the meantime, he joined the research and teaching staff at the University of Missouri.

Both as a writer and speaker, Dr. Albrecht served tirelessly as an interpreter of scientific truth to inquiring minds and persistently stressed the basic importance of understanding and working with nature by applying the natural method to all farming, crop production, livestock raising and soil improvement. He always had a specific focus on the effect of soil characteristics upon the mineral composition of plants and the effect of the mineral composition of plants on animal nutrition and subsequent human health.

Dr. Albrecht strove not to be an ivory tower pontificator trying to master and defeat nature, but to be a leader of true science and understand the wondrous ways of nature so we could harness them for the lasting benefit of all. A man of the soil, William A. Albrecht summed up his philosophy as such, "When wildlife demonstrates the soil as the foundation of its health and numbers, is man, the apex of the biotic pyramid, too far removed from the soil to recognize it as the foundation of his health via nutrition?"

Dr. Albrecht was a true student of the characteristics of soil and wasn't timid about his views — be they to a farmer in the field, an industry group or to a congressional subcommittee.

Respected and recognized by scientists and agricultural leaders from around the world, Dr. Albrecht retired in 1959 and passed from the scene in May 1974 as his 86th birthday approached.

About the Albrecht Papers

When the first volume of these papers was issued, no one could foresee the possibility of recovering and publishing all the papers of this great scientist. For this reason the organization of these papers has not followed Dr. Albrecht's work in a calendar sequence, meaning the order of study and investigation. Instead the papers have been organized into topic themes.

Here the papers have been grouped to best focus attention and allowed to reciprocate the values upon which all of Albrecht's work.

About the Editor

Charles Walters was the founder and executive editor of *Acres U.S.A*, a magazine he started in 1971 to spread the word of eco-agriculture. A recognized leader in the field of raw materials-based economic research and sustainable food and farming systems, this confirmed maverick saw one of his missions as to rescue lost knowledge. Perhaps the most important were the papers of Dr. William A. Albrecht, whose low profile obscured decades of brilliant work in soil science. Albrecht's papers, which Walters rescued from the historical dustbin and published in an initial four volumes, continue to provide a rock-solid foundation for the scientific approach to organic farming. Additional volumes of Albrecht's papers were organized and edited by Walters for later publication — the result is shown here with this book. During his life, Walters penned thousands of article on the technologies of organic and sustainable agriculture and is the author of more than two dozen books (and co-author of several more), including *Eco-Farm — An Acres U.S.A. Primer, Weeds, Control Without Poisons, A Farmer's Guide to the Bottom Line, Dung Beetles, Mainline Farming for Century 21* and many more. Charles Walters generously shared his vision, energy and passion through his writing and public speaking for more than 35 years and made it his lifelong mission to save the family farm and give farmers an operating manual that they couldn't live without. *The Albrecht Papers* are an important part of this message. Charles Walters passed on in January 2009 at the age of 83.

An Albrecht Vignette

Between the founding of Acres U.S.A. and the death of William A. Albrecht in 1974, the editor of this volume taped about 100 hours of conversations with the great Professor. During one of the last taping sessions, Albrecht handed over some 800 papers and a few have turned up since then. This volume contains papers closely identified with the human health factor. Dr. Albrecht came to this editor's attention during an editorial stint at *Veterinary Medicine* magazine. Albrecht had rare insight into the chemical equation of soils — as well as physical and biological connections. These understandings led him to pull the soil sample from which was isolated Aureomycin. In the mid-1940s this new "medicine" literally leaped into the nation's headlines as an antibiotic. It held great promise as an instrument to beat death-dealing viruses and as an answer to gram-positive bacteria.

It was the soil of Sanborn Field that held answers in escrow, both as soil fertility and human health — and animal health also.

From the Publisher

A large part of the Acres U.S.A. mission is to preserve and promote the wisdom of those who came before us. Prof. William Albrecht was such a visionary. A collection of his papers was the first publishing entry toward this mission, that book being *The Albrecht Papers*.

Charles Walters, our founder and longtime editor — and my father — sought out Dr. Albrecht not knowing what lessons were there to be learned. The name Albrecht appeared in journals around the world, yet officials at the University of Missouri where the retired professor kept an office discouraged a meeting citing his age, poor hearing, and the like. Charles Walters visited anyway. What came from these meetings, which soon grew into weekly sessions, was a mentor/student dialogue. Albrecht, ever the patient pedagogue, dispensed the logic, elegance and simplicity of his agricultural systems to an eager mind. And Charles Walters, the publisher and writer, picked up the charge and spread the timeless wisdom of William Albrecht around the world to a new generation of farmers and agronomists.

It's hard to say whether Dr. Albrecht's work would have found its way to light through the efforts of others or if without the republication of Albrecht's papers they would have remained just that, papers to eventually fall into the dustbin of history.

Four volumes of *The Albrecht Papers* eventually came forth. Each had a style and character of its own and each brought new lessons from the master soil scientist to life, but only the most disciplined students of the soil tended to seek out and study these dense works.

Late in his career, semi-retired and legally blind, Charles Walters undertook the Herculean task of reading and sorting the hundreds of remaining papers and articles in Albrecht's archives. He completed that task a few years before his death in 2009. What was left to accomplish was the monumental job of converting damaged and faded copies of articles, some 80 years old, into formats compatible with modern publishing and readable by all.

From file cabinets full of faded photocopies came forth several new volumes of *The Albrecht Papers*, each with a specific focus and theme. It is our goal to produce these works in a timely fashion. In your hands is the beautiful collaboration of the visionary research of Professor William Albrecht and the deft editorial eye of Charles Walters. We hope you enjoy this new creation of William Albrecht and Charles Walters.

— Fred C. Walters

Foreword

William Albrecht was not only a distinguished scientist and brilliant scholar; he was also a true visionary and committed humanitarian. He was still chairman of the Soils Department and a familiar name in the College of Agriculture when I first arrived on the University of Missouri campus in the fall of 1957. I recall a friend being somewhat offended because Professor Albrecht seemed to question the intelligence of people like him who been raised on food from the "worn out" soils of south Georgia. We students weren't aware at the time of the larger controversy that surrounded Albrecht's work linking the health of soils to the health of animals, including people. While president of the Soil Science Society in 1938, he had written in the Yearbook of Agriculture "A declining soil fertility, due to a lack of organic material, major elements, and trace minerals, is responsible for poor crops and in turn for pathological conditions in animals fed deficient foods from such soils, and mankind is no exception."

The instructor in my beginning soils course stuck pretty close to the physics, chemistry and biology of soils. I don't recall him ever mentioning Albrecht's work linking soil health and human health. Perhaps he did, and I just don't recall. Or perhaps he didn't want to endure the professional criticism Albrecht endured for venturing beyond the narrow bounds of his academic discipline. The University had plant and animal scientists who were studying the health of plants and animals and an entire medical school studying the health of people. Professor Albrecht was admonished to restrict his observations and conclusions to the health of soils and crops and leave questions regarding the health of animals and people to others.

Perhaps his most controversial and most important study was his review of World War II era dental records of 70,000 U.S. sailors. He linked the health of sailors' teeth to the health of soils in their native regions of the U.S. In those days, people for the most part ate foods grown in home gardens, on local farms, or at least grown in their respective regions of the country. He concluded, "If all other body irregularities as well as those of the teeth were so viewed, it is highly probable that many of our diseases would be interpreted as degenerative troubles originating in nutritional deficiencies going back to insufficient fertility of the soil." With the end of World War II, Albrecht called for a major national initiative to restore the health and fertility of America's "worn out" soils.

Instead, the nation's agricultural priorities shifted to producing more agricultural commodities and producing them more efficiently in a quest for cheaper food. Albrecht anticipated that the growing reliance on commercial fertilizers to increase productivity would degrade soil health, which in turn would diminish animal health and human health. He was particularly concerned that the overemphasis on nitrogen, prosperous, and potash (N, P, & K) would lead to the depletion of trace minerals, such as manganese, copper, boron, zinc, iodine and chlorine, which are essential to both plant and animal health. He wrote "N P K formulas, as legislated and enforced by State Departments of Agriculture mean malnutrition, attack by insects, bacteria and fungi, weed takeover, crop loss in dry weather, and general loss of mental acuity in the population, leading to degenerative metabolic disease and early death."

Albrecht ventured into economics in the late 1950s, at about the same time I discovered the discipline of agricultural economics as an undergraduate. He wrote, "The costs of growing healthy livestock and healthy people do not fit themselves readily into our economics where costs and earnings must always be matched in monetary values (dollars). We are slow to realize that good health is not a purchasable commodity. Health of plants, of livestock and of humans via proper nutrition... will not submit to solution by monetary manipulations." Over time, he became increasingly concerned and outspoken about the potential negative impacts of profit-driven farming practices on the health of the land. He wrote: "We are slow to study the importance of soil fertility to the quality of food, for this is not yet to our economic advantage in the marketplace."

After retirement, as an emeritus professor, Albrecht continued to explore and write about the link between soil health and human health. In 1966, he pointed out that the health of the soil affects the nutrient balance between proteins and carbohydrates in both feed and food crops. He concluded only healthy organic soils with the proper balance of macronutrients and micronutrients could produce the complete proteins necessary for good human health. He distinguished between the "grow foods" grown on healthy soils and "go foods," which were filled with carbohydrates for energy but lacking in the complete proteins needed for growth and health. "Go foods" make humans fat; it takes "grow" foods to keep humans healthy. I doubt Albrecht would be at all surprised by the epidemic of obesity and other diet related health problems confronting Americans today.

These few references provide but a brief glimpse of Albrecht's work linking soil health and human health and barely hint at the enormous body of less controversial work that brought William Albrecht to the pinnacle of his profession as a soil scientist. He didn't present his conclusions as proof, but instead as compelling challenges to soil scientists, agricultural scientists, and scientists in general. He presented what I call the Albrecht hypothesis that *human health is inseparable from soil health.* This is not a proven fact but a proposition or hypothesis that has yet to be thoroughly tested, at least by the respected research institutions. Albrecht didn't claim to have the final answers regarding soil health and human health. He suggested it would take at least a half-century to unravel the mysteries he had begun to explore.

Unfortunately, few scientists since have had the courage to venture outside of their academic disciplines to explore the broader implications of their work for society and humanity. Many consider themselves to be soil scientists, plant scientists, animal scientists, medical scientists or economists — period. Albrecht knew he needed a basic understanding of all these fields if his work as a soils scientist was to fulfill his public responsibility to society and humanity. His work reportedly was dismissed by the academic community because he refused to restrict his work to soil science and he eventually was forced into retirement. Today, American society may well be suffering the ecological, social, and economic consequences of the failure to explore Albrecht's hypothesis linking soil health and human health.

When I ventured into agricultural sustainability in the late 1980s, I discovered that Albrecht's stature among those in the sustainable agriculture movement was higher than his stature among agriculturalists at the peak of his academic career. He was and still is considered to be among the best of a small group of soil scientists who have contributed anything of real value in restoring sustainability to American agriculture. Other soil scientists have since taken on the task of exploring soil health and sustainable productivity. However, Albrecht's work still represents a voice of authority on all matters related to soils for many farmers, even though he is still controversial among academic soil scientists. For many sustainable farmers, *The Albrecht Papers,* a series compiled and edited by Charles Walters of *Acres U.S.A.,* is the bible on all matters related to soil fertility. Volume 8 is but the latest in that series. The lasting value of Albrecht's work has been validated for many by the restored health of many soils, crops, farms, and farm families who have followed the "Albrecht method" of soil management.

Though still unproven, the legitimacy of the Albrecht hypothesis linking soil health and human health also has been validated by more than a half-century of American history. A French contemporary of Albrecht,

André Voisin, paraphrases the Albrecht hypothesis as: "Animals and men are biochemical photographs of the soil." If we Americans are biochemical photographs of the soil, we are the picture of a nation whose food is grown in increasingly unhealthy soils.

The declining physical health of Americans is perhaps most obvious in the growing epidemic of obesity. Obesity is not simply a matter of personal inconvenience or embarrassment; it is closely linked to a number of diet related diseases, including diabetes, heart disease, hypertension, and a variety of cancers. Recent statistics classify two-thirds of adults and nearly one-third of American children and teens as obese or overweight. Since 1980, the number of obese adults has doubled. Since 1970, the number of obese adolescents ages 12-19 has tripled and the number of obese children ages 6-11 has quadrupled. According to a 2010 report of the Robert Woods Johnson Foundation, *F as in Fat; How Obesity Threatens America's Future*, the tendency toward obesity has continued unabated in spite of a host of programs mounted by government and nonprofit organizations to combat it, the latest being President Obama's White House Task Force on Childhood Obesity.

In terms of economic costs, obesity related illnesses are projected to claim about one-in-five dollars spent for health care in America by 2020 — erasing virtually all of the gains made in improving public health over the past several decades. Health care costs in America now consume more than 17% of the total GDP or economic output, nearly twice as much as in 1980 and more than twice as much as the costs of food. If current trends continue, health care will claim more than one-third of all U.S. economic output by 2040. Obviously, there are multiple causes of obesity and other diet-related diseases, including sedentary lifestyles. However, one significant cause might well be decades of preoccupation with economic efficiency with declining soil health, animal health, and human health, as Albrecht anticipated.

Some recent scientific studies have begun to confirm that an agriculture driven by economic values has depleted the nutritional value of the nation's foods. A particularly revealing study was published in the *Journal of American College of Nutrition* in 2004. It compared nutrient levels in 43 garden crops in 1999 with levels documented in historic benchmark nutrient studies conducted by USDA in 1950. Declines in median concentrations of six important nutrients: protein -6%, calcium -16%, phosphorus -9%, iron -15%, riboflavin -38%, and vitamin C -2% were observed — even when measured on a dry weight basis.

Other studies have since found similar results showing diminished nutrient density of foods over time.

Some of this loss of nutrients may be due to changes in food processing and distribution. However, numerous studies have shown significant reductions in the nutrient density at the farm level associated with increasing use of modern yield-enhancing technologies — fertilizers, pesticides, high plant density and irrigation. This so called "dilution effect" apparently is well known among plant scientists, although rarely mentioned in relation to diet and health outside of organic circles.

Organic farming provides a convenient contrast to conventional agricultural practices. A review of 97 published studies by *The Organic Center* comparing organic and conventionally grown food indicated that "on average" organic foods are more nutritious than conventional foods. Conventional foods often contained more macro nutrients — potassium, phosphorus, and total protein — but organic foods were consistently and significantly higher in vitamin C, vitamin E, polyphenols and total antioxidants, which are frequently lacking in American diets. Admittedly, some of the studies were inconclusive and others favored conventional foods. Farms can be certified as organic after refraining from use of inorganic fertilizers and pesticides for only three years. It may take decades of organic farming to fully restore the chemical and biological health of "worn out" soils.

Compelling evidence in support of the Albrecht hypothesis also can be found in USDA statistics documenting long-term consumption patterns in America. During the first half of the twentieth-century, as people became less physically active, they ate fewer calories. Americans were consuming roughly 10% fewer calories per person per day in the late 1950s than in early 1900s. Per capita calorie consumption leveled off during the 1960s. In the early 1970s, the number of total calories in the average American diet began a persistent upward trend, while physical activity obviously continued to decline. Between 1980 and 2004, total daily calories per capita from all sources, including alcohol, increased by 21%. The logical consequence is the alarming increase in numbers of Americans who are overweight or obese.

Why did Americans eat *less* as they became *less* active during the first half of the century but eat *more* as they became even *less* active during the second half of the century? The human species obviously didn't evolve that much over a 100 years, but the food system most certainly did. The over-consumption of calories closely parallels the industrialization of the American food system, including the industrialization of agriculture, which was driven by economic efficiency. The increase in consumption was not simply a response to lower food prices, as the percent of income spent for food dropped more from 1939 to 1969 than from 1969 to 1999. We appear to be seeing the consequences of an agriculture driven by a quest for economic efficiency rather than the health of the land and the health of people — as Albrecht predicted.

In summary, the credibility of the Albrecht hypothesis linking soil fertility with human and animal health has withstood the test of time and has become even more compelling with the rise of obesity and the related decline in human health. It is quite fitting that Acres U.S.A. would choose this time to publish this new volume of The Albrecht Papers linking soil health with human health. This new volume provides a solid conceptual and analytical foundation for Albrecht's conclusions linking soil health and human health, as well as a collection of papers linking soil health specifically with the health of farm animals.

This volume includes some of Albrecht's early analyses of geographic patterns of soil health and human health. He attributed the diminished fertility of soils in different regions of the country to leaching of minerals in high rainfall areas and depletion of organic matter by tillage, particularly in regions with higher temperatures. He pointed out that human populations were able to expand beyond areas of higher natural soil fertility to more marginally fertile soils as chemical fertilizers became available to maintain crop yields of the poorer soils. Although crop yields were maintained, or even increased, through fertilization, the nutritional value of crops produced on the less naturally fertile soils declined. The dominant crops produced within regions also changed in response to declining natural fertility to crops that allowed farmers to maintain total tonnage per acre of production. Invariably, the nutrient values of the new crops were inferior to those previously produced as natural fertility declined. The result has feed and foods crops higher in carbohydrates but lower in the complete proteins essential for growth and health of animals and people.

In this volume, Albrecht emphasizes that: "Every kind of creation starts with a handful of dust, or with the five percent of vegetation, and finally of our bodies, that is the ash." The rest is made up energy from the sun linking carbon, hydrogen and nitrogen from the air. The former he referred to as biosynthesis, the latter photosynthesis. Photosynthesis produces the carbohydrates essential for quick energy, with excess energy stored as body fat. Biosynthesis produces the proteins essential for the growth of strong muscles and bones — essential for good health. The "handful of dust" from healthy soils is also essential for secretion of the hormones that regulate various human functions, including metabolism, growth and development, tissue functions, and psychological mood. With the depletion of natural fertility, production methods have relied increasingly on photosynthesis to produce high yields while neglecting biosynthesis, which is necessary for the nutrient-dense crops essential for the growth and health of both farm animals and humans.

This volume includes a number of papers linking soil health with the health of farm animals. Albrecht believed that livestock are the best soil chemists. He observed that animals in the wild are able to select a healthy, balanced diet from the variety of plants available to them. Each plant species has a different nutrient potential with its actual nutrition levels additionally affected by the quality of soil in which it grows. Wild animals selectively choose plant species higher in potential nutrient density and plants of the same species growing on soils with a healthy balance of macronutrients, micronutrients and biological organisms.

Albrecht observed that domestic livestock have this same capacity as wild animals for choosing healthy diets from crops grow on healthy soils. Grazing livestock selectively avoid plants growing in soils that are "worn out" and soil areas that are either deficient in or oversaturated with specific nutrients, such as areas around manure patties. His classic example is the consistent preference of cows for grass on "the other side of the fence," along roadways and railroads, where the soils have not been depleted by cultivation. He believed the only way scientists could accurately assess the health of soil was to assess the health of animals that ate the crops grown on the soil, including the health of people who ate the animals that ate feed crops grown on the soil.

He and other scientists of his time observed that when livestock are fed pre-mixed rations, they would eat excess amounts of some nutrients in order to get their minimum requirements of others. If we humans have this same capacity, perhaps we are a nation of people who are "overfed" but "undernourished." Using Albrecht's terms, Americans may be overeating "go" foods only because they don't have ready access to "grow" foods, resulting in too many calories and too few of the complete proteins essential for good health. The sedentary lifestyles of many Americans obviously contribute to the growing epidemic of obesity. However, excessive eating and the resulting excessive weight obviously contribute to sedentary lifestyles. Many Americans may be overfed and undernourished because their foods are produced on unhealthy soils.

I recently participated in an extended interview for a Home Box Office video-documentary series dealing with the issue of obesity: "The Weight of the Nation." The producer of the segment dealing with agriculture seemed to be intrigued with the Albrecht hypothesis. She even convinced the producer of the series to send a videographer to record my presentation of the "Albrecht Lecture" at the University of Missouri. However, the final version of the documentary contained no mention of the potential link between declining soil fertility and the growing epidemic of obesity. Apparently, the "more-credible scientists" on their panel of experts convinced the producers that any link between soil health and human health was negligible, or at least too controversial to defend. I mention this only because Albrecht frequently addresses the failures of modern scientists to appreciate the public health implications of soil health.

In this volume, Albrecht writes about those who approach soil science as the "industrial manipulation of dead materials" to gain economic advantage. "People who approach agricultural research in this way have lost sight of agriculture as a biological demonstration by forces of nature, where man is more a spectator than a manager in complete control of soil and produce." He continues, "They seem unaware that the soil of our planet is a complex material development through many centuries, having the power of creation, not only for plants, but for everything that lives, moves and has being upon the earth."

Albrecht explains the lack of scientific interest in his hypothesis linking soil health and human health as follows: "The life of the soil is not attractive. The death of it is no recognized disaster. Hence, it may seem far-fetched to anyone but a student of both the soil and nutrition to relate the nutritive quality of feed and foods to the soil." Apparently, the increasing specialization and narrowness of scientific disciplines has left us with few if any students of both soil and nutrition. Regardless, as Albrecht points out, ignorance of a fact does not negate its validity: "To say that we don't believe there is a relation between nutritive values of feeds or foods and the fertility of the soil is a confession of ignorance of all that is to be know of this fact and is not a negation of it."

Apparently, *The Albrecht Papers* will have to serve the needs of those of us who are concerned with both agricultural sustainability and human health a bit longer. This new volume is certainly a timely and worthy addition to the others. I hope the thousands who read it will spread the word about the logical connections among soil health, animal health, and human health until it grows into a public demand for fundamental change that is as compelling as it is necessary. That change must begin with a restored respect among both farmers and scientists for the importance of soil health. From this respect, a commitment to restoring the natural fertility and productivity of the soil must arise as a means of restoring health to humanity. Perhaps then, William Albrecht also will receive the respect he so richly deserves as a distinguished scientist, brilliant scholar, true visionary and committed humanitarian.

— John Ikerd, author of Small Farms are Real Farms
and Sustainable Capitalism

Preface

The end product of agriculture has to be human beings capable of thought and reason. That mankind stands at the top of the title pyramid was both an Albrecht logo and a dictum. During World War II Dr. William A. Albrecht made his famous fitness studies, relating draft eligibility to the availability of soil nutrients, always citing calcium, magnesium, sodium and potassium as prime cations, with anions structured to accommodate life in the soil. Albrecht's findings were disturbing to the twin precepts that had swept the republics of learning, namely, N,P and K fertilization and toxic rescue chemistry. That partial and imbalanced fertilization meant toxic rescue chemistry became an Albrecht given. His reports on dental caries as related to the soil nutrient norm were published all the way from Europe to Australia, with papers in German dominating. Some have been presented in earlier volumes, it being impossible to relegate very much of Albrecht's work to the airtight compartments required by single factor analysis.

It always disturbed Albrecht that modern agriculture seemingly could not keep up with its science. Through a long career he proved beyond the shadow of a doubt that the N, P and K system worked only by accident when it worked at all. His observations became secure when the electron microscope first came online. For the first time the marvel of mineralization known as the cell came into view. Here was the missing link in understanding metabolic activity and the chemistry of growth.

The seed, of course, comes alive by imbibing water. It is then that the desiccated colloidal content becomes soaked. The seed swells. Fantastic forces are put into motion. It has been said that 2,000 miniature atmospheres function. Sailors know this, especially if they've ever shipped on a leaking tub with grain in the hold.

It also takes air to trigger metabolic activity. Without oxygen growth stops. If oxygen is cut off for too long, the seed dies.

Soil fertility suggests the requirement for oxygen, both to accommodate the seed and the livestock in the soil.

Many of Albrecht's papers could be laced into a volume such as this, and all of these papers could be installed properly in earlier and later volumes, it being understood that the end product of farming be kept in mind.

The point here is that the chemistry of growth involves the cell, first, last and always. This may seem odd, but odder still is the fact that the farmer seldom if ever sees a cell, the appropriate microscope being unavailable. Yet what happens at the cellular level will determine the bottom line at the end of the year. This cell, this key to prosperity unlimited, can be plate-like, concave, spherical, whatever, according to the role assigned by the Creator. Any diagram is both a fiction and the truth, a bird's eye view of creation.

We will not further elaborate by considering the catalytic nature of enzymes, or embarking on the rest of the journey Albrecht has sketched out for us. The subject is mentioned here because that bird's eye view prompted scientists to attempt random saturation of cellular substrate. This was all to produce bins and bushels of resultant food that did not support plant, animal and human requirements. This at first became a breathtaking observation, then a scandal, finally a monument to the stupidity of man, and at this writing a disgrace to a civilized society.

Since the single cell requires several hundred enzymes to even function, many being molecular, plants incapable of developing their own hormone and enzyme systems due to a shortage or marked imbalance of nutrients cannot furnish the upscale requirements of the human being or animal.

Soil Fertility & Animal Health was the second volume in this series. It codified a series of articles Albrecht wrote for the *Angus Journal*. A few of the caboose papers in this volume properly belong in that second volume, but were not discovered for several years after its publication. They are presented as an add-on to the human health factor.

Maurice Wilkins and Rosalind Franklin did not identify the DNA molecule until late in Albrecht's career, that identification being prompted by the explosion of an atomic bomb over the crowded city of Hiroshima, Japan. Albrecht and his associates knew that the world was changed forever by that explosion, a change that could be measured and compared using soil samples sequestered before the event. Unfortunately nature and institutional arrangements decreed that this great scientist, Albrecht could not stay around and see the next great chapter in the story of *Soil Fertility & Human and Animal Health*.

Collectively, all the Albrecht papers seem to say that the balance of health in crops, animals and human beings depends on more than the balance of mineral elements. It is never enough to suggest that the ratios between calcium, magnesium, sodium and potassium totally govern the health profile. Those ratios nevertheless stand as a gatekeeper for soil tests and consultants for the simple reason that the Albrecht equation works — in the tropics, temperate zone, everywhere, with limiting factors being the life in the soil, tillage, decay management, water in the soil, capillary return and the several other considerations extension of those ideas would account for. Research not beholden to fossil fuel technology has validated Albrecht ever since his ideas were first published.

Single factor analysis is the mark of an amateur. Yet too much research is pursued with that orientation in mind.

The research plots on Sanborn Field at the University of Missouri served up the life form refined by science as Aureomycin. Plots left undisturbed went to poverty weeds. Others detailed for science the beneficial effects — and hazards — of monocultures, nitrogen fixation via legumes, and of course the foundation principles for health in plants, animal and humans based on several Albrecht ratios assisted by the precepts of eco-agriculture.

Insight into the farming craft is best attained when soil fertility is related to human health.

— Charles Walters

Section 1

Introduction

CHAPTER 1

Plant, Animal and Human Health Vary With Soil Fertility

THERE IS AN AGE-OLD saying which tells us that "To be well-fed is to be healthy." All of us appreciate human health, but, unfortunately, more when we do not have it, than when we do. Plants and animals should be healthy also when well fed. Wild animals "know their medicine," as it were, not by knowing how to cure sickness, but what to choose to eat so as to be healthy. Grazing wild animals do not discriminate much between different plant species on a fertile soil, but they will discriminate between the same plant grown on different fertility of soils, or on the same soils treated differently. The animals are "seeing" their good nutrition, then, according to what the soil offers via any plant species. It is the soil fertility and not the plant's pedigree that is the distinguishing feature of the forage, and the criterion of the choice by the animal. Nutritional value according as the soil makes it, is the animal's means of being well-fed and therefore being healthy.

Immunity of Healthy Plants

The plant's health fits into the same category, namely, if the plant is "well-fed" — not necessarily in terms of yielding big bulk of vegetative mass — it can protect itself against fungus attack and also against insect attack. Healthy plants, then, in what you might want to call healthy in their "resistance to attack by fungi, or insects" result from soil fertile enough to make those plants carrying higher concentrations of proteins within themselves. The physiology of the plant, determined by its nutrition, is the distinguishing feature. If the plants are well-fed, then, they are healthy — that is, fungi or other microbes (lower life forms) do not attack them.

Protein Builds Resistance

It is significant that we point to the higher content of these plants, when they are "healthy." It is protein by which our bodies get protection. Our bloodstreams must have the protecting proteins, either already on hand or soon made, if some foreign proteins like a bacteria, fungi, or parasite entering our body is to be destroyed by our body (or we be destroyed by it). Animals protect themselves by proteins, but animals must get their proteins by eating the plants. Plants (and microbes) are equipped to make proteins from the elements, animals are not. Thus, animals get their proteins and protection from the plants. Plants get their proteins to the degree that the soil fertility helps them create these compounds. Healthy animals and healthy plants, then, are so because they have proteins, or are well-fed in what comes about because of the soil. It is the soil, then, which is the foundation of good nutrition, especially complete proteins, thereby building good health.

Protein Basic to Life

Good health of animals and plants calls for (1) cell multiplications, cell repair or replacement, or just simply body growth — fat is not growth in that sense, even if it increases weight of body; (2) protection against invasion by other life forms like bacteria, fungi, virus, etc., and consumption of our cells by those other cells against which we must generate our antibiotics, antibodies, antigens, or protective compounds; (3) reproduction of the species. In all of these there are the proteins, and all that is associated with them, viz., the enzymes, vitamins, hormones, etc., which render the services. Being well nourished is then mainly a problem of proteins, and their creation by plants and microbes, according as the soils permit.

Protein and Reproduction

In this geographical area, i.e. Missouri, we know that the soils do not grow the protein-producing crops unless some soil treatments are used. We should, therefore, expect protein problems in nutrition in this area. We should, also, expect health accordingly. We can grow the carbohydrate crops for fattening. We **fatten** hogs and cattle here, but have troubles with their **reproduction**.

Crops Reflect Protein

Since soils fit a climatic pattern of differences in the degree to which the rocks have been developed into a fertile soil, or excessively developed into one washed out, as it were, we have crops making proteins and carbohydrates to be "grow" food, or we have crops making mainly carbohydrates to be not "grow" foods, but only energy or "go" foods. These latter soils then do not feed us well and may, therefore, give us poor health. Some correlation of the condition of teeth, of rejectees from the armed services, of fungus attack like histoplasmosis, etc., suggest that health patterns of the country go back to the soil patterns via the proteins and all that is required to grow them.

Vital Soil Elements

Since the air and rainfall serve to supply the carbon, hydrogen, and oxygen, namely, the components of the carbohydrates or energy foods, we do not worry about those three essential elements our bodies need. They, coupled with nitrogen, also coming originally from the air but taken by most crops from the soil, constitute about 95 percent of the crops, of our food and animal feed, but the 5 percent coming from the soil includes a much larger list of elements, namely, calcium, phosphorus, potassium, sodium, chlorine, sulfur, magnesium, iron, iodine, fluorine, manganese, copper, boron, zinc, cobalt, molybdenum, and possibly others.

Of these, the "trace" elements, namely, manganese, copper, boron, zinc, iodine, chlorine, and molydbenum have just recently gotten attention.

Evidence of Soil Deficiencies

Our limited knowledge has been extending itself. By means of bioassays, that is, the use of experimental animals, the science of biochemistry and its refined methods have helped us learn of the importance not only of the possible deficiencies in our soils of the major elements as they bring about deficiencies in health, but also the deficiencies in our soils of the trace elements as potential deficiencies in health via plants and animals as our foods.

The major elements as materials of construction permit us to locate them in their functional places. But the trace elements, serving much as tools, cannot always be found in the finished product or in established functional positions in the body.

We are slowly coming around to see the soil fertility pattern as the determiner of our health pattern as our life lines of nutrition are shortened or cut off by (a) increasing population, (b) dwindling acres per person, and (c) declining depth of surface soil as declining fertility supplies.

Section 2

Soil Fertility and Animal Health

CHAPTER 2

Soil and Livestock

GOOD BULK is registered by satiation and the relief of hunger. Food quality, when defective, remains unregistered by these means, but gives us the hidden hungers that may be lifetime torments.

These hidden hungers originate in the soil and reach us by way of plants that also suffer hidden hungers. So also animals suffer their hidden hungers, and so humans, in their turn, consuming the products of starved plants and animals, suffer. This whole series of torments is caused by nutrient shortages in the soil. It should be exposed and possibly cured by soil treatment.

Proper nutrition is an enemy of "disease," in plants as in people. Fungus attack on plants, the "damping off" disease, has been demonstrated as related to a hidden hunger for lime or calcium. More recently potato scab has suggested its connection with insufficient calcium in relation to potassium in the soil fertility offered the potato plant. The potato plant demands much calcium in its tops which duplicate red clover in content of this nutrient.

Plant health in the humid temperatures is doubtlessly declining as the soil is declining. As we fail to return manures, fertilizers and nutrients in the equivalent to those taken off in the crops, we are invoking hidden hungers in the plant and encouraging plant diseases.

Man's nomadic habits have covered much of what a life in a limited location might eventually reveal. He has moved to new soil. But now that rubber shortage and gasoline rationing are putting fences about us as we have done to our livestock, our own deficiencies or hidden hungers will lead us more quickly to consider the soil.

Calcium and phosphorus deficiencies soon show up in livestock. In some localities animals born in early winter develop rickets by late winter or early spring. Their bones break readily and the pelvic-spine joints separate. The animal "goes down" when the farmer believed "it was doing well."

Disturbed reproduction processes are another consequence, the record of hidden hungers for calcium and phosphorus. Shy breeders among the cattle are increasing.

On some of the less fertile soils farmers are wondering why their cows breed only in alternate years. It is not suggestive that on many of these same soils the calves show malformations enough to make them less true to breed type? The backbone of a cow reared in such a herd reveals she had sacrificed part of her backbone for foetus production and used the succeeding year to replace her backbone rather than to indulge in another reproductive cycle. (She was originally a regular breeder but became a shy breeder and died all too early in her life.)

Males, too, may lose breeding capacity on deficient forage feeds grown on deficient soils. Male rabbits under experiment with forage grown on calcium-deficient soils became impotent. Their litter mates, on feeds grown on soil given calcium, retained their capacity to serve as fathers. When the feeds of these two lots of rabbits were interchanged for the second period of the experiment, the situations were reversed. Those originally made impotent by lime-deficient forage recovered their male potency, while the lot put on forage from lime-deficient soil, lost it.

Reproduction, as a delicate physiological mechanism — if its late arrival and early departure in the individual life cycle is any suggestion — may possibly be disturbed by other soil deficiencies not yet considered dangerous to this process of maintaining the species. Hidden hungers by way of decreasing fertility in the soil may be the quiet force by which species of animal life have become extinct. Nature's warnings allow time for us to heed them against our own extinction if we will look to the soil and conserve its fertility against the forces of exhaustion as well as its body against the forces of erosion.

One might well say that the moods of Mother Earth are not always constant and kindly toward those creatures whom she nurses. The rates of delivery to the plants of exchangeable nutrients by the soil vary with different parts of the year, or the seasons. Because plant growth stops during the winter season, this need not imply that chemical reactions within the soil cease during the same period. In fact the rapid exhaustion of the exchangeable supply by rapid plant growth should occasion restoration of equilibrium with cessation of plant growth. In the absence of plant growth, nutrients may move into the absorption atmosphere of the colloid to accumulate for ready removal by contact with plant roots during the next growing season.

Spring plowing facilitates these adjustments of concentration of available nutrients by rearranging contacts between colloids and mineral crystals. Consequently, the spring plant growth into this larger supply of fertility and through root extension for its rapid absorption, means a liberal supply of soil nutrients in contrast to the lower rate at which the plant is building its carbohydrates. Further, this means luscious plant growth of which the lusciousness is contributed by the soil more than by air and sunshine. Such plants are mineral-rich and protein-rich, to say nothing of their contents of vitamins or other growth-supporting essentials.

As the plant growth extends into the summer season, the store of exchangeable nutrients in the soil has already been lowered. At the same time, the increase in sunshine and in temperature bring greater rate of carbohydrate production. Thus, spring growth of plants means high mineral and protein concentration of nutritive value as body construction, but later growth in the summer suggests woodiness and fuel value.

When with each mouthful of luscious grass the animals ingest growth-promoting nutrients assembled by extensive root action through the soil, rather than mere woodiness from an extensive plant top collecting sunshine and fresh air, is it any wonder that the shaggy winter coat of hair is shed, and that a sleek animal condition comes on in early May? Should there be any wonder that animal thriftiness is lessened by August, and shall we accept the oft-given explanation that it is wholly because of the heat and the flies? Some of you may have heard cattle feeders remark of the steers in the drylot in February, "They ought to go to the market soon, because they are licking themselves." Some even say that this licking behavior is an index of feeding efficiency. It would perhaps be better to view it as a danger sign that recommends sale before disaster comes. Have you ever asked yourself why cattle do not continue to lick themselves, or each other, after they have been on spring pasture for a few weeks on fertile soil?

It may not be out of place to give some theoretical consideration to vitamins as a possibility in connection with this particular animal behavior of licking their own body coverings. Might it not be possible that after a long period of winter on dry feeds of low mineral and vitamin contents that the body needs for vitamin D become greater than the ingested supply? Might not the animals fatty secretions by the skin become activated in the sunshine with sufficient resulting equivalent of vitamin D which the animal by chance has learned to keep going through the cycle of excretion, activation and ingestion? As a suggestion for this theory, it has been demonstrated that the yolk of the sheep fleece for the fat of the wool is more prominent on sheep fed hays grown on land that was limed and phosphated than on those fed hays grown on soil without lime. Sheep growth per unit of feed consumed was also better by from 25 to 50 percent on the former. The better body growth and more prominent skin secretions may both be connected with the same physiological improvements connected with the soil treatment. Soil fertility is not flowing into the plant at constant rates at all periods of the season. These differences through the year and in variable soils make for different plant compositions but exert still larger influences on the animals consuming the plants. Naturally, the question implied is this, do the humans escape these subtle forces of the soil?

That seasonal differences in soil fertility exert themselves on animals is not so difficult to understand when we recall that nature has put the birth time of animals so commonly in the spring, or the time when the heavy calcium load of lactation can be met more widely by the luscious vegetation for the survival of the species. Unless the soil supports the vegetation, the vegetation cannot support the animals. Human births are not seasonally concentrated, yet in December (1941) issue of Human Biology, reports from a survey of ten thousand students of the University of Cincinnati (birth dates 1904-21 inclusive) that those born in the spring are taller, heavier, and smarter than those born during the summer. Here may be further evidence to the more direct relation of soil fertility to the animal and the human species. Here is human evidence that Mother Nature nourishes more efficiently in the spring than in the winter. The fact that life forms carry the reproductive load of foetus development on the dry feeds in the winter, may make many a maternal animal endure hidden hungers, and even sacrifice itself where some help through better forages on improved fertility of the soil might save.

Leguminous crops have been one of the great feeds to bring breeding animals through the winter in good health and with a generous crop of offspring. They have been fine means of growing young animals with good bone and straight back lines. Farmers all want plenty of legume hays but can't grow them, as they say, because their "soils are sour." Legumes need lime on the soil, to remove what is commonly called "soil acidity." It has only recently been demonstrated that the soil acidity is not injurious of itself. The so-called "plant injury by soil acidity" is largely a matter of a deficiency of the plant nutrient, calcium. It is, in truth, a deficiency of many items in soil fertility of which calcium is the one so pronouncedly deficient on the list that confusion has long persisted in our explanation of the benefits from putting limestone on our soils. We have believed that liming gives benefits because the carbonate of calcium removes the acidity. In reality the benefits come about because the calcium carbonate puts the calcium into the soil to satisfy the plant's needs for this nutrient in its body building requirements. After we have come to understand the function of liming, we shall be putting calcium back to the soil and drive out some of the hidden hungers in our livestock. When once we are fully accustomed to putting calcium into the soil to feed our plant and animals, we shall be more ready to do the same for phosphorus and all the elements that we will eventually put back to relieve the animals and ourselves of all these hungers. When only a few hundred pounds per acre of limestone, less than that of phosphate and less than tens of pounds of other nutrients are all that must be put back to make normally healthy plants and the resulting healthy animals, we should shake off our pessimistic views of the problems involved, likewise dispel our fears of the hidden hungers and go to work optimistically in restoring the soil fertility that drives them all away.

Soil acidity has so commonly been considered as a disaster that perhaps you may not be ready to believe that the soil acidity, so prominent in the temperate regions, may in reality be a blessing. The highest degrees of soil acidity occur in regions of moderate temperature and moderate to higher rainfalls. Maximum concentration of human population occurs in those same temperate regions. We have been inclined to believe that disturbed body comfort relative to temperature militates against denser populations in the frigid or the torrid zones. But when human movements like those of our armies are so much "on the stomachs," we must look to their increased chances to be fed there as the cause of concentration of people in the temperate zones. Soil acidity represents these greater possibilities. The very property of the clay enabling it to hold much hydrogen to make it acid, is the same property that enables it to hold many kinds of, and large quantities of, the nutrients for plant production. Soils of the frigid zones do not develop much clay content, or a clay that is able to supply much plant nourishment. Soils of the torrid zone, particularly, the humid tropics, have a clay product formed from such complete mineral breakdown that the resulting clay compounds have little holding, or little exchange capacities. So the acidic property of the clay, and of its associated humus, formed in the temperate zone may be the reason why we live in greater numbers in the temperate zone.

Soil fertility, then, controls the concentration and localizations of the human species within the humid-temperate belts of the world, rather than the necessary mass of clothing (or lack of it) required for human comfort. Our soils have the ability to take up and deliver nutrients if we will manage those nutrient supplies by maintaining them through fertility return to the soil rather than mining the soil continually and then moving on.

I say, then, that soil acidity in the presence of liberal supplies of soil fertility is beneficial. High concentrations of people and the food to guarantee them have been supported where soil acidity mobilizes the nutrients into the plants more effectively than under soil neutrality. Recent studies, using spinach as the test crop, have demonstrated that this vegetable took more calcium, more magnesium, and others from the soil when these exchangeable nutrients were accompanied by acidity.

We must not console ourselves too quickly, however, with the belief that soil acidity is always beneficial and that we need to do nothing about it. It is beneficial only when accompanied by nutrients. As these nutrients become exhausted, hydrogen or acidity replaces them, and when acidity is all that remains the plants must suffer starvation.

Such was the situation in our virgin soils. They were acid but fertile because of high humus contents in which fertility had been hoarded by virgin vegetation. These stores have now been mined. With the increasing acidity and the declining crop yields, or legume crop failures, the acidity was considered as the cause of them. It was not the presence of acidity but the absence of fertility, that was the cause. We now know that nutrients in fertilizers put into the soil are taken by plants more effectively in the presence than in the absence of soil acidity. The crusaders against soil acidity may now desert that cause and march under the banner of soil conservation by restoring soil fertility.

That some of the hidden hungers in animals and in plants can be driven away by putting the nutrients, calcium and phosphorus, on the soil as fertilizers has been demonstrated experimentally only recently. Such is true if increased growth on the same amount of nourishment or within the same time period may be considered as absence of serious hunger. Sheep, as test animals fed the same amount of hay and of grain per head per day, gained weight differently according as the soil had been given phosphate, or lime and phosphate. The plants had some of their hidden hungers routed too, as judged by the different yields per acre. The internal physiology of the plants must also have been changed since they were not widely different in chemical analysis, yet served widely differently in the efficiency with which their offerings in bulk served to be converted into meat as mutton.

Viewed more specifically, if the sheep gains are calculated as coming wholly from the two pounds of hay taken a day, the soybean hay from untreated soil made one pound of gain per 9.7 pounds of hay consumed; that soil given phosphate produced a hay of which 5.4 pounds made one pound of sheep; but when the soil was given lime and phosphate as a means of more properly satisfying the soybean plant hunger, then 4.4 pounds of this hay were all that was needed to give one pound of lamb in return. As an economic consideration of the grain needed to supplement the hay, if one puts all the gain on the basis of grain supplement, the grain requirements per pound of animal gain were 4.2, 2.3 and 1.7 pounds according as combined with the hay from the acid soil without treatment, with only phosphate treatment, or with limestone and phosphate as nutrient returns to the soil, respectively. Even if we should not be moved out of sympathy for the animals that are suffering hidden hungers, there are economic bases that bid fair to have consideration for them. In the last analysis, the most economic animal gains can not be made by animals enduring hunger, either visible or invisible.

Rabbits have been used extensively as forage eaters to test the hay crop for its dangers as an inducer of hidden hungers or conversely its efficiency as a producer of healthy animals. This miniature form of livestock is serving as excellent biological assay of the soil's store of plant nutrients. Calcium and phosphorus, in their mobilization in the body from the intestine to the blood stream, to the bones for storage, or in the reverse direction from the skeletal storage into the blood, the body, a foetus, or milk, manifest their deficiencies and unbalanced relations in terms of enlarged parathyroid glands. Here in these small bits of tissue, the soil fertility shortages as calcium and phosphorus are recorded in the same manner as iodine shortages in food are recorded by goiterous developments of the thyroid glands. Post mortem weights of the parathyroid of the rabbit reveal in some measure the magnitude of the hidden hunger of the animal for calcium and phosphorus. They tell of the torment the animal was enduring while confined by a pen or a fence to the quality of forage feed that itself in turn was confined to the low fertility of the soil.

Animal hungers for energy-supplying compounds are not so common as they apparently are for the growth-promoting substances, such as protein that contains nitrogen and phosphorus, and for calcium and other elements going into the plant from the soil. Plants reflect the same shortages, in their changed composition and lowered seed yields, within which the nutrient concentration must be constant to guarantee the next plant generation. When these soil-given nutrients are denied the animal, it may be even possible that the animals are not using their energy foods efficiently. Growth-promoting foods do more than serve as building blocks. Energy-producing foods do more than deliver heat and power. They have interrelated effects. There are suggestions that lime and phosphate on the soil may play some role in aiding the animal metabolism to use its energy supplies more efficiently. This is the suggestion by acetoneaemia in the pregnant cow, by forms of acidosis or incomplete combustion of energy foods, by pregnancy diseases of sheep. When some good green alfalfa hay or an injection into the blood stream of calcium gluconate represent relief for a case of acidosis in conjunction with the animal's body shortage of calcium and phosphorus in foetus building, the question may well be raised why the failure to burn the energy foods can be temporarily relieved by a blood treatment carrying calcium, and cured by feeding a legume that demands so much calcium and phosphorus in making a vitamin-rich forage of itself. Perhaps the efficient body metabolism of burning energy foods is in some way influenced by these growth-promoting foods that are so significant in the soil fertility-plant relations. Further research alone can supply the answers to these questions. Possibly the helps from the soil may make a contribution to their solution.

While the *modus operandi* of our hidden hungers may still be partly unknown, or at least not fully understood, it is consoling to know that much can be done to the nutrient quality of forage feeds for animals and of the vegetables for humans by looking to the soil fertility. Wild animals and our domestic ones, where possible, have exercised unique choices in selecting their herbage with fine degrees of discrimination according to soil treatment. Hogs have demonstrated their choices of the grain according to soil treatments, and it took many years of study and is still a confession to be wrung from some hog feeders with difficulty as Professor Evvard has put it, that "a pig will make a hog of himself in less time — if he is given a change — than we can."

Applications of limestone and phosphate to the soil have been pointing themselves out as the main nutrients involved in animal troubles. It has often been demonstrated by choices of many different animals that we need no longer hesitate to see in these two soil treatments a significant help in making the forage feeds from many soils more efficient for animals in growing their own bodies and in producing their offspring. By the time these become common dosages on soils to relieve plant and animal hungers in the humid soil areas, there may follow shortages of other nutrient items as potassium, magnesium and others to bring up hungers again. If their addition to the soil can set in motion the microbial service within the soil, and the manufacturing business within the plant above the soil to give complete foods, certainly this method of preventing hunger by natural routes working from the ground up will be far more simple than searching for drugstore dosages as antidotes against hungers, bad health and impending death. We need to see in the restoration of the soil a means of demonstrating the age-old truth that an ounce of knowledge applied as prevention is worth libraries of information serving as the pounds of cure.

Conservation of soil fertility and its regular return to restock the soil to the level where it grows its own cover against erosion before erosion is disastrous, needs to be more than ideas. It must be action out on the soil. Our lands given treatments of lime, phosphate, and, in many instances, complete fertilizers, for one or two tilled crops, must regularly be put up for the rest and recuperation under sod crops with their fertility restoring effects. The metabolism within our soil has been over stimulated. While the soil has been burning itself out, the crop quality has declined to bring on hidden hungers. Judicious attention to the soil for the better understanding of it as a complex biochemical performance, and of the plant as an equally complex phenomenon, can offer hope against what today may seem like starvation by degrees. Soil conservation as a national effort has begun to lead our thinking in that direction. Better nutrition is taking us there also. As we get the fuller knowledge about the soil and the role it plays in making Mother Nature a better nurse of us all, our present prodigality toward soil will change to a reverent conservation.

CHAPTER 3

Soils — Their Effects on Nutritional Values of Foods

WHEN NATURE PUTS different species of plants into different places so that grasses grow luxuriantly in some areas, and trees, shrubs and brush in others, she is demonstrating the different plant-nourishing qualities that exist in the soils. Nature produced forests, built primarily of cellulose (woody fibers) with little value as food for warm blooded animals, on the well-watered calcium-deficient soils of the eastern United States. She produced tall grasses on the younger soil of the eastern prairies where the rainfall was moderate; she grew short grasses on the still younger semiarid soils of the western plains.

The American bison, a beast noted for its massive bony structure and great strength, was the animal product characteristic of the plains area soils on which, a generation or so later, wheat was grown that was high in protein and in the mineral elements required to support the manufacture of protein by plants. Protein is an essential food substance, basic in the functioning elements of all animal bodies. The starch also present in the grasses represents only stored energy, and it plays a part in the building of excessive and abnormal fatty layers in domestic animals, fat that is bad for the pocketbook and for the health of the consumer who buys the animal as meat.

Organized knowledge about the locations and relationships of plants, animals, and human beings and their interactions with their environments is the basic outline of the expanding biological science called ecology. Among the chief environmental factors is the pattern of the fertility of the soils which fundamentally maintain all life.

Nature's array of various interrelated life forms has been telling us for countless generations that the soil of each region is best suited to supplying the needs of the specific plant and animal life which thrives in that region. Each of nature's crops (plant or animal) represents a survival of the fittest, determined basically, if there are no disturbing factors, by what the local soil provides in nutrients. This fact was emphasized by Darwin a century ago.

The wisdom of the animal body

Animals search out their feeds for quality in terms of health and growth. They test and choose soils according to the nutritive qualities of the plants which grow on them. That there are soil differences which underlie variations in the nutritional values of crops is indicated every time a cow breaks through the fence to get out of her pasture. She is prompted by more deeply seated causes than a mere desire to get to the other side or to escape confinement.

Careful observation of the cow's misbehavior, as she seeks to eat where she is not supposed to, is very revealing. One finds that usually she is expressing a preference for grass growing on the virgin unharvested soils along the highway or the railroad right-of-way, as compared with the grass growing in the long-used, time-worn soils inside the pasture area. The cow's wisdom in seeking soil that grows feed of high quality carries an important lesson for men. When men moved their grazing animals such as cows, sheep, and goats to the fenced-in well-watered lands now customary, they failed to realize that animal physiology is such that the animals were not necessarily feeding well and living in good health. There were deficiencies, due to the insufficient fertility of the soil in the enclosed pasture areas, and continuing unplanned use of the land often increased the deficiencies and caused additional ones to appear. In due course, farmers often came to face the need of purchasing protein supplements for animal feeding, even for the abnormal castrated animals that are fed only to be fattened for slaughter.

When it comes to judging the nutritive value of various grasses available for feed, appearances may be deceiving. Thus, in a fenced-in, humid grazing field where the soil has been largely depleted, lush green grasses may grow in certain spots fertilized by a cow's droppings, and it might seem to a man that these grasses ought to be desirable and especially nutritious to the cow. But the beast, in its natural wisdom, knows better, and avoids the greener grasses which are not really as nutritious as they seem. (See Figure 1.)

Fig. 1. Although the hummocks of grass in this field appeared lush and green, the cow which fed here instinctively preferred the surrounding forage which, as explained in the text, was more nutritious despite its less succulent appearance. (Photo by G. E. Smith, Department of Soils, University of Missouri.)

In current agricultural practice, there is often an attempt to grow dark-green grasses of the sort that the cow does not prefer by fertilizing humid soils with chemical nitrogen. We labor under the delusion that a higher concentrations of nitrogen in the fertilized vegetation is proof that the grass must contain higher concentrations of protein, but unfortunately, protein is not fully measured by nitrogen content, which may be but a crude and unreliable chemical symbol of the nutritive quality of feeds. Those who contend that the crude protein in the grass grown by such fertilization with nitrogen duplicates the nutritional quality of the protein which is grown by legumes fail to manifest the wisdom exhibited by the cow.

On the semi-humid soils of the Plains and Western Prairies, the cow's droppings as fertilizers do not exhibit the disturbing effects that have been mentioned on the growth of the grasses, nor on the cow's choice of food, and no dark green spots in the pasture are in evidence. On the dryer soils, under only low to moderate rainfalls to change the character of the soil, little organic fertility has been leached away. Plenty of plant-nutritive material is left to balance the added nitrogen. The crops actually growing, on account of the scant rainfall, have not acted to remove important elements of the fertility supply.

Soil Quality, Not Plant Pedigree Alone, Determines the Nutrient Balance in a Crop

Those who contend that a given plant does as well on any soil on which it grows as it would on another soil except for the volume or weight of crop produced, have a wrong understanding of the nature of plant inheritance. In one experiment, potassium (potash), recognized as an essential factor for the plant's production of carbohydrate and needed often for increased yield of plant material, was added in various amounts to all but one of four plots of soil which were otherwise alike. Seeds from the same mother plant were used to give a constant genetic background. Of three crops, the first was not given legume bacteria for nodule production, while the seeds for the other two were treated with bacteria which established prominent root nodules.

In terms of crop yields, the first crop was a bountiful one, varying in quantity with the amount of applied potash. Nevertheless, in terms of total nitrogen, it gave back no more in the total crop (both tops and roots) than what was in the seed originally planted.

The second crop took nitrogen from the atmosphere to increase nitrogen in the plants over the total in the planted seed. However, the third crop did not give more nitrogen than was present in its seeds because removal of the tops and roots of the plants had *depleted the soil* to such an extent that even with the root nodules, the third crop was not able to utilize atmospheric nitrogen. The third crop gave larger yields of dry matter (plant material with moisture removed) than the second. Although the seeds for the second and third crops were identical in every way, *nutritional properties of the crops were quite different because of differing soil characteristics.*

In the same experiment, measurements were also made of the amounts of sugar and starch in the various crops. The results (see Figure 2) show that within each group of identical and identically treated seeds, characteristics of the *soil* had an important effect on the proportions of sugar and starch in the crops. (In the diagram, "B" and "C" indicate the seeds that were inoculated with nodule-forming bacteria; the "A" seeds were not so treated.)

These observations show the serious error of those who argue that soil is of no importance in determining the nutritional value of the crops grown on it. It *is* the soil which determines nutritional value. The genetic factor present in the seed and transmitted to the growing plant merely sets limits to the range of variations the soil factors can produce. To argue, as have government officials, that the soil, however deficient in natural fertility, is of no significance in determining the quality of the crop is a confession of misinformation, not of scientific knowledge.

Animals, Too, are Greatly Affected by Soils

Experimental work with rabbits has shown that the body growth of the animals and their body physiology, even the maintenance of sexual vigor, varied according to differences in the fertility of the soil on which crops for their feed were grown.

Tests were made with hay grown on soil with no nitrogen, and other hay grown on companion lots, otherwise the same, which were treated with various sized doses of commercial fertilizer nitrogen.

In repeated trials with lots of five rabbits (two males and three females), the animals were offered for choice equal amounts of four different hays along with constant quantities of corn. The rabbits regularly chose to consume the most hay from the check plot which had no nitrogen treatment, and consumed decreasing amounts of the hay crops that had been grown with larger amounts of chemical nitrogen used as fertilizer. Thus the rabbits demonstrated an ability to recognize differences in the nutritive values of the several crops grown on differently fertilized soils. Naturally enough, the animals which chose to eat less hay showed smaller gains in weight than the others. Thus the properties of the soil samples had an indirect but definite effect on the characteristics of the animals fed with the forage grown on them.

The data indicated that the animals were struggling with poor nutrition and body growth and avoided the supposed protein supplement in the form of the artificial high nitrogen content in the hay, which, though it was nitrogen, did not correspond to the high quality protein which they needed. The unbalanced nutritional quality of the feed obtained by some of the rabbits even produced sexual infertility, which was not present when the animals were on a diet which was known to be complete for growth.

The facts that have been outlined will be observed in nature by those who do not have preconceived ideas about plant growth. The professional agriculturist unfortunately often views the effects of soils on the growth of plants with a distant outlook, as if the only problems were those of industrial manipulation of dead materials, with emphasis on the various technologies for *economic* advantages only. People who approach agricultural research in this way have lost sight of agriculture as a biological demonstration by the forces of nature, where man is more a spectator than a manager in complete control of soil and produce.

Such unrealistic views of agriculture have led to the expressions by high governmental officials of the view that soil is but a chemical and physical agent for the production of larger quantities of crops; they seem unaware that the soil of our planet is a complex material developed through many centuries, having the power of creation, not only for plants, but for everything that lives, moves and has its being upon the earth.

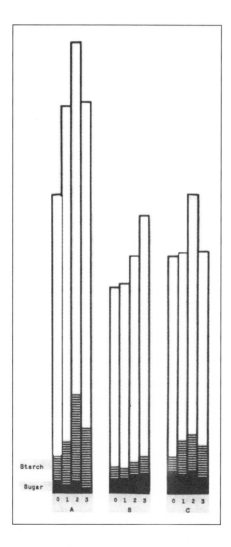

Fig. 2. The three groups of bar graphs show the effects of different soil treatments on three successive crops of soy beans. The height of each bar indicates the total yield of dry matter from a given quantity of seed. The solid section at the bottom of each bar represents the amount of sugar in the crop as determined by analysis, and the cross-lined section represents the amount of starch. Within each group the seeds used were identical, and the soils used were identical except for increasing amounts of added potassium proportional to the numbers, 0, 1, 2, 3, shown at the bottoms of the bars in each group. Note that differences in soil treatment affect not only the total yields but also the relative ratios of sugar and starch to each other and to the total yields. This demonstrates clearly that characteristics of the soil do have a marked effect in determining the nutritional qualities of the foods grown on it.

CHAPTER 4

Soil Builders Build Better Cattle

YOU TOO, like many others, may have been asking, "Just what do we mean when we say better soils; better for what?" Grazing on one soil may be better for growing the calves while on another soil it may be better for fattening older animals. Pastures are too commonly considered as good merely because they are providing considerable tonnage per acre of certain crops. We are coming, however, to see that feed quality depends on the soil fertility, and those cattlemen who are rebuilding and maintaining their soils are also building better cattle.

As agronomists, we have been juggling the various grazable crops into many schemes of crowded successions of them in their seasonal propriety. Then, too, when the better forages of longstanding reputation for high feed quality, like alfalfa and red clover that are commonly reputed to be "hard to grow," have been failing, we have taken to the search for, and the importation of, other crops to replace them. If these immigrant substitutes produce tonnage where their predecessors fail in this measure, we seemingly hail the newcomer as a grand success.

Our eyes have been fixed on the crop, on its tons of forage, and on its bushels of grain. Our eyes and minds have not gone deeper. They have not looked below the crop to recognize the soil and its insufficient delivery of fertility as the possible reasons why bluegrass pasture, for example, does not come on early in the spring; why it fails to carry well into the summer before it becomes weedy; why alfalfa does not yield more heavily and last longer before grasses take it; and why the cattle and other livestock don't do as well as they once did. Our measures of better pasture crops have been only quantitative. They must also be qualitative.

In feeding the cattle and other domestic animals, we have thought mainly of the question "How much?" and not often enough of "How well?" We have seen each pasture as a certain crop variety and the bulk it produces. We are just coming around to recognize that it is the soil and its fertility that determines the quality or nutritive value as feed which any crop variety can attain. We are coming to see that it is the better — the more fertile — soils that are the better grazing in terms of carrying more animals per acre, more animal growth per ton of feed, more animals in terms of better reproduction, and a better business in total.

Increased grazing pressure that brought a decline in soil fertility because of the decreasing return of organic matter to the soil has resulted in mesquite coming into this once cattleman's paradise. The upper photograph was taken in 1903 while the same pasture as it appeared in 1943 is shown below.

— Photographs courtesy of U.S. Forest Service.

It has been the discriminating selection by the animals, as we observed them grazing one part of a field given soil treatments in preference to another not so handled, that has slowly brought us to think about using and depending more on the animal's judgment of the quality of the forage. We have been slow to believe that a calf given the chance will make a cow of itself quickly. Yet for hogs we are generally following that very belief as Prof. J. M. Evvard of Iowa, the inventor of the self-feeder, gave it to us when he said, "If you will give the pig a chance it will make a hog of itself in less time than you will."

Cow Before Plow in Westward March

We have been too prone to think of the grazing herds as mowing machines when, more significantly, they are physiologists and not economists or farm managers. They are not concerned with tonnage production per acre, nor are they disturbed by a slow rate of their laying on of fat. On the contrary, they are searching for mineral-rich, protein-rich forages that give good body growth, of strong bone, of much muscle and of fecund reproduction for maintenance of their species. We have failed to observe their breaking through the fence in the spring, not to go from one cultivated field to another, but instead to go from a cultivated field to the unfarmed highway and to the untilled railroad right-of-way where the virgin soils are growing grass crops that manufacture more than just woody bulk.

Our cattle are trying to tell us that, (a) the fertility of our soils is declining, (b) that crops are less proteinacious and less mineral-rich as a consequence, and (c) that the better quality of the feeds must be grown into them from the soil and not thrown in from the chemist's shop. They are passing judgment, quite different from the way we do, primarily on the soil and secondarily on the varieties of the crop.

Changes from Lowered Soil Fertility

The declining soil fertility has been responsible for shifts downward of the protein and mineral concentrations within the crops more common formerly. It has been responsible for shifts to newer kinds of them imported without recognition of the low fertility of the soils growing them indigenously. The declining soil fertility has been pushing the hard wheat, that is, the high-protein wheat, westward. It has brought the soft wheat, that is, the starchy or highly carbonaceous wheat, following behind it. It has pushed the cattle and the sheep, that is, the animals of highly lean carcasses, farther west. It has left the hogs, as highly fat carcasses, trailing them in this westward march of livestock.

When Kansas City recently became the major cattle market of the United States did it occur to you that declining soil fertility on the longer-farmed soils farther east meant that crops not higher in protein but consisting primarily of the carbohydrates high in fattening value became predominant. Lower levels of soil fertility in the more acid, and, therefore of necessity, less fertile, soils of the Eastern United States have pushed the grass-eating, domestic animals westward. It has crowded them more and more into that longitudinal soil belt where that native herbivorous feeder, the buffalo, had selected the soil fertility that grew him well and multiplied him to the large numbers in the thundering herds reported by the forty-niners. He was not a synthesizer of fats. He was a builder of bone and brawn.

Barley planted in this field was first grazed in the areas where the drill had turned around in finishing the corners thus nearly doubling the amount of fertilizer applied. These areas were grazed closely while the rest of the barley in the field was disregarded. This photograph was taken by E.M. Poirot, Golden City, Mo.

Herefords and Hard Wheat

Take the soil map, if you will, of the United States and also the map of the population of Herefords to see on what soil areas they are concentrated. You will note that they and the hard wheat are together in our mid-continent. Do we not see that our less-leached, more calcareous soils give high-protein wheat, make mineral-rich and protein-rich other grasses, and thereby can grow animals — rather than merely put on fat — today as in the virgin past? Can we see a soil-fertility pattern outlining the growth-power for cattle and sheep centered in one natural soil area of lesser rainfall and less bulk of crops, while in another soil area of higher rainfall and much tonnage of forage per acre there is located the fattening power?

The soil-fertility picture on the map and the pattern of livestock distribution of the United States demonstrate the cattle growing themselves on the lime-laden, more fertile soils, or on those not highly leached, while they are fattening themselves on the acid or more severely leached soils. This same relation is verified in Argentina, in the Australia-New Zealand area, and in South Africa. All of these are in the temperate zones with the specific climatic soil pattern duplicating that of the United States.

Building Soils to Build Cattle

If it was the declining soil fertility, in spite of the calcium now going back in limestone in the eastern United States as correction for the increasing failures of legume crops, that started the beef cattle marching westward, we might well ask whether that march is still in progress. For a positive answer to this question one needs only recall that the grazing troubles, and breeding difficulties are not new today in what was once the buffalo plains. One needs only to recall bulls of impossible reproductive powers in verification.

Soils under the low annual rainfalls in the temperate zone have meant grass that grows animals efficiently. But it has also meant small annual tonnages in the crops of grass. Unfortunately we have not taken cognizance of the soil fertility conditions by which the virgin grass makes beef cattle grow well and reproduce well. Such nutritious grass is produced from the fertility released by mineral breakdown and by the decaying organic matter. It was stocked in the soil from the countless crops of virgin grasses that had dropped back to build up that rotating supply of nitrogen and mineral fertility. Rainfall is sufficient to decay the organic matter, but too little rain comes to break down much rock or minerals annually and to bring it out from the unavailable forms.

An early spring invitation to livestock is the green clover on one side of the fence. No temptation is offered by the broom sedge, still dry and drab, on the other side. Treatments that built up the soil to a level that would support clover made the difference. Photograph taken at the farm of James Evans in Boone County, Missouri.

This situation under intensive grazing means rapid depletion of the organic store of fertility. When cattle are harvesting the grass, they carry off its high-protein and high-mineral contents instead of allowing these to drop back to the soil in their cycle of keeping good grass growing by means of the organic matter assembly line of the soil.

Heavy Grazing Depletes Fertility

Increased grazing pressure on the "short grass" country is depleting rapidly the active fertility in the accumulated organic matter. Short-rooted grasses in shallow surface soils soon find too little nitrogen and mineral fertility from which they can manufacture their former high concentration of proteins and mineral complexes within themselves. In their stead there come deeply rooted plants. Those that can penetrate down extensively enough to find minerals sufficient for wood making in a sparse population of tree or bush crops, and being legumes, as many of them like the mesquite are for example, can provide enough nitrogen from the air and the little in the soil to give them their slow growth. Even in the grass country, the good grass, too, is on a westfard march seemingly with the mesquite following in its trail.

Hereford Herd Built by Soil Builder

While our cattle population is seemingly being pushed westward as the declining fertility is crowding out the nutritious grass, and while mesquite and broom sedge are coming in, this is not the universal situation. There are plenty of cattle growers on farms where attention is going to the fertility of the soil.

The reader can think of some Here-ford breeder, perhaps, just as we can, who spent 50 or more years in building a wellknown herd. In his late years the man I have in mind found his cows becoming shy breeders. Their top lines suggested soreness in the back as it was up and the head down. Their coats were less glossy and, worst of all, less callers were coming to purchase his surplus.

His experience as a cattle breeder, through study of pedigrees and purchases of bulls, had built itself up well. But his appreciation of the declining soil fertility of his farm had not grown sufficiently for him to realize that while he was pushing his cattle breeding upward, the internal strength of his soil — the foundation supporting both him and his herd — was letting him down. It should have been no surprise that buyers of young Herefords were passing him by and going only a few miles farther to another Hereford herd. Perhaps we should say the same herd, since part of his herd was purchased by a novice farmer and hopeful cattlemen who as a city business man, found himself with some land suddenly on his hands.

This newcomer, who was started in the cattle business by this "old timer's" surplus of one year, had treated the grassland as well as the tilled soil of his farm with limestone and other fertilizers. He brought his soil up to the fertility level that was needed to produce alfalfa. He was subscribing to the belief that mineral-rich, protein-rich forages would grow better cattle. He was convinced that if he built fertility into the soil it would build the cattle for him.

In testimony of the soundness of his judgment, his cows are not shy breeders. His entire calf crop comes during a short season. This simplifies management. His calves are a uniform lot. The animals are active, of good body lines, and easily kept in fine condition. He is filling the market now that his near-by colleague formerly filled. These two are cases where disregard of the soil fertility of his farm put one man out, while restoring and maintaining the soil fertility of his farm put the other man in and gave him the market reputation for that community. Building the soil built his cattle business.

Outgoing Fertility as Weeds Come

Weeds in our pastures are evidence of the neglect of the soils. They are crops that are manufacturing so little of feed value that the cattle disregard them. It is necessary to support the palatable herbage by soil fertility to enable these crops to manufacture what complexes of carbohydrate and protein nature the cattle must have in order to get energy and build their protein-containing tissues. When cattle are confined by fences, we need to appreciate our responsibility of providing all the nutrient essentials in such a limited area which the animals ranging over much more territory are collecting by means of their discriminating choices.

If the eye of the master is to fatten the flock, he must see (a) the fertility of the soil, (b) the nutritive quality of the herbage in terms of it, and (c) the selective grazing behaviors of the animals as they condemn or approve his judgment and management of the first two of these three essentials in cattle growing. He must see that the animals are selecting according to the nutrient values of the feeds and not according to the particular crop variety or the tonnage per acre.

We are thinking much about soil conservation as it is calling for grass cover to keep the soil from washing away. But when we ask the cows to eat that grass cover, it is far more important to think of the nutritive quality in terms of soil fertility of the soil growing that protection. If the soil is built up in fertility it will grow its own cover quickly. It will granulate itself. This improved soil structure lets water go in rather than off. Soil so improved holds its granular form in spite of the rain. It takes in more water. It extends the grazing season at both ends. It grows a feed of quality that makes healthier and more fecund animals.

If we are going to conserve our soil, the restoration of its fertility is the first step. By this we shall grow grass quickly and abundantly of such feed quality which grows cattle too. The conservation of the soil almost will be incidental. By starting to think and to work on the fertility, the men who build up their soils through a grass agriculture will be building up good cattle at the same time.

CHAPTER 5

Our Livestock — Cooperative Chemists

IN HIS STUDIES and world travels extending over twenty years or more and reported under the title1 "The Origin of Species," Sir Charles Darwin emphasized the many details by which each life form seemed to fit into the several supporting factors which characterized the environment. His studies prompted the lessening importance of the pedigree, however regal, and the increasing emphasis on environment, particularly the nutrition, as a factor determining the healthy survival of any species.

His publication, of more than a century ago, resulted from what one pair of eyes could see and one mind could organize about causes and effects. That memorable research occurred almost unaided by any of the techniques presently extending our visions of the animal physiology as that can be supported by the many crops which grow on the farm, or are available as feed (and medicine) in the market place. Darwin summed up, on a broad scale, the cause and effect relations between the soil that creates the plants and thereby the animals consuming them. Vice versa, there are also the effects of animal manures on the soils and the plants, as one of the cycles in Nature's conservation. We are, but slowly, coming to recognize what Darwin called "The struggle to survive." We need to appreciate that struggle, exhibited even by our animals under domestication and to recognize all that is included in his expression "The healthy survival of the fit."

Age-old facts. The basic principles, according to which every kind of life today becomes fit and able to survive, are no different than those in control in Darwin's time. Each kind, whether microbe, plant, animal or man must be nourished well enough, (a) to grow a healthy body; (b) to protect that from diseases as well as from predators; and (c) to reproduce its kind with prolificacy. Nourishment equal to that responsibility depends, in simplest consideration, on the fertility of the soil making up the environment of the species.

As livestock owners, we need to remind ourselves that during the past ages all wildlife has been searching out and balancing the items of its diets. Those include water, carbohydrates, proteins, inorganic essentials, various vitamins and possibly many other organic and inorganic essentials, yet unknown. That instinctive search by the individual has demonstrated a success in the health of the wildlife species which certainly transcends that allowed our hogs, for example, which Professor Loeffel of Nebraska College of Agriculture told us "bring in a new disease about every two years."[1]

Accordingly, when the wild animals are such capable connoisseurs in feeding themselves for their good health; and when our domestic ones in reaching across, and then breaking through, the fence to get to feed on the grass on virgin soil along roads and railroads are telling us that they have not lost a similar instinct after centuries under domestication; should we not follow and pay tribute to the animal's ability for assaying its own feeds? It was years ago when Professor John Evvard of Iowa paid his tribute to that rare ability of the hog when he said, "If you will give the pig a chance, it will make a hog of itself in less time than you will."

Natural Laws. When the herds and flocks of the primitives and pioneers moved from good feed for themselves to more of it as chosen nutrition for their fitness to survive, their master followed their crooked pathways in his confidence and success of survival of himself and his family. He accepted their capabilities as biochemists (mainly ruminants) assaying the higher qualities of the crops established naturally by the balanced fertility of the soils to which the animals led him for the succession of harvests from seasons to seasons. He survived because of this animals as cooperative chemists whose judgements he accepted. History has some valuable lessons here.

A discussion of those lessons from livestock divides itself logically into four parts based on the following facts:

I. Our Domestic Animals, as Well as Wildlife, Are Struggling to Comply With the Evolutionary Laws Controlling Their Healthy Survival.

II. The Chemical Composition, i.e., The Nutritional Value, of Our Feedcrops and Products Therefrom. Varies According to the Balance

---

[1] *A late announcement cites hemophilia (bleeding disease) of hogs as a new disease. Missouri Farm News Service, 53: No. 27, March 4, 1964.*

and Inbalances of Their Plant Diets Available in the Fertility Elements and the Organic Matter of the Soils.

III. Feed Choices by the Animals Represent Their Reported Bioassays of the Effects by the Soil Fertility on the Nutritional Qualities Grown Into the Crop and Not on Its Yields per Acre.

IV. Animals Are Connoisseurs of Feeds for Their Health With Successes Transcending Those of the Laboratory Chemist, Prone to Emphasize "Crude" Protein.

If we are to "sell" our crops to our livestock for the price of their good health, must we not consider their choice for that result in which they have demonstrated so much more wisdom than we have?

I. Climatic Pattern of Differing Degrees by Which Rocks are Developed Into Soils Gives the Pattern of Animal Distribution

Cattle. The geographic location in good numbers of any particular animal species gives us also the location of soils growing feed crops which meet amply the animals' nutritional requirements of proteins as well as of carbohydrates and other items of a good ration. Beef cattle production in the United States duplicates the geographic area where the American Bison was naturally most concentrated. That is the area along the longitudinal line between the soils of the Prairies and the Great Plains. That marks out their adherence to regions of virgin grasses, mainly the short ones.

But in terms of the soils creative potential for proteins, they were staying on those with annual rainfalls of near 25 inches. That is where the rocks and minerals have not been excessively developed as are those under higher rainfalls which produce scant protein but mainly carbohydrates as do soils growing forest crops. The climatic forces of 25 inches of rainfall have not depleted the soil of major available nutrient elements like calcium, magnesium, potassium and others. Instead, the soils still carry ample reserves of them in the pulverized rocks to be weathered sufficiently during the growing season. That mineral reserve is renewed periodically also by the dust storms. These make deposits on the soil's surface of unweathered, well-mixed, silt minerals brought along by the Missouri River deposits in its winter-dried flood plains to be picked up there or from drier areas to the West.

Thus, the organic matter in the grassy sods is an effective weathering agent. By its decay, coupled with the mineral, or loessial, deposits on the land surface, there is the regular renewal of high-protein potential in the crops. While those effects may have been viewed as scant ones in forage yields per acre, the abundance of the crop yields is not the criterion of choice by the beasts which take to grass on naturally fertile, still highly-calcareous soils producing legumes abundantly among other native vegetation. It is on such soils, delineated by the buffalo, where our choice protein food of beef grows itself. Such was a Western cattleman's implication when he said, "No we don't grow beef cattle, we only count them."

Pigs. While the area in the United States where beef grows is naturally to the west of the 98th meridian of longitude and under lower rainfalls, the area growing the pigs is to the east of that line and under higher precipitation. Our porkers mark out the more highly developed soils east of a line

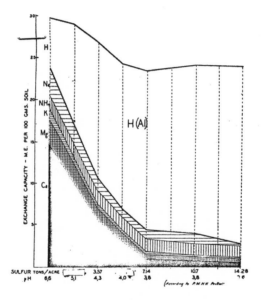

Fig. 1. Losses of available nutrients (calcium, Ca; magnesium, Mg; potassium, K; ammonium, NH4; sodium, Na) and of total exchange capacity (T) with increasing development of a soil given sulfur (Schwefelmenge) as increasing tons per acre but decreasing pH values under high rainfall (leaching).

Even the first two units of sulfur brought about (a) losses of Ca-50%; Mg-70%; K-50%; NH4-40%; Na-60%; total exchange capacity-8%; and (b) increase of hydrogen (aluminum) saturation from 20 to 68 percent. Each vertical line, considered as the ratios of the vertical elements, shows the changes in those to each other, most markedly to the decreasing calcium and to the increasing acidity (hydrogen saturation), as the soil was more highly developed.

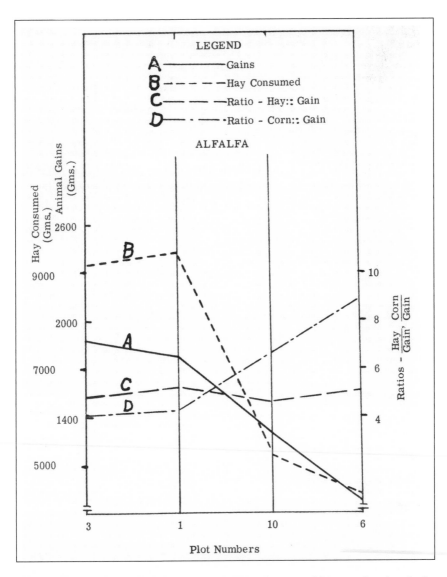

Fig. 2. *The amounts of alfalfa hay consumed by the test-rabbits put the plots in the same order as in the preceding tests of choice amongst four alfalfa hay samples from different soil treatments. The gains in weight follow the amounts of hay consumed. There are the nearly constant ratios of hay taken to gains, even if in some cases the rabbits held consumption near saturation. Also, the ratio of corn to gain was higher as the quality of hay (by rabbit choice) was lower. The rabbits voted in opposition to the soil manager's choices of soil treatments for bigger yields of alfalfa hay per acre. (Data from Mo. Agr. Expt. Station.)*

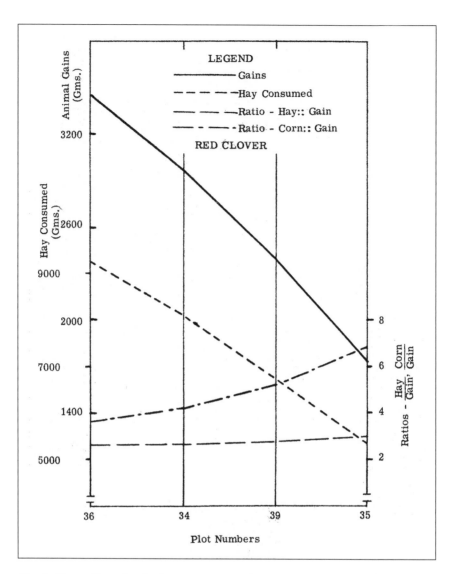

Fig. 3. Test-rabbits, by the hays consumed, duplicated the order of their choices of the same hays according to soil treatments growing the red clover samples (Sanborn Field, 4-yr. rotation since 1888). The gains by the weanlings were closely related to the amounts of hay eaten. There was nearly a constant ratio between hay taken and resulting gains with more of the latter as the choice was higher. According as the quality by animal choice went lower, so the ratio of corn to gain went higher. The weanling animals preferred to gain as the protein quality of the legume hay determined by choice, rather than to fatten by the corn as the carbohydrate part of the ration.

extending from the western edge of Minnesota to the southern tip of Texas. That line divides our "pedocal" soils (high in calcium or lime) from the "pedalfers" (high in acid-, aluminum-, and iron-clays).

Born, as our pigs are, for a short life-span of near six months, sorely beset by prompt castration and rapid onset of a severe case of obesity, they serve prominently as an economic fit (not necessarily a naturally healthy one) into the eastern mid-continent. That is the climatic soil setting where corn as an excessively high-carbohydrate diet for the fattening pigs (much as it is for France's Strasburger geese of "pate de foie gras" fame), is blended with the minimum of protein supplements. That practice gives us a ton-litter per sow-mother and much-desired farm mortgage lifter in the hog's brief life time of a half-year. It is that same region of the hog to which the cattle come from the West for a duplicate fattening treatment or "finishing" experience. They are the quickly-accepted companions of the hogs following in close company to which the ruminants give delectable dietary supplements of ample vitamin B12 and possibly other similar fecal contents of values not yet catalogued.

Limited Area. The mid-continent is a limited area, but has the unique climatic forces developing soils which grow both proteins and carbohydrates in its West, but mainly carbohydrates only in its East. This mid-continent is our country's great natural food asset. About ninety percent of its soils are in farms. Under recent technological soil treatments, many of them have pushed up their grain yields for feed concentrates as much as one hundred percent. Surprisingly too, that area is the most efficient in radio reception. That is a natural correlation with healthy plants chosen as feed for healthy animals when that means of wireless communication by electrical phenomena finds its higher efficiency on the fertile and more productive soils which are, by that character, simultaneously better conductors of electricity for broadcasting. Also in terms of the most universal human ailment, tooth decay, the mid-continent has the lowest numbers of caries of teeth per human mouth.

The figures for those increase on going both to the west and to the cast of that unique agricultural soil area.[2]

When the feed choices of warm-blooded animals seem to fit them so healthily into their environment; and when the lowly and fixed forms of life exhibit a similar natural relation between their healthy existence and

---

[2] *Wm. A. Albrecht. Our Teeth and Our Soils. Ann. of Dentistry, 6:199-213, 1942. Also Mo. Agr. Expt. Sta. Cir. 333. 1948.*

the degree of soil development under particular climatic forces; must we not recognize those many interrelations and the interdependencies of all life forms (including livestock) all resting on the soil as the creative force and foundation?[3] Accordingly, isn't it high time to consider managing the health of farm animals by managing fertile soils for protein according as the carefully observed choices by animals (and our soil test arranged for such) make suggestions? Likewise, must we not guard against pollutions of the environment, so common when man takes over the extensive management of that also, but under emphasis on the advantages of economics and technologies and disregard of the biotic requisites of the many life forms which help to feed him?

II. Nutritional Value of Feed Crops Depends on Organic and Inorganic Fertility of Soils Growing Them

Proteins vs. Carbohydrates. The soil's control of the chemical composition of the crop it grows transcends any guarantee of nutritional value as feed by the pedigree of the planted seed. Our plants, like the animals, are also struggling for proteins by which they grow, protect themselves and reproduce. They, too, require a balanced diet, i.e. of soil fertility in definite portions, if they are to be healthy enough to survive.

When our main concern has been about crops for their big yields of bulk and so little concern has gone to their nutritional value, we would little appreciate the natural law which tells us that as our soils vary in their degree of development, so they deliver varied plant compositions, either (a) as one of largely carbohydrates with mainly fattening feed values for older animals on highly humid soils, or (b) as one of both carbohydrates and ample proteins with many other nutritional uplifts connected with the latter as nutritional guarantee of growing younger animals on the semi-humid and semi-arid soils.

Calcium vs. Potassium. As a simple illustration of the above law, there is the balance of calcium (magnesium), which is a relatively high requirement by crops growing on soils under 25- inch or less rainfall, against that of potassium. The requirement of the latter is relatively high by crops growing

---

[3]*Those interdependencies of the life forms rather than only on the physical forces may well be expected when "it took less than an hour to make the atoms, a few (say three hundred million years to make the stars and their planets, but three billion years to make man." George Gamow. The Creation of the Universe. The American Library, 501 Madison Avenue, New York 22, New York.*

on humid soil in contrast to their demands for calcium, when yet they emphasize big yields of crop bulk under ample rain as water for such. It is commonly granted by the farmers, that calcium is important in growing legume crops of high - protein and rich - mineral contents. That is a natural fact well established by laboratory and field research. That potassium is physiologically important in the plant's synthesis and mobilization of its carbohydrates is an equally well established natural fact. Accordingly, the higher concentration of protein in the natural vegetation bespeaks a much higher supply of available calcium (magnesium) than of available potassium in the soil. The effects of that higher ratio of the former to the latter in the soil fertility are modified by the soil's supply of active phosphorus and particularly the latter's association with soil organic matter. Thus, the plant nutrition from the soil, in either balance or imbalance, decides in the main whether the nutritional feed value we grow is one for either growing healthy young livestock or mainly for fattening older animals.

Chemical analyses of crops grown commonly, (a) on the slightly developed soils under scant rainfall of the West, (b) on those moderately developed ones in the mid-continent, and (c) on those highly developed soils of the Northeast and the Southeast, have mean percentage contents of calcium (CaO) in the following respective order, (a) 1.92, (b) 1.17 and (c) 0.28. If we set the values for calcium and potassium in the highly developed soils (c) at unity or the value of one, then the respective values for contents of calcium for the differently developed soils become (a) 6.8, (b) 4.1 and (c) 1.0, while for potassium they are (a) 1.9, (b) 1.6 and (c) 1.0. These latter two sets of figures tell us that as a promoter of protein production in the forages of the slightly developed soils of the West, the calcium in the soil is in a wide ratio to the potassium there as it is also in the forages. Consequently, when the calcium weathers out of the soil relatively so much faster than does the potassium, that natural fact moves the crops from those of higher protein and nutritional contents to those of lower ones. It brings in the call for protein supplements, even for fattening purposes.

When plants merely pile up carbohydrates, they build big yields of crops as bulk. But in growing proteins, they burn much of the carbohydrates to accomplish the syntheses of them. They also use the carbohydrates as starter compounds for that process. High nutritional values are not naturally associated with big yields as the natural rule.

The above relation of declining concentrations of protein in the crops to the higher rate of depletion of the calcium than of the potassium in the soil was shown by an experiment. A highly fertile soil given increasing applications of elemental sulfur and exposed to leaching conditions of humid soils decreased the ratios of available calcium to potassium very decidedly and of that calcium to each of the other nutrients measured (Figure I).

The significance in modifying the crop's composition shown here by the balance and imbalance between only two of the nutrient elements, viz. calcium and potassium, can be expected as well between any pairs, triples, or more of the essential nutrients listed to date. Research is multiplying to report such variations in compositions of crops due to soil treatments reported promptly by animal choices and discriminations. Those are also being verified by biochemical tests even to variation in amounts of amino acids as measures of the completeness of the proteins as nutrition. Only a few reports about interactions of nutrient elements recognized in the soil, in the plants and the animals will be given here.

Potassium and Sodium. Since these two are monovalent alkali elements and highly soluble, they are not held strongly as part of the proteins within the cell. They are, therefore, in its liquid contents and outside of it. They influence other elements highly. In the husbandman's language "The plant gorges itself with potassium." It is accumulated in the cells more rapidly and to a higher degree than the bivalent calcium and magnesium.

If one makes up a nutrient solution of equivalent concentrations of potassium, sodium, calcium and magnesium, their respective uptakes will be widely different should one use five plants like buckwheat, sunflower, maize (corn), potato and plantain (marine), as has been reported.[4] The percentage of the plant's total cations made up by each element will vary widely amongst those crops, as do the totals. Sodium, as the percentages in the plants listed above varied from 0.9 to 28.5; potassium from 39.0 to 70.0; calcium from 11. to 33.; and magnesium from 11 to 27.

That the cells of the plant tissue are each a biochemical institution in its own rights is further shown when the roots of one plant exclude sodium while those of another take it abundantly. Yet the plant that excluded sodium took magnesium two and one-half times as abundantly as the one that took sodium so generously. Maize (corn) was the highest in uptake and concentration of potassium but lowest in calcium. That dilemma in quality is a sequel to our selection of that crop for the maximum of vegetative bulk resulting from maximum output of carbohydrates but the mini-

---

[4] *Runar Collander. Selective Absorption of Cations by Higher Plants. Plant Physiology 16: 16:691-780. 1941.*

mum of proteins; all with little of nutritional value as growth potential for young animals.

Most grasses duplicate corn in its luxury consumption of potassium. Consequently, the herbivora may ingest per day 500-600 gms. of the element potassium which is 10 to 12 times their requirements. On the other hand, the amount of sodium ingested rarely exceeds half of the requirements, according to studies in the Netherlands.[5] Accordingly, herbivora excrete significant quantities (85 percent of uptake) of potassium, mainly in the urine, to raise the active potassium in the surface soil layer.

Potassium tends to reduce magnesium absorption by the animal unless the forage is high in the latter. But its absorption is favored if the forage contains liberal concentrations of phosphates and/or crude proteins (nitrogen). The reduction of magnesium absorption is encouraged also by low sodium in the feed, but saponins (soaps) in plants have the opposite effects.[6]

As additional elements, calcium and magnesium demonstrate their interplays and antagonisms with the plant's nutrition and that of the animal. High concentrations of calcium in the forage usually raises the needs for magnesium. These two as exchangeable amounts in the soil are recommended in a ratio of at least seven of calcium to one of magnesium. So, similarly, high calcium in the feed raises the need for magnesium. This need is accentuated as the phosphorus there is higher. The increased concentration of phosphorus also modifies the effects of the ratio of calcium to potassium.

Balance for Plants, Thereby for Animals. Imbalances, and interactions in the soil which modify the nutrition of the plants and consequently of the animals by other sets of elements might be cited. But the preceding ones are sufficient to remind us that every plant is; (a) limited to drawing carbon for nutrition in photosynthesis of carbohydrates from a small zone in the atmosphere according to diffusion and air transportation; and, (b) confined to that limited soil volume encompassed by the extent of roots' contact for requisites of all other synthetic processes. It, too, is struggling to be nourished by a balanced diet of (a) inorganic or "ash" elements and (b) organic compounds of its own synthesis and of such by both fungi and bacteria within the root zone and the rhizosphere of the limited root surface.

It is the microbes, within those soils containing ample organic matter, that correct and alleviate imbalances and antagonistic effects between the

---

[5] B. Sjollema et al. Investigations into Hypo. magnesemia in Bovines. Tydschr. Diergeneesh 80:579-604, 1111-1134, 1955.

[6] Andre Voisin. Grass Tetany. Part II. "Mineral Balances of Soil and Mineral Balances of Grass." Crosby Lockwood and Son Ltd., London. 1963.

several nutrient elements when excessively ionic effects occur from any one of high solubility. Such high availability makes it quickly taken over by the microbes in advance of its uptake by the plants. It is put by them into organic compounds exhibiting its non-ionic behavior because of chelation into larger molecular units. That is a unique service in plant disease prevention by the soil microbes scarcely appreciated when we are so prone to believe microbes the causes of disease. According as we keep provoking the soil microbes into hasty and excessive consumption of the reserve soil organic matter through use of salt fertilizers, the soil's buffering capacities against our imbalanced treatments will be reduced to where the hidden dangers to healthy animal nutrition will become more baffling. We do not yet appreciate the soil microbes as shock absorbers via soil organic matter as the counter-acting energy source.

III. Discrimination Between Feeds Reports Animal Assays of Nutritional Values According to Soils Growing Them

Choice — A Natural Phenomenon. Any grazing animal is a natural phenomenon of one form of life struggling to survive. It is not a demonstration, so much, of our capable management. Wild animals do not choose to be fattened when that is a sickening process which we admit so widely when in case the human struggle to survive it results in obesity and the sextette of degenerative ailments which are a sequel of it.[7] Why does an animal first reach over and then break through the fence to the highway or railroad right of way? Isn't it the higher quality of feed offered by the virgin soils and so reported by the beast that risks its life in demonstrating its choice by going there?

Conversely, the animals demonstrate their refusal and voluntary starvation when they do not take the green grassy spots of tall plants resulting from fecal and urinary droppings. When it is said so commonly that "a sick sheep is as good as a dead one" are we not demonstrating how poorly we have been feeding them while they have been politely protesting under starvation without showing readily evident symptoms right up to the point of their death?

---

[7] *Blake F. Donaldson. Strong Medicine. Dobbleday; New York. Lists the "obesity sevtette" as hardening of the arteries, arterioscleroses, heart failure, osteo-arthritis, diabetes and gallstones, none of which is classed as an infectious disease.*

When the cow comes through a mile of southern piney woods on the coastal plains soils to get the limited grazing along the edge of the highway serving as calcium fertilizer, are we recognizing what a capable assayer of quality of her feed that head of livestock is? We indict ourselves when we do no more than erect highway signs asking the motoring public to avoid killing the animals.

Organic Values. Even the hog, considered so voracious, is a very keen discriminator if you will put the corn grains of the same soil given different treatments into the separate compartments of the self-feeder to measure the different consumptions of each under repeated trials. It was under such test conditions that the hoggish beasts refused to take the corn grown where sweet clover was turned under as green manure ahead of the corn planting. But they took decidedly of that grain where the ripened sweet clover residues were turned under simultaneously.

In that demonstration, the difference in the quality of the grain as feed because of that slight difference in the organic fertilizers was enough to let the pig report its ability to recognize the difference in what it chooses to eat as food for survival. Knowing now that green sweet clover contains the drug, dicumerol, which prohibits blood-clothing and invites the injured animal's bleeding to death, shall we say the animal avoids that drug which may possibly be moved as organic compound from the soil, through the corn plant, and into the corn grain from the green manure but not the fully matured one turned into the soil ahead of planting the corn?

Numerous other discriminations by animals, both wild and domestic, could be cited of difference in the feed unnoticed by the feeder. We are prone to disregard the suggestions of the fastidious animals. We remain unmindful of the simple fact that they are feed customers of our best possible feed service with highest pay by them for such. They have no alternative but to take our decisions on quality in disregard of theirs. Should we be surprised and alarmed then, by the many animal disasters, like sterility, diseases, pests, feed poisons, deaths, etc., from the malnutrition we perpetuate under technologies and economics but in disregard of the biotic laws of nature to which the animals try to adhere in spite of us?

IV. Animals' Choices Represent Values Beyond Laboratory Measurements

We are slow to believe that the health troubles of our livestock may be connected, (a) with the plant species we choose to grow for feed, and

(b) with the declining fertility of the soils on which the chosen crops are grown. Instead of aiming at better animal health by choice of plants of higher protein potential and by supplying the soil fertility conditions required for those as their virgin crops had them, or even as the best known practices grow them; we are prone to bring seed from anywhere without careful observation of the soil conditions growing it in its choice climatic setting, and to plant it anywhere without duplicating the soil fertility level to which the crop was truly natural. Emphasis is strong on the crop pedigree but weak of the soil fertility to create it. When a crop makes much bulk for yield on a poor soil, and is of such low feed value (possibly poisonous) that the animal develops a deficiency of vitamins etc., suggesting "hoof disease" the ailment takes the name of the crop, *e.g. "fescue foot."* We are slow to see the depletion of soils bring on a succession of substitutions making less and less of nutritional values of crops but in satisfying yields of bulk. Emphasizing fattening values for quick gains in weight, we miss the need to keep the animal healthy for the survival time required for even that process.

Animal Wisdom. Research, relating the fertility treatments of the soil to the crop's nutritional values as animal-favored choices was begun at the Missouri Agricultural Experiment Station in the early forties. Two experiments deserve citation here in which domestic rabbits were the test animals. Those trials established the animal's choice as one of unusual biochemical accuracy in assaying the quality of the hay according to the fertility balances or imbalances of the soil growing the forage.

Four plots of a series in alfalfa were harvested and used for feeding trials with weanling rabbits as cooperating chemists. The plot numbers and soil treatments were as follows: plot 3, none; plot 1, 60 pounds nitrogen per acre in spring and after each cutting; plot 10, 100 pounds ammonium nitrate, 200 pounds superphosphate, 60 pounds muriate of potash and 2 tons limestone on the acre basis every six years, and plot 6, the duplicate of plot 10 but every two years.

The order of choice was first determined by offering constant amounts of each of the four hays along with a given weight of corn and measuring the daily consumptions of hay and grain. That soon established the order of choice in which they were listed above for the plots and soil treatments, namely plots 3, 1, 10, 6.

As a sequel, in another test, each hay was fed separately with corn grain from the same lot to measure (a) hay consumed, as well as grain, (b) gains in weight, (c) ratio of hay to gain, and (d) ratio of corn to gain.

Since plot 3 was the choice, it gave the highest gain in weight of animal; was next to highest in hay consumption; and was lowest in ratio of hay to gain, and likewise, in ratio of corn to gain. Accordingly, the rabbit's choice was definitely the selection of the hay for the most rapid growth of the weanling animal and at the combination of soil treatments for hay of the highest quality as growth potential. (Figure II)

In terms of gains the rabbits reported the values of the four hays in the following order with first choice as 100 percent, and the others as 90, 65 and 50 percents of that. The amounts of hay taken, demonstrate a self-denial of both hay and corn according as the hay was of lesser choice, in the order of first choice as 100 percent, namely, 100, 102, 55 and 50. These animals used the choice of the hay to decide on starvation but that of corn also according as it balanced the hay.

Such a report casts decided doubt whether as managers of soils and of crops, or as feeders, we have been pleasing our animals as producers growing them under confinement, on rations of our specifications, and grown on our fertilized soils. In this case of alfalfa, already so widely grown, and with so many kinds of soil treatments, the rabbits voted against all of the three offered for their consideration under assay.

A second and similar test used red clover hays from four plots on Sanborn Field grown in a four-year rotation of corn, oats, wheat, and red clover since 1888. The procedures were similar to those used in the first test reported here. The order of choice established by the rabbits for these plots and soil treatments were the following; plot 36, full soil treatment according to soil test plus magnesium limestone; plot 34, 6 tons manure annually; plot 39, full soil treatment plus calcium limestone; and plot 35, no treatment.

Big Lesson from Livestock. Here again the choice by the animals represented the highest efficiency of the red clover and corn in combination to grow weanling rabbits at the most rapid rate. Again, regardless of the possible threat of starvation, the animals consumed the corn at a certain balance with the hay. More significant was the choice of the hay as a daily quantity to be taken, regardless of whether that resulted in added growth or not of the body. (Figure III)

Such data are undeniable evidence that the animal is a most capable biochemist in assaying feed values for its growth (not for fattening) and in selecting those according to differences in quality of the crops (not as yields per acre) as nutrition for healthy growth of the animals. Such data given us by rabbits as cooperative test-chemists tell us, to our chagrin, that what we have been doing to our soils may not have been under-girding, or meeting the animals' approval in, their natural struggle for healthy survival. Simultaneously, the data tell us that we have big lessons to learn by using them as cooperators in selecting their rations. They have here shown that they are most capable biochemists, who do not interpret their data of livestock feeding for advantages in economics only. Instead they tell us that the animals will cooperate with us in livestock production if our goal, like theirs, is the growth of healthy animals via the fertility maintenance of the soil for that kind of biotic service, within which man can also be included.

CHAPTER 6

Livestock Can Teach Us a Lesson On Nutrition From the Ground Up!

WHEN A COW BREAKS THROUGH the fence, you perhaps ask (in one way or another) "What's in her mind?" If you correctly answer that question, there is a mutually beneficial solution to the broken fence problem.

If not, there is conflict between Mother Nature and you ... conflict in which Nature strikes back with a recoil damaging to both you and the cow. For the fence-breaking cow more than likely is demonstrating her recognition of the higher quality feed growing "on the other side of the fence."[1] Grass on virgin soil along the highway or railroad right-of-way is better nutrition, in her judgment, than what is growing on depleted soils in her pasture. By such discrimination, animals were surviving naturally and in good health long before domestication.

Careful study of some of the soil and plant facts related to livestock behavior, and the behavior of all other living things, reveals that animals carefully consider their nutrition "from the ground up." And accurate interpretation of such behavior is essential to the progressive stockman.

Organized knowledge of the distribution patterns of different kinds of life on the earth's surface is the science of ecology. The search for reasons why a particular kind of life is in a specific place has yielded a list of possible responsible factors that includes rainfall, temperature, geology, topography, soil acidity and many others. More recently, however, we have realized that all factors can be summed up in the word "food" as the major determinant of any ecological pattern. Of the various food components, proteins are the major constituents which life struggles to obtain.

---

[1] *Phillips petroleum Co., Bartlesville, Okla. Motion picture title.*

Soil science in its recent remarkable development, with much help from other sciences, has pointed to variations in yield and quality of proteins according not only to the different crops but to any crop according to differences in fertility of the soil growing it. Those differences in soils' capacities to create living proteins in crops and animals result from variations in the climatic forces of rainfall, temperature, topography and other weathering agencies acting on the rocks to produce soil. Consequently, "We are what we are because of where we are" and "We are what we eat" ("Mann ist was er esst"), in the words of a geologist and a German geographer, respectively.

In observing animals, plants and microbes as life forms in that order below man in the biotic pyramid where all rest on the soil as their creative foundation, we need to be reminded that when man came on the scene he was met by each of these forms as healthy "climax crops" (Figure 1). By natural evolution, each was probably at its height of (a) growth, (b) self-protection and (c) fecund reproduction. They were discovered and domesticated only because they had achieved natural healthy survival through their own instinctive nutritional struggles. In other words, they had proven fit to survive in a climatic and soil setting responsible for a particular degree of soil development that undergirded their survival with proper nutrition. It was for each a case of ecology at its best.

Unfortunately, we have no "natural climax crops" left as standards of "fitness" and excellence for plants and animals in agriculture. We have transplanted from anywhere to everywhere, and healthy survival has not been among the objectives of such reshuffling. This has brought more life forms into conflict with the natural instincts and struggles that originally kept them healthy. Transplanting, but with neglect of the virgin soil as to its origin and climax, is now gradually resulting in malnutrition and failing health — deficient nutrition from the ground up. Some observations in support of this thesis will be discussed under the headings of (a) interdependence, a natural law, (b) survival depends on selection of foods according to soil fertility and (c) the struggle for proteins and evolution of helpful body organs.

A. Interdependence, a Natural Law

I. Legume Plants and Soil Bacteria

The biotic triumvirate of (a) the soil as foundation, (b) microbes as decomposers and (c) plants as major producers of energy and growth sub-

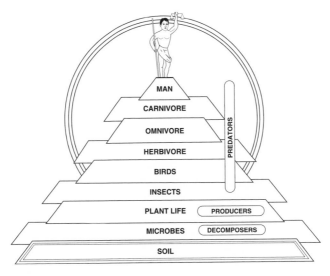

Fig. 1. The many life forms arrange themselves in a biotic pyramid illustrating the decreasing population of each life form according to its increasing bio-chemical complexity. All rest on the soil as their creative foundation.

stances emphasizes their own essential interrelations and interdependencies as linkages, cooperations and symbioses by which they are the foundation of all other higher and more complex life strata. But the latter also have interdependencies with microbes and plants, thereby with the soil.

It was as late as 1888 when we first recognized the interdependency, nutrition-wise, of legume plants and the nitrogen-fixing soil bacteria in their root nodules as a case of symbiosis or mutual benefit. We discovered years later that legumes are not nitrogen fixers purely because of pedigree. They are such only because of ample soil supplies of their delicately-balanced requisites for many inorganic nutrient elements, of which calcium (not listed among contents of commercial fertilizers) is the foremost.

When the soil failed to supply calcium more abundantly than any of the many other soil-borne inorganic nutrients, soybeans when first transplanted to the United States produced much vegetative matter but no seed. Disregarding fertile soils to guarantee reproduction and, thereby, survival of the species, superficial thinkers pronounced this plant immigrant "an excellent hay crop but not a seed crop." They overlooked the undernourished crop's low feed value when the forage plant could not even synthesize the necessary proteins to be mobilized later into seed for reproduction and procreation of the species. It required research by colloidal clay techniques to demonstrate that such soybean hay crops (roots and tops combined) contained less nitrogen, less phosphorus and less potassium (only ones tested) than were in the planted seeds.

II. Non-Legume Plants and Soil Fungi

The nutritionally advantageous alliance between either non-legume or legume plants and soil microbes (fungi) on soils well stocked with organic matter is not even yet significantly appreciated. Attention has been intensely focused on soil fungi lately because they are the commercially-lucrative source of the many antibiotics, death-dealers to bacteria. But the bacteria in soil are secondary microbes there. Fungi are the primary ones, more capable of obtaining food for both energy and growth from the woody carbonaceous organic matter of crop residues, the main energy source for all life within the soil. Much like any other higher life form, soil microbes are also struggling for proteins.

Accordingly, since bacteria have narrower carbohydrate-protein ratio requirements than fungi (as we know from manure-making, composting practices and commercial mushroom production), nitrogen will be conserved longer and held in insoluble organic forms rather than in water-soluble forms when there are more highly-carbonaceous residues in the soil. While fungi are holding nitrogen in their cellular compounds along with residues of less solubility or wider carbon-nitrogen ratios, bacteria are using organic matter of narrower ratios to make their nitrogen highly soluble. Soil rich in natural nitrogen must also be relatively rich in carbon compared to nitrogen to hold the latter there.

It must also follow axiomatically that the addition of nitrogen salts to the soil works against natural nitrogen conservation in soil organic matter. Soluble nitrogen is used by microbes, both fungi and bacteria, to help build their cellular protein tissues (provided carbon of soil organic matter as food energy is present). But while that process occurs, about twice as much of the combined insoluble carbon in the organic matter is respired or converted into gaseous carbon dioxide that escapes into the air.

III. Microbes Give Nitrogen but First Take It

According to such natural laws, we can understand why 25 years of continuous wheat on Sanborn Field, fertilized by either ammonium sulfate or

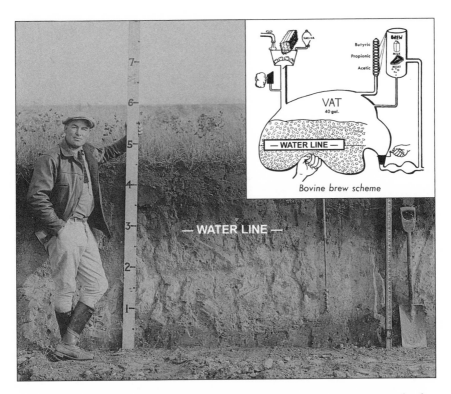

Fig. 2. The bovine paunch at top right is similar in many respects to the fertile prairie soil profile. Neither dare be water-logged to allow only anaerobic fermentation and its intoxicating by-products. Each must offer aerobic and oxidative conditions above the water line where constructive microbes can build protein compounds to be plants' organic food and the animal's protein supplements. Unlike the soil, however, the bovine rhythmically shifts its paunch profile to put roughages through anaerobic and then aerobic treatments.

sodium nitrate only, lowered the totals of both nitrogen and carbon (organic matter) in the soil below amounts in similar soil given no treatment — when in both cases all crops were removed. Simultaneously, the use of 6 tons of manure per acre annually under similar continuous wheat increased both nitrogen and carbon as constituents of organic matter in the soil. We dare not forget that not only plants but all life forms are interdependent in one way or another on soil microbes. All are supported by the soil; but microbes, the lowliest and simplest, always eat at the first sitting.

Just as fungi are more capable than bacteria in decomposing insoluble carbohydrates, allowing bacteria to profit by using secondary fungi products as bacterial nutrition, so we find fungi more capable than bacteria in decomposing rock minerals. Fungi are more powerful in separating the cationic elements like potassium, calcium and magnesium from the anions like silica. Fungi in symbiosis with algae, in the form of the lichen, live on what appears to be clean rock. In this living combination, fungi supply the inorganic essentials and the green algae provide the organic carbohydrates (possibly proteins, too), so this union again supports a distinct flora of bacteria. This is, then, a unique almost cellular or microscopic association of fungi, bacteria and plants (in very close contact) converting rock surfaces into soils to support all three. It is a case of the lowest three strata of the biotic pyramid reduced in concept to symbiosis and interdependence at cellular dimensions. It represents almost twice as much thermo-dynamic potential for chemical mineral decomposition as any plant root contact with rocks.

We apparently have not appreciated the ability of fungi to hydrolyze insoluble cellulose into simpler carbohydrates like sugars, to hydrolyze proteins into available amino acids or to weather rock minerals for plant use, since scientific studies of this order have not seemed potentially as lucrative as many other avenues of organizing natural facts into sciences. Nor have we regarded agriculture as biological performances first and economics second, with the former the cause of the latter.

Instead we have searched for economic opportunities even at the cost of dire conflict with matters biotic. By that view we have created Frankensteins within biology that are now giving us so-called "health problems." We apparently don't realize that the so-called "dangerous" soil microbes or "germs" are not demons of destruction ... save as failing health invites their natural acts of premortal decomposition. Instead of recognizing ourselves as responsible for the conflict with Nature, we are designing by means of our technologies the most powerful chemical poisons to destroy lower life forms completely. We have most seriously accepted Pasteur, so capable in his public relations during his time, but are not familiar with Bechamp, the scientist on whom the former as publicist depended.[2]

We are trying to destroy the lowest life forms, those next to the soil from which all creation takes off. We are learning that microbes give but, under our seeming ingratitude, we are slow to learn of Nature's recoil when microbes also take — and we call it "disease."

---

[2] E. Douglas Hume. Bechamp or Pasteur. A lost chapter in the history of biology. C. W. Daniel Co., Ashingdon, Rockford, Essex. 1923, 1932, 1947.

IV. Higher Life Forms Dependent on Microbes

Insects, as one of the lower animal strata of the biotic pyramid, are also in symbiosis with microbes when the latter must be harbored internally or be "nursed" by insects. Termites (wood-eating roaches not considered strictly insects though a corresponding low-life form) harbor a number of species of cellulose-digesting protozoa in their highly-developed hind intestine. These roaches depend on the protozoa for their major food supply, while most of the protozoa are dependent on their roach hosts for their restricted habitat and for food of wood particles.

Another group of insects dependent on microbes includes the screw-worm larvae, the sheep maggots of several species and the special ones discovered and used in World War I for cleansing badly-infected wounds, including bones. It has been established that those maggots feed not so much on the infecting bacteria but rather on the protein products resulting from microbial digestion of protein tissue. It is said that the "wounds are cleaned," and the specific fly maggots used do not seriously harm living tissues.

In one experiment, a house fly laid its eggs on wood shavings in the corner of the cage where an experimental cancerous white mouse was regularly urinating and manure was accumulating so as to result in a composting process. It was observed that the mouse was very cautiously searching out and eating the house fly maggots regularly. Soon thereafter the cancerous tissue of the mouse began to atrophy, with increased activity of the mouse resulting.[3]

Such natural behavior suggests the stages of dependence and the chain of interrelated struggles for protein building upward to warm-blooded bodies by means of (a) the decomposition of organic matter supporting microbial synthesis of their own proteins from the cellulose composted with urine of the mouse, (b) the maggots' required proteins supplied by the microbes and their digested products and (c) those proteins required for the mouse supplied by the house fly maggots via initial urinary body wastes of the mouse in cycle of re-use via that catenation of the several biotic strata. Through them, man at the apex of the pyramid is able to hoist his nutrition from the soil upward.

Like that of the termite, the hind intestine (or the large one) of all higher life forms harbors microbes, particularly bacteria, of many kinds. That holds true for all the strata above plants, including insects, birds, herbivora, carnivora and man. That those microbes render services of nutritional and survival value is a slowly-growing conviction. The "sterilizing" effects of

---

[3] Paul O. Sapp, Ashland, Mo. Reported in person.

TABLE 1. Carbon and Nitrogen Content of Soils Under Continuous Cropping to Wheat and Timothy

(Sanborn Field, Missouri Agricultural Experiment Station)

Plot Number	Cropping Periods	Crop and Soil Treatment	Carbon % (1)	Nitrogen %	Ratio C/N (2)
		Tilled Soil, Continuous Wheat			
2	1st 25 years	Commercial fertilizer	1.13	0.107	10.5
	2nd 25 years	Commercial fertilizer	1.02	0.100	10.3
5	1st 25 years	6 tons manure (3)	1.52	0.140	10.8
	2nd 25 years	3 tons manure	1.27	0.119	10.6
20	1st 25 years	6 tons manure	1.38	0.145	9.5
	2nd 25 years	Ammonium sulfate	1.07	0.081	13.2
30	1st 25 years	6 tons manure	1.61	0.171	9.4
	2nd 25 years	Sodium nitrate	1.30	0.094	13.8
		Sod Soil, Continuous Timothy			
23	1st 25 years	No treatment (4)	1.32	0.141	9.4
	2nd 25 years	No treatment (4)	1.45	0.135	10.7
22	1st 25 years	6 tons manure	1.69	0.177	9.5
	2nd 25 years	6 tons manure	2.04	0.195	10.4

(1) Percent of dry soil.
(2) Ratio of carbon to nitrogen in the soil.
(3) Tons per acre of barnyard manure.
(4) Except for periodic plowing of both plots after plot 23 became foul with weeds.

antibiotics taken either orally or hypodermically, often with serious health disturbances, support this fact.

Products of both microbial decomposition and synthesis in the large intestine are currently lending themselves to fuller elucidation and recognition. Those include synthesis of vitamins, enzymes, recycled compounds and other reactions not yet completely cataloged.

V. Microbial Biochemistry Favored in Special Body Structures

The herbivora are a unique case of close connection with soil microbes at both the anterior and posterior ends of the digestive canal. At the anterior end, the true symbiosis of the ruminant with microbes occurs in three alimentary organs especially designed for advances microbial services before digestion by the true stomach takes place. This arrangement is highly essential for ruminants, which are nourished so extensively by bulky high-cellulose vegetation. The rumen is particularly equipped for microbial digestion and synthetic services by which the microbial substance itself is a very important nutritional factor, digested en route through the animal and supplying many essential nutrients not initially ingested. Thus the significance of soil fertility[4] is connected with the fore as well as the rear anatomy of the animal in biochemical ways still unknown (Figure 2).

These facts suggest that the ruminant is clearly a warm-blooded summation of its creation through a series of all the biosynthetic services from the soil via microbes, plants and the animal itself. Should we not, in consequence, accept the chemical picture of the blood of such an animal as the best index of the fertility of the soil? Should we not expect deficiencies in the latter to be reflected as irregularities in the nutrition and health of the former?

B. Survival Depends on Selection of Foods According to Soil Fertility

I. Animals Discriminate Among Compounds, Not Elements

For survival, any animal must respect its relation to all other biotic strata on which it either is dependent or with which it is competitive.

---

[4]W. H. Plander et. al. Rumenology. Missouri Agricultural Experiment Station Bulletin 619. 1954.

Evolution tells us that no species can or dares extinguish another completely. Accordingly, an animal must capably assay what it chooses to consume. Since variable soil grows foods of variable quality, the animal's successful discrimination must rest on its highly refined ability as a "connoisseur of soil fertility."

In agricultural practice, then, we can premise better husbandry on our confidence in the cow's choice of feed components and their qualities according to fertility of the soils growing them. Soils must be managed by us as caterers to livestock and not as dictators compelling animals to accommodate themselves to our technologies and economics of simple business transactions.

II. Calcium

Livestock often reach across the fence or graze one certain area in the pasture, telling us that the element calcium is perhaps the first soil fertility requisite for quality forage on soils in humid areas. The importance of calcium in the synthesis of proteins of pulses, clovers and other more nutritious forages (according to the animal's choice of them as supplements to non-legume forages for balancing its diet) was emphasized in the Old World since the early days of the Romans and in the New World since Benjamin Franklin. Unwittingly and for many years, calcium has served to build proteins, though lately it is emphasized mainly for its carbonate serving to reduce the degree (pH) of soil acidity. In both respects, magnesium plays a similar confusing role ... but less prominently because of the lesser quantities involved.

Animals naturally are not expected to be capable of assaying the ash content of forages. But rather we expect livestock to recognize the organic compounds created from inorganic elements in the soil. Animals in desperation will consume even crushed limestone and other inorganic elements to make up mineral and salt deficiencies in the soil on which they graze. Since calcium plays a major role in the synthesis of required amino acids composing proteins, we are apt to emphasize the individual nutrient element (calcium) of the soil rather than all the synthetic food substances, especially proteins, for which it is responsible.

It has been recently reported[5] that, by assembly of proper laboratory chemicals under specific conditions, the energy of an electric discharge will

---

[5] Melvin Calvin. Communications: From Molecules to Mars. Bulletin, American Institute of Biological Sciences, XII 29–44 (5). 1962.

synthesize a whole series of requisite amino acids. But it will occur only if calcium, even limestone, is present as the catalyst. The establishment of calcium's role in amino acid synthesis helps us to see the animal's choice as a most important instinct, antedating by eons the knowledge we have of it.

It should, then be no surprise that livestock graze first on the limed portion of a field and neglect that which has not been limed. Nor should it be a mystery why cattle in the southern piney woods will travel for miles to graze along the edge of a cement highway (Figure 3).

III. Magnesium

That animals should discriminate between magnesium and calcium as soil factors responsible for their choice might not readily suggest itself. But such was demonstrated some 15 or more years ago[6] when a dairyman noticed that his Guernsey calves ate the second coat of plaster, containing magnesium, in a particularly sanitary barn but did not mar the first coat containing the calcium or the lime plaster. Suffering seriously from white scours, the calves (which had to be housed in the autumn before the new barn was completed) discriminated in what might well be considered an act of desperation.

Their observing owner — mentally prepared for this accidental discovery — noticed the damage to the second coat of plaster on the finished stall but none to the first coat in the unfinished one. His analytical mind caught the implication of magnesium missing in the calves' fodder because of magnesium deficiency in the soil growing it. Dosing the calves with magnesium salts and later treating the soil with dolomitic limestone eliminated white scours and calf fatalities.

Magnesium is a divalent alkaline element and a close companion to calcium. It is also the ash element core of some presently-known two dozen enzymes (protein-like chemical structures). Accordingly, animals also struggle for life-promoting magnesium. This is emphasized even in our thinking of magnesium as an ash element only and as if the animals were discriminating between only the inorganic elements of plant delivery from the soil. We need to see that it is rather a manifestation of needed major synthesis by plants, struggling for organic compounds like the proteins, in which any one of the deficient essential inorganics will lower nutritional quality of the nitrogen-carrying compounds apt to be considered as proteins.

---

[6] E. R. Kuck. How Guernsey Calves Helped Solve a Feed and Crop Fertilization Problem. Better Crops. December 1946.

IV. Phosphorus

During the early period of increasing use of agricultural limestone and other fertilizing materials, the practice of drilling superphosphate with the wheat-clover seeding brought many reports of farmers observing the livestock taking clover in the part of the field given the phosphate on limed soils but neglecting the same legume where no phosphate was used. Similar observations were reported where rock phosphate was the fertility uplift on unlimed soils.

Acid phosphate supplied not only the required phosphate in such cases but supplied also gypsum, a compound of both calcium and sulfur. Hence, one might believe the animals were choosing in favor of one or both of these last two elements also connected with (or retained in) protein synthesis. But since limestone had already provided calcium and since rock phosphate supplies no sulfur, it was established that phosphorus was the element limiting the nutritional qualities the animals were assaying. Since phosphorus so commonly limits growth, is also connected with the energy-transferring feeds and is becoming more limiting as soils are more depleted of their virgin organic matter by which insoluble phosphorus is made available, animals are more and more emphasizing phosphorus by their discriminations.

V. Sulfur

In similar situations we can recognize livestock's emphasis on deficiencies in sulfur when this element, measured in amounts by analytical procedures like ignition, duplicates phosphorus in soils and crops very closely.

VI. Potassium

Since potassium — a highly soluble, monovalent, alkaline element — is more intercellularly than intracellularly distributed in plant tissue and since within the cell it is found in the vacuole rather than within the living cytoplasm (protein), we would not be so prone to emphasize the animal's common discrimination in favor of forages growing on soils given extra potassium treatments to affect plant protein directly. But in experiments with legume forages on heavily-limed soils, with heavy infestations of root-rot on corn given phosphate but showing low exchangeable potassium by soil test, animals showed decided preference for forage grown with extra potassium.

In this case again, the legumes were improved through possible help in their synthesis of carbohydrates as forerunner compounds in the synthesis of proteins or other essentials preferred by animals rather than just by increased concentrations of inorganic alkaline potassium. Potassium gives indirect support to protein production.

VII. Nitrogen, Only a Symbol of Protein

The element nitrogen is normally a gas. It appears inorganically in combination with hydrogen as the positive ammonium ion and with oxygen as the negative ions of nitrites and nitrates. Organically, its extensive combinations with carbon and hydrogen make up 16% (as a mean) of the living protein tissues and fluids. It is readily transformed analytically and synthetically by microbial life, especially in the soil, from either organic to inorganic forms and vice-versa by many kinds of chemical and biochemical reactions, with its final simplification through oxidation or even by reduction to gas that returns to the atmosphere. In animal metabolism of proteins, its simplification results in its elimination in the form of organic urea.

In the struggle for nitrogen for proteins, only microbes (when amply supplied with energy foods) can combine elemental gaseous nitrogen with carbon and hydrogen to produce proteins. Hence, all higher forms of life, so far as we now know, ultimately depend on the lowly microbes for their combined nitrogen.

The fact that animal choices are determined so generally by proteins more than by other feed components is not evidence that nitrogen is the element characterizing the choice. Rather it is the organic nitrogenous compounds that are responsible. Animal choice is not guided by the ash element nitrogen.

In support of that contention, one needs only to see the spots of lush green grass in a pasture that mark the urinary droppings, which liberally fertilize the grass with nitrogen broken down by soil microbes into either ammonia or nitrate form. But livestock refuse to take this forage so heavily fertilized with nitrogen, though they crop closely around the distinguishing spots. In spite of animals' refusal of that much greener and more abundant growth, there is an increased concentration of nitrogen in it. Though measured by chemists as more "crude" protein and considered quality feed worth eating, it is simply "too crude" for the cow customers to buy.

That ignition analyses do not show us the determiners of animals' choices among the soil-borne nutrient elements was shown by making bio-assays and chemical analyses of alfalfa hay grown with different soil treatments. The hay was grown on four plots given:

(a) No treatment, plot No. 3.

(b) Nitrogen, 60 lb. per acre in spring and after each cutting, plot No. 1.

(c) 100 lb. ammonium sulfate and 200 lb. superphosphate per acre annually plus 60 lb. potassium chloride in alternate years, plot No. 6.

(d) 100 lb. ammonium nitrate, 200 lb. superphosphate and 60 lb. potassium chloride per acre annually, plus 2 tons of limestone every six years, plot No. 10.

The four lots of hay were offered for measured consumption by choice as supplements to a single lot of corn. Four weanling rabbits per pen in five pens were used in five trials — the equivalent of trials by 100 animals. The data is assembled in Table 2.

The test indicated that rabbits do not recommend chemical nitrogen as soil treatment for legume hay. Their consumption (quality evaluation) varies, because of those soil treatments, as widely as five to one. That variation was not correlated with order of nitrogen concentration, hence not with "crude" protein as measured chemically. Nor was it correlated with concentrations of calcium, magnesium or phosphorus. Nor were those correlated with each other. The rabbits simply preferred hay grown from nitrogen supplied by microbial decomposition of soil organic matter and by microbial nitrogen fixation on the roots of legume plants. Since the much larger portion of nitrogen in any legume crop comes from the former source rather than the latter, it is evident that the animals prefer protein nitrogen which comes from soil organic matter rather than from chemical salts. The animals distinguish between protein qualities to such a fine degree that they may separate them according to amounts of their components, i.e., their values in terms of nutritional balance of the required amino acids.

In another similar assay by rabbits, using fescue hay grown with only increasing additions of ammonium nitrate to the soil, the first increment of fertilizer brought about first choice; no treatment was second choice; and, with higher increments applied to the soil, choice dropped more and more below no treatment. Daily total consumption by choice in two trials with this non-legume hay was but 6.1 and 10.5 gm. hay per rabbit. By contrast, in two trials with alfalfa the corresponding figures were 31.1 and 33.9 gm. hay per day per rabbit.

The one plant species was apparently chosen under duress of starvation when the ratios of amounts consumed were as wide as five to one in

Fig. 3. This cow may have traveled miles for narrow strip of grass along this highway.

favor of alfalfa over fescue. The animals separated differences in quality by spreads far wider than any shown by chemical analysis. When animals are such capable connoisseurs of the rations we offer, why not cater to their choices? Why not use them in research to discover the criteria by which animals judge what they want, with soil fertility as the major factor in the choice?

C. The Struggle for Proteins and Evolution of Helpful Body Organs

Anatomical and functional designs of the alimentary canal and other organs helping it pass food through for preparation, digestion, absorption, chemical censoring, metabolism, excretion, etc., impress one quickly with the complexities of body organs as they digest and conserve proteins in contrast to the relatively simple task of handling carbohydrates and fats.

I. Lower Life Forms

Anatomical arrangement of the digestive organs of sucking insects vary widely for separating low concentrations of proteins out of the plant saps and juices composing their diets. The protein-poor but carbohydrate-rich solution is not put directly into the stomach, arranged to attack proteins with strong acid (as is also the case with warm-blooded bodies). Instead, the liquid diet is shunted first through auxiliary canals and pouch-like structures adept in filtering out the proteins and other nitrogenous materials, while the sugary liquids are moved on for excretion. But the proteins are returned to the major alimentary canal for digestion.

One needs only to cite the common aphid as an illustration, with its sugary excretions collecting like mist on auto windshields or serving the honey bee, in seasons of low nectar flow, with resulting honey of little use save for its fermentations and thereby self-clarified alcoholic solution.

II. Warm-Blooded Animals

All ruminants, as herbivorous feeders, are particularly unique examples of the modification of the anterior portion of the alimentary canal into three extra pouches for treatment of food before digestion by the true stomach. Increasing acidity in that sequence to the very acid condition of the stomach suggests more complete hydrolysis of proteins into amino acids and increasing rates of many other reactions. It lengthens the incubation time under warmer temperatures for microbial syntheses before treatment of the microbes themselves by strong acid. It favors many other chemical reactions under nearly anaerobic conditions for initial fermentations and other attacks on more stable carbohydrates. That succession of increasingly drastic treatments seems necessary to handle high-cellulose feeds as well as proteins.

The pig and the chicken, habitually close followers for the droppings of cattle, reveal wisdom and unique nutritional values in their choices. These two non-ruminants pay tribute to the microbial synthetic services performed in the ruminants' anatomy but not in theirs. They search out vitamin B12 (and possibly other essentials), because ruminants' symbiosis with intestinal microbes synthesizes it. The uniqueness lies in the fact that this vitamin is required in only micro-units. Hence, with bio-assays of that refinement, discriminations between quantities of amino acids should not be an animal endowment beyond our imagination when survival by evolution is considered.

Perhaps a more challenging evolutionary adaptation of body organs for more favorable management of the struggle for proteins is exhibited by the camel. Because it inhabits the deserts, our attention focuses first on shortage of water. But such arid ecological settings forcefully remind us that equally as (or more) hazardous is the shortage of proteins in any vegetation rooted in salt-saturated soils and with its tops in an atmosphere of maximum temperature and near-zero humidity.

That the camel can tolerate severe water depletion of its body by going without water for days is well known. It has been reported[7] that this domestic animal can deplete its body's water content to the extent of a body loss of one-fifth its weight. Then by drinking once it can restore that weight and body appearance to normal in a very short time.

But the camel's metabolism includes a practice of conservation rather than excretion and later intake as is true for water. Urea, as the end product of protein metabolism, is not sent from the liver to the kidneys for excretion. Instead, urea is retained in the system by recycling from the liver back into the rumen. Thereby this metabolite of previously-ingested feed is merely the chemical nucleus passed up front again to be built into microbial protein, then later to be digested en route through the alimentary canal and become urea again for the repeated process.

In this particular case, evolution has given us Nature's practice of adding urea to the feed of the ruminant, possible at least under duress of near-starvation. This is done by a simple modification of the anatomy in the form of a vessel from the liver to the paunch. By that method, we believe urea is protected against the rapid changes to ammonium carbonate or to ammonia, carbon dioxide and water as moist urea salt does on atmospheric exposure. The amino nitrogen of the urea would remain linked to the carbon and save the synthetic costs of restoring that connection distinguishing the protein nitrogen and that is so costly in laboratory synthesis.

In case of the camel, Nature has long been feeding urea for maintenance of the body proteins. Much is yet to be learned about what the ruminant herds and flocks of primitive man may have been doing for survival of man in his closer connection, via the animals, with his own nutrition from the ground up.

---

[7] Knut Schmidt-Nelson. The Physiology of the Camel. Scientific American 201: 140-151 (6). 1959.

TABLE 2. Animal Assays (Weanling Rabbits) and Chemical Analyses of Alfalfa According to Soil Treatments (Putnam Silt Loam)

Plot No. (and order of Consumption choice)	(100 grams)	Chemical Analyses (Percent of dry matter)			
		Nitrogen	Calcium	Magnesium	Phosphorus
3 (1)	25.6	2.627 (3)	1.100	.319	.237
1 (2)	22.2	2.523 (4)	1.290	.325	.218
6 (3)	9.2	3.024 (1)	.959	.256	.294
10 (4)	5.1	2.748 (2)	1.260	.236	.299

Plot 3, no nitrogen; plot 1, 60 lb. nitrogen in the spring and after cutting; plot 6, 100 lb. ammonium sulfate and 200 lb. superphosphate annually, 60 lb. potassium chloride biannually; plot 10, 100 lb. ammonium sulfate, 200 lb. superphosphate, 60 lb. potassium chloride annually plus 2 tons limestone per six years.

D. Summary

Much is yet to be learned by studying microbial metabolism in its primordial setting, namely, on rocks and within the soil. Nutrition of the microbes, as the first forms of life, started there on simple minerals mixed with microbes consuming their own dead bodies, all as life in single-cell stages.

This discussion emphasized the simple natural fact that all life is dependent upon (or is in symbiosis with) microbes when the provision of nutritive substances, especially proteins for growth rather than carbohydrates for energy, is considered. The symbiosis so universal in the lower end of every alimentary canal has not occupied much of our thought (so shadowed by "fear of germs"), but it is a requisite for health to which life forms lower than man cling.[8]

Biotic strata other than man are gifted in assaying their food intake according to (a) different plant species and (b) different degrees of rock development into soil on which plants grow. While this has been animals'

---

[8] William A. Albrecht. Guest editorial: Nature Teaches Health via Nutrition journal of Applied Nutrition 12 (4). 1959.

means of survival by evolution during the ages, we humans are just beginning to recognize the ecological patterns of various strata in the biotic pyramid that reflect the soil as the major factor underlying food quality and, thus, health. According to the degree that such natural facts are accepted as essential truths by which man must also survive, so will the soil be more carefully and completely conserved; and thereby higher quality nutrition for more abundant health of all life will be the result.

CHAPTER 7

Soil Fertility and Animal Production

The Cow Ahead of the Plow

NOW THAT WE are talking more and more about a "grass agriculture", especially as it is to help in combatting erosion, we are moving back to the ideas given us by earlier history. We are coming to see that it has always been well that man should be closely associated with the animals that eat grass. In the earlier days of nomadic agriculture the cow went ahead of the plow.

The nomad moved his tent in the direction taken by his grazing cattle and flocks. The cow searched out the grasses for their higher nutritional values according to the higher fertility of the soil. She was making a biological assay of the fertility of the soil as registered in the quality of the feel suitable not only for herself but correspondingly also suitable for man as well.

As long as man was following the grazing cow, he was using the best assaying agent to select the land where he might well put the plow and establish his arable agriculture. If the cow chose it to assure her future offspring he might well accept that soil and its output as security for his.

However, in our settlement of the United States and our movement westward across them, we have reversed that procedure. We didn't follow the previous choice of the areas by the grazing animals. Rather, we put spurs into the horse and sent him galloping westward. We put the whip on the team, the plow on the wagon, and with cow tied behind it, dragged her westward. We put the soil under the plow without the advance biological assay by the cow to tell us of the fertility of the soil as she assessed it by the high quality of the vegetation growing on it.

As long as the cow went ahead of the plow, not only the health of the cow but the health of man as well was under better assurance. It was when we reversed that combination and put the plow ahead of the cow that we moved into troubles in nutrition and troubles in the health of both beast and man.

Man is Dependent on Foods Synthesized by Life Forms Below Him

Man is at the top of the biotic pyramid. Immediately below him are his animals; just below them are the plants; then below them are the microbes; and finally below all of these is the foundation of all life, namely the soil, Located at the top, as man is, we are interested in what happens in all the life forms below us. Man depends on the animals as the gathering, assembling and synthesizing helps in providing his food.

By means of his animals he can feed, as it were, over more extensive areas of different soils. He brings together the different required nutrient elements from wider sources and has them manufactured into his foods by other body agencies physiologically similar to his own.

Man is one life form that cannot be nourished by taking the separated or simple elemental forms composing his food. This must be passed to him in the form of the more complex compounds. The animal is an agent in performing that service of building it more nearly of the particular complexity as he needs it. The animal, in turn, depends on the grass, which synthesizes from the simple elements, the compounds that feed the animal.

Man is engaged in a strenuous struggle for his foods. He is using the help of the animals, the help of the plants, and the help of the microbes. All of these bring from the soil the simple but essential elements of inorganic origin to be compounded with those from the air and water to be his organic food.

Energy Foods for Fattening Service

Food serves us in two major functions. The first of these, which stands out more prominently and has been more commonly emphasized, is the provision of energy. Food serves in supplying the necessary calories, and in the storage of energy laid away on the body as fat.

Different soil areas are different in the readiness with which the animals feeding on the crops grown there put on fat. While older animals are more commonly expected to put on fat, some soil areas encourage this even in younger animals, with the resulting hindrance rather than help in animal production.

In the human species, there are body differences too in the different soil areas in the United States. Perhaps you do not look at folks as a judge of their body forms much as a performance in judging livestock. But have you not seen crowds in which the prevalence of obesity, corpulence, rounded, massive, body lines and accompanying characters suggested the slang term "corn-fed" as fitting description?

Have you not seen groups of folks in other parts of the country where you considered it appropriate description to speak of "the slim, trim boyish figure" and where the speech was slow and musical? Do you perchance see in the face the register of the development of the skull indicating the poorer or better nutrition from the soil areas over which the individual has roamed?

When we are nourished by foods that supply mainly energy, mainly bulk, then some of the body characters become irreguarities, if not even deficiencies with damage.

Fattening the animal has been a prominent one among the agricultural practices and feeds have been considered mainly for that service by them. Too little attention has been given the service by feeds and foods in growing a body so that it can use energy feeds and that it can carry on reproduction of its own kind.

Protein Foods for Body-Building

Foods must serve another function, namely they must grow the body. This function is not secondary, but primary, in importance. One must construct the furnace before we can burn the fuel in it. One cannot grow a body by means of energy foods only, such as starches, sugars and other carbohydrates. Bodies are built of proteins, mineral and organo-mineral compounds.

Dairy feeds to supply proteins are a problem because our crops that synthesize proteins more prominently, such as the legumes, require a generous supply of fertility from the soil. They have not grown successfully everywhere. Protein production is a struggle for the plant just as it is a problem for the feeder of animals to provide it for his herds and flocks.

Getting its protein in the case of the plant means that as a forage it is rich in "grow" food values. It means that later in its growing season this highly elaborated food constituent is assembled out of the plant body and

"TO BE WELL FED IS TO BE HEALTHY"
Merely more clay put into the pure sand, even though the clay was very acid, protected the plants from fungus attack (right), while those grown in mainly sand (left) were harmed badly. (Photo by Missouri Agricultural Experiment Station.)

concentrated in the seed. It means that reproduction by the plant is favored since that process depends on protein.

Protein production, therefore, unlike the production of carbohydrates, which are made mainly from air and water, is possible only when the soils are fertile, and when the fertility helps the plants to convert their carbohydrates into proteins and all else that means growth. The struggle for proteins is universal. It means a struggle by man, by the animals, by the plants and by the microbes, all of which can get them only as the fertility coming from the soil to all these life forms makes their reproduction and growth possible.

The creation of any form of life, then, is possible only when the warm moist breath is blown into the handful of dust that is truly a fertile soil. All the requisite elements must be present there, lest we finish the creative process and have nothing but energy foods, carbohydrates or little more than warm air. We need to emphasize the soil fertility as the basis of protein synthesis.

This synthesis is the difficult part of our agricultural creative activities. It is becoming a problem of national and international scope with more implications than is commonly appreciated. Protein provision is more than a matter of purchasing it as a supplement. It is a matter of having the fertile soils to grow it as quality in the feed along with the bulk of it.

Plant roots find the clumps of manure buried in the soil and develop many extra roots there where the extra fertility can be had. In this manner the plant balances its own diet if the areas of different nutrients can be found within root reach. (Photo by courtesy of Dr. A. R. Midgeley, Vermont Agricultural Experiment Station.)

Climatic Forces Give Pattern to Soil Development

Perhaps you have never thought that the pattern of the climatic forces that develops our soils from the rocks is the pattern of our soils according as certain areas produce mainly carbonaceous crops with much bulk yield per acre, while another area produces mainly mineral-rich, proteinaceous crops less bulky.

If one looks at the map of the rainfall of the United States and omits the area west of the Coast Range, then the plant life, the animal life, and the agriculture take to a distinct pattern as one goes from the west to the east; that is, as one goes from almost no rainfall to the higher amounts of it in the east and the southeast.

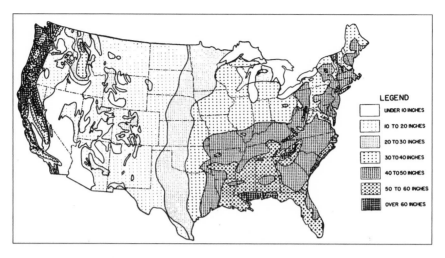

RAINFALL MAP OF THE UNITED STATES
The rainfall map gives the basis of the pattern of the fertility of our soils.

It is the water that breaks the rock down to form the clay and smaller rock fragments which compose the soil. The increasing rainfall in western United States means an increase in the clay and consequently there is more soil as the annual amount of rainfall goes higher in that area.

In the mid-continent, the soil contains a good amount of clay. The rock has been broken down and its losses have stocked the clay with these fertility elements held there in the exchangeable or available form. Plenty of calcium or lime and other fertility is left in the soil to grow legumes, to fix nitrogen, to make the soil black, and to granulate it to a good depth as we think of it in the more fertile "prairie" soils.

It was those "prairie" soils that grew grass and not forests. Those grasses were good pasture for the American bison. As a consequence we may mistakenly believe that grasses anywhere are good feed crops to make bone and brawn as they did for the buffalo.

But grasses are good feed crops only when they grow on soils equally as fertile as those chosen by the buffalo. The buffalo did not crowd into the eastern limits of the prairie where annually much more bulk of grass was produced. Quite the opposite, he stayed on the soils that were under lower amounts of annual rainfall; were richer in calcium or lime; and were therefore richer in nitrogen and and all else of fertility that encouraged growth of more protein and less of carbohydrates. He selected his feed according to its nutritional quality and not its quantity.

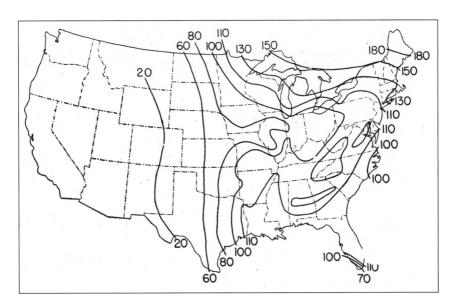

RATIOS OF RAINFALL TO EVAPORATION

Where the rainfall is more than 100 percent of the evaporation, the soils are highly leached of their fertility. The relatively low ratios of the Cornbelt suggest that it has its higher rainfall during the growing season but yet has soils not excessively leached. (Map by Prof. Transeau, Ohio State University.)

In the eastern half of the United States with annual rainfall of 40 inches or more, the rocks have not only been broken down to form much clay, but so much rain has fallen to go down through the soil to leach the available or exchangeable nutrients off the clay and to leave the clay fraction of an acid reaction. The soil is not only acid, but so much woody or carbonaceous vegetation grows that it adds much carbonic acid to the soil by decay and is keeping the soils in the northern half of the eastern United States in that acid condition.

Adding the higher temperatures to the higher rainfalls in the southeastern states breaks the rocks down more completely and forms a different clay. It is one that doesn't even hold the acid or the hydrogen; much less will it hold fertility in the form of calcium, magnesium, potassium and the other elements commonly held on the clays under lower temperatures farther north.

The soils of the South are not so acid then. Unfortunately, they are not so fertile either, since if they will not hold much acid or hydrogen, they will not hold other elements having the same electrical charge and being plant nutrients which the hydrogen is not.

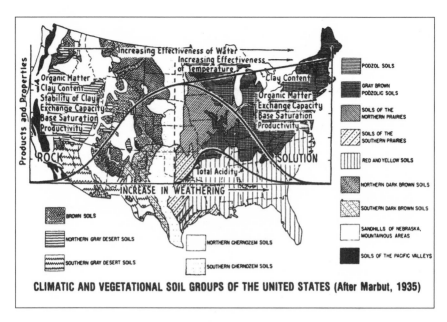

Soil Map of the United States and Curve of Soil Development. Soils in the west are under construction, while those in the east are under destruction in terms of production of protein-rich crops and body-building feeds and foods.

Soil Fertility Controls the Economics

Fortunately for the central states, much of the rainfall comes in the summer when there is also much evaporation, encouraged particularly by the winds blowing from the Southwest. As a consequence, there is rainfall to break down the rock. But instead of it going down through the soil to carry the dissolved rock products away, the water evaporates to leave them held by the clay in the soil. Thus the soils of the Cornbelt were made more fertile than many others with no more rainfall but with less evaporation.

It is the differences in the climate within the United States that makes the soils in the west different from those in the east. In the latter they are different in the north from those in the south. We have a west and an east then because the crops, animals, and peoples differ accordingly as the soils feed them differently We also have a north and a south for the same reason.

One needs only to look at our beef production to be reminded that it is in the west central states. Sheep production is there also. These highly protein bodies with less propensity to generate fat of their own choice are on the soils that are still well stocked with minerals. They are where the soils are not so highly leached and acid, where the soils still contain plenty of calcium, and where they still grow legumes "naturally".

If we look at our pork production, this fat-supplying animal power is in the region of the more leached soils. It is on the so-called acid soils which grow mainly carbohydrates and fuel values.

It is on these soils where protein supplements are a problem to the point of their being rationed in wartime. If one goes South there is cotton production and sugar production, but there is animal production only with many troubles accompanying it.

These differences in agricultural production are apt to be considered by some folks as due to differences in the economics. Yes, it is more economical to produce protein where the fertility of the soil is sufficient to do it "naturally". Yes, conversely it is less economical to produce proteins where the fertility of the soil is so low that mainly sugar and fiber crops are the natural output by it. Beneath what may be called economics are the great natural forces of creation that control even the economics.

It is wise then, or good economics, to know the fertility of the soil we are using for production of only carbohydrates to be sold as bulk, or of both carbohydrates and proteins, the latter of which demands more soil fertility for its basic services in reproduction or multiplication of the living things which agriculture creates.

Virgin Vegetation and the Soil Fertility Pattern

One needs only to recall where the virgin forests were and where the grassy prairies were, to be reminded that there was a reflection of the soil fertility pattern by the virgin vegetation. The forested soils of the eastern and southeastern states were so highly leached already then that the Creator himself could make only wood. This was possible only because the trees were putting back to the soil much of their used and reused fertility in their annual drop of leaves.

Forest soils now cleared for agriculture can scarcely be producers of protein, much less so after we have burned out by cultivation the humus residues originally left by the forests. It is those soils that can be acres for catching sunshine, fresh air and rainfall for assembling calorie values for us in fruits, sugars, vegetable oils and other fuel foods. Unfortunately,

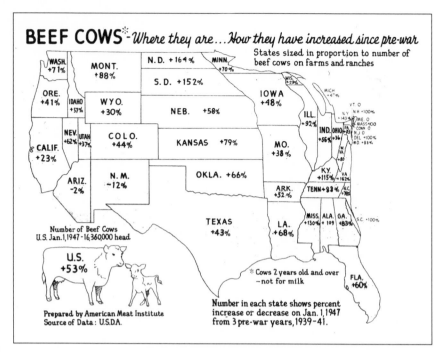

Beef production concentrates itself on the soils where lime in the soil and its pro-tein-producing power make it possible for this high protein food to be synthesized.

for good nourishment of man and beast, we need more than acres of soil. We need depth of it and much more do we need fertility in it to make proteins as well as carbohydrates.

Agricultural Crops Fit into the Climatic Pattern of Soil Fertility

Not only the virgin vegetation but also the agricultural crops in the United States divide themselves into those rich in minerals and proteins growing on the less weathered soils in the western states, and those poor in minerals and protein — therefore high in carbohydrates — in the eastern and southern states.

We have a "harder" wheat, one higher in gluten as its protein, as one goes west from the Cornbelt. We once had hard wheat in the eastern states when the Geneseo River valley was the "bread basket" of this

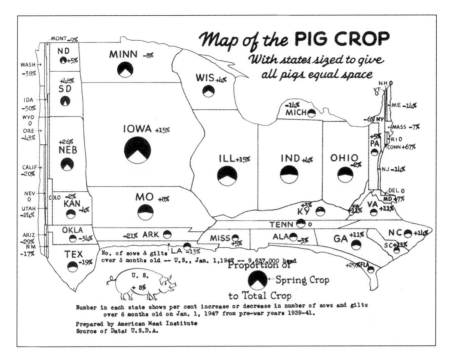

Hog production is concentrated in the cornbelt where the soil fertility encourages the crops to synthesize starch and its fattening values for mature animals more abundantly than the complete proteins for body-growing values of younger animals. (Map by courtesy of American Meat Institute.)

country. But with the exploitation of our soil fertility, our wheat goes soft.

One needs only to study the wheat of Kansas, which, in 1940, contained 10 percent of protein if grown in the eastern or wetter part of the state, but had increasing concentrations of protein going as high as 18 percent of protein in western or drier Kansas.

Only recently have we come to see that it is not the low rainfall directly that makes hard wheat, or the high rainfall directly that makes soft wheat. We have learned that it is the fertility of the soil still left in the areas of low rainfall to make proteins, and washed out of the soil to make it impossible to synthesize proteins but still possible to make carbohydrates in areas of higher rainfall.

These facts have now been demonstrated experimentally. By lowering the calcium content of the soil in relation to the potassium content, the protein synthesizing activities by the plants, depending on the calcium as the protein catalyzer become less. But the carbohydrate synthesizing activities depending on the potassium as their catalyzer remain prominent.

Since the lime goes out of the soil relatively much faster than the potassium under the climatic forces, it is this particular change in the ratio of calcium to the potassium, and changes in other ratios also, that brings changes in the food-synthesizing activities by the plants.

In this fact we have the basic principle underlying the different compositions, not only of the different kinds of plants on different soils, as illustrated by the forest trees in contrast to the prairie grasses, but also of differences within a single species, as illustrated by the differences in concentration of protein in wheat varying from 9 to 18 percent from Missouri to western Kansas.

Here then in the differences in the fertility of the soil as developed by the climatic forces, and not in the differences in the rainfall and temperature themselves, is the reason why the plants within a single species may look alike but yet be widely different in their services either as "grow" foods or as "go" foods.

Animals Balance Their Own Diets

When in the pasture of mixed herbages, we find the cow grazing some plant species closely while she allows others to grow tall, we may well believe that she is demonstrating her capacity to balance her own ration. She is probably balancing the protein in the clover against the carbohydrates in the bluegrass. She is carrying out her selections just as far as our confinement of her inside the fence and our inclusion of different herbages in the pasture permits.

If the fertility in the pasture soil has declined seriously, she reaches through the fence — or breaks through it — on to the highway or railroad right-of-way for the grass growing there where the soil has not been depleted through crop removal. On the soils of the Coastal Plains of the southeast she is on the highway grazing right along the edge of the concrete roadbed to get the more proteinaceous herbage growing on that strip of soil that is saturated by calcium and other fertility coming from the concrete.

She will select the strip in the pasture where limestone or other fertilizers have been applied. Here in these instances she is doing just as she did when her selections once led the plow of the nomads to the fertile soils. She is assaying the forage for its quality according to the fertility of the soil that is making feeds of service for body-building rather than for fattening only.

Pastures Should Consider Soil Fertility and the Physiology of the Cow

In attempting to manage the seasonal grazing program by providing the crop successions that give rye in the early spring, sweet clover next in order, bluegrass later, lespedeza after that, and so on through until the end of the season, we are forgetting that the cow is not a substitute for the mowing machine.

Pasturing is a matter that must consider the physiological performances by the soil fertility within the plants so that this forage output by the soil satisfies the physiological demands by the cow. She too is in the business of creation with a natural instinct to know the creative help she can expect from the handful of dust on which she depends for this.

Much as our cattle select their particular grazing areas in accordance with the fertility of the soil, so does the selection of plants by fungi and insects for attack and destruction suggest a correlation between these behaviors by different lower life forms and the fertility of the soil growing their victims in question. Careful observation of fungus attacks on soybeans growing on soils differently treated suggests that the attacks are made on plants that are low in lime and unable to build the protein for their own protection.

Another study suggested still more strongly that the insect, known as thrips, was attacking the spinach plants according as they were growing on soils low in either calcium or nitrogen, the two nutrient elements associated with protein production by the plants.

Such demonstrations suggest that, for the plants like for the humans, it is the protein that is protection against microbial invasions and even against insect attacks. We protect ourselves against disease by means of certain protein compounds — some injected directly into the blood stream. We call on the proteins for just such help when we cure tuberculosis by rest and a high-protein diet.

Conversely, then, can we not consider that the increasing disease, whether originating in deficiencies or in microbial attacks, is merely tell-

Hogs demonstrated their ability as judges of the quality of the corn grain when they went through this 40 acre field and hogged down first the corner where the soil had been treated to make alfalfa growth possible. (Photo by Virgil Burk, Columbia, Missouri.)

ing us that we are being given less of the kind of protection that must be built from the ground up? Isn't it possible that the decline of the soil fertility — for protein production — is registering its effects in the increasing problems of bad health and disease in both animals and humans?

Soil Fertility Controls Animal Nutrition

In order to give partial answer to the question of how far the soil fertility controls animal nutrition, three lots of seven lambs each were fed on soybean hay for a period of time followed by the feeding of lespedeza hay. Each of these hays was grown on three plots, given the following soil treatments, (a) none, (b) phosphate, and (c) lime and phosphate.

The growth of these lambs on these hays after nine weeks showed that, in the respective order of the above soil treatments, they had gained 8, 14, and 18 pounds respectively per head. They had eaten the same amount of hay per head per day, hence the differences in growth must be ascribed to the differences in nutritional values of the hays brought about by the treatment put on the soils growing them.

In addition to these differences in growth, there were wide differences in the quantity of their wool. Those sheep fed the hay from limed land produced a wool that scoured well, carded nicely, and came through as excellent fibers. Such was not the case with the wool from the sheep fed the hays from the soils not limed. Then too the lambs that had been fed hays grown on the soils given lime and phosphate were ready to be bred by the next autumn, but the others were not.

Here are significant effects, namely the better reproductive powers premised on the better fertility of the soil. Truly the creative powers reside in the handful of dust.

We are coming to see that the big agricultural problem is one of understanding — and then managing — the productive powers of the soil. These powers are reflecting their decline in the increasing difficulties in raising our animals and in keeping them reproducing regularly at high levels of fecundity.

Quality of the Same Breed Varies with Different Soils

Perhaps you have not thought that soils are widely different within an area as limited as a state like Missouri. But in order to let the animals themselves demonstrate the fact that different soils grow different animals, even of the same breeding, ten lots of lespedeza hay were assembled from the five outlying experiment fields representing the five soil areas of Missouri. The hays represented each area with the soil given (a) no soil treatment, and (b) soil treatment, or a total of ten lots of hay.

Ten rabbits were fed on each lot only to find that the originally uniform group of 100 rabbits was changed to ten different groups. Each group now reflected the soil and the fertilizer treatment on which the hay had been grown. Here it was not the breed but the feed that determined the animal characteristics; that is, the appearance, the blood picture under test, the weight of their bones, the breaking strength of these, and other body and physiological characters not so commonly considered as under the control of the fertility of the soil growing the feed.

Our Teeth and the Fertility of Our Soils

The bones of our own bodies suggest that their qualities are correlated with the quality of the soils growing our foods. This may seem to be a stretch of the imagination. However, if we consider the teeth as an exposed part of our skeleton, and if we use the data of the condition of the young men of the nation as revealed by the inductees into the Navy, the numbers of cavities of our teeth reflect the climatic pattern of soil fertility.

Those inducted from the mid-continental belt along the Mississippi river, that had the prairie grasses and the soil fertility with pronounced protein-producing power in it, had the lowest number of cavities in the teeth per individual. In going east or in going west from the soils of this area and its more pronounced fertility, there was an increase in the numbers of cavities and fillings per mouth of the young men taken into the Navy, as reported for some 70,000.

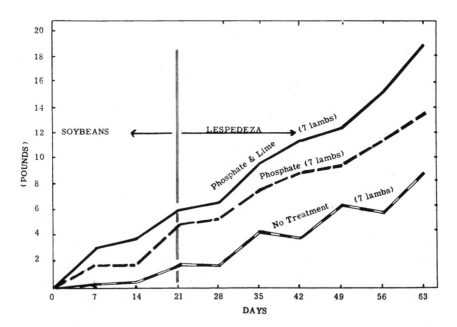

CURVES OF GROWTH OF SHEEP
Experimental trials with lambs demonstrated that even though they consumed the same amounts of lespedeza hay per head per day, they made more growth according as the soils growing the hay were given more fertility treatments. (Photo courtesy Missouri Agricultural Experiment Station.)

One scarcely needs to be a chemist or a plant physiologist to see the climatic pattern of fertility reflected in the soil and the vegetation. That pattern was being reflected more clearly by the young men of the Navy as they opened their mouths and told us that we humans, like the animals and the plants, are a part of the ecological array of all life that reveals its pattern of characters according to the fertility pattern of the soil by which these are created.

Soil Fertility Pattern and the International Food Problem

The pattern of soil development and its corresponding fertility pattern is larger than a national pattern. It may be one that will be helpful in seeing the pattern of soil fertility and the quality of food as basic to the present food problem of the world.

One needs only to look at the soil map of the world and search out the soil areas similar to ours that produce the proteins in the wheat and the meat as we have them in the United States. When one finds that these soil areas are located in the Soviet Republic, and in the outlying dominions of Great Britain, one can find good suggestion why these countries, along with the United States, are the present major world powers.

We can also understand why Japan went into North China (into South China only under war), Mussolini went into North Africa, and Hitler wanted to go east into the Ukraine of the Soviet Republic. When the leaders of their respective countries did not have the necessary fertility resources to produce the foods that truly satisfy, might we not anticipate their military movements in certain particular directions under compulsion of the force of hunger?

Perhaps we can see the present world problem not as one provoked by politicians, but rather as one of an exhausted fertility and thereby one of producing food that does more than deliver calories.

Perhaps we can project into the future to see our own own problems as threatening duplications of those of the Old World, and realize very soon how significant the conservation of the soil and its fertility is in preserving our own freedom and democracy.

These much-mentioned characters of a well governed group of people cannot be imposed on the hungry group. They must be inherent in the group because of the contentment that comes with the security of better food and which cannot be supplied except by ample fertile soil.

It is this broader aspect of animal production, pointing to the human just above the animal, that gives significance to the fertility of the soil. Shall we not, each one of us, undertake our separate responsibilities in conserving the soil and its fertility so that thereby we may preserve ourselves, our freedom, and our democracy, all at the same time?

Soil treatment for the growth of lespedeza hay brought about a decidedly better growth of the rabbits, and bigger size and strength in their bones. (Photo by Missouri Agricultural Experiment Station.)

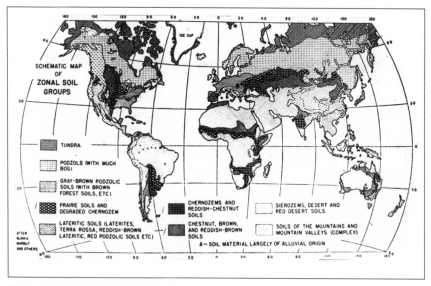

SOIL MAP OF THE WORLD
By using the soils of the United States as a guide, it is evident that the soils of the world similar to our hard wheat and beef area are limited and in control of mainly the "Three Powers".

CHAPTER 8

Soil and Livestock
Work Together

LIVESTOCK IS THE SOURCE of many of our best food proteins. These are the result of complex life processes in the soil, in the microbes, in the plants, and in the animals. All these add up to good food, provided all the essential raw materials are supplied at the starting point, which is the soil. Livestock and soil work together with the soil in control. As a phase of this natural performance of manufacturing proteins, we may well study first the soils under their general fertility pattern as this is suggestive in solving the problem of giving us plenty of protein in the form of meat.

The provision of protein as food is not only a struggle for us humans, but is one for animals and for plants as well. Reproduction — the very purpose of existence — depends highly on this food and body constituent. The stream of life flows, not from one grain of sugar to another, not from one starch cell to another, not from one globule of fat to another, but only from one molecule of protein to another protein molecule. Consequently, if life exists and multiplies itself, it must succeed in appropriating unto itself plenty of protein. This must be done either by the direct synthesis of it from the elements in the weather and those in the fertility of the soil, or by consumption of the amino acids already synthesized by some other living agency. Obtaining protein sufficient for body growth and reproduction is a strenuous struggle, whether it is by the simple microbial cell or the complex human body.

All Life Forms Obtain Their Proteins According as the Soil Fertility Permits

For the human, the protein problem is one of providing both the proper amount and the proper quality of it. As to the amount, this is a problem very often of the economics of purchase. As to the quality, this problem solves itself more readily by choice of those produced by life forms higher in the biotic pyramid, such, for example, as the animal proteins in meat, milk, eggs, and fish. Plant proteins, originating lower in the biotic scale, often leave doubt as to their sufficiency in quality or their completeness in all the amino acids. Fortunately some proteins originating in some forms as low as the yeast, contribute specific qualities coming now to be highly appreciated.

Quality of proteins is a bigger problem according as we consider those given us by life forms of less complicated physiology. The proteins of the complex synthetic potentialities in our meat animals are more nearly like those of our own bodies. They are therefore more nearly complete in quality. Meat is therefore such a universally desired food. Plant proteins too often represent a problem of supplementing them with animal proteins for our proper diet. Microbial proteins have food and feed values too as we recognize in well-ripened cheese for ourselves, and in those synthesized from urea, for example, by the microbial flora in the upper part of the animal intestinal tract for later assimilation during the conversion of feeds in digestive transit.

The problem of proteins for the wild animals is one of finding in the plants all the required amino acids. For this reason the deer browse on only the growing buds, that is, the highly reproductive parts with the higher mineral and protein concentrations than the rest of the plant. For this reason deer and other herbivora search out the fertilized fields and cultivated gardens to be considered such terrible marauders. The protein problem for our wild life is serious enough to be a potent force bringing on wildlife extinction against which we are holding out hope while struggling to combat it by other means and in disregard of the soil fertility in control.

For our domestic animals we say it is a problem of "purchasing" protein feed supplements. For some farm animals these can be wholly vegetable in origin. For others they must be both vegetable and animal. For blockaded Britain, this problem meant almost the elimination of hogs and poultry while the farm animals of strictly herbivorous feeding habits were maintained. Here the longer animal gut that permitted more extensive symbiotic services by the microbial synthesizers of protein within it was almost a second Dunkerque in saving that country. The microbes, a life form so low in the biotic scale as to be right next to the soil, played a larger role in solving Britain's protein problem than we are wont to recognize.

The problem for the plant of providing its protein parts represents a still larger struggle. The plant is fixed in place. It must start with the simple elements, and possibly some limited compounds within root reach. From these it synthesizes first its amino acids and then synthesizes the proteins from them. Such is the problem of constructing its body by cellular multiplication, possible only through protein of its own complete elaboration.

Only the plants and life forms lower in the biotic pyramid, according to present knowledge, can synthesize amino acids. It is this plant process, in the main, which makes higher life forms so dependent on plants and through them dependent on the elements of fertility in the soil. It is this dependence of man and his animals on the amino acids — the building stones of the life-carrying proteins — synthesized by the plants generously only on the more fertile soils, that gives a pattern of the protein problem in agriculture. This pattern, in turn, is premised on the pattern of the fertility of the soil.

Synthesis of Carbohydrates by Plants is Mainly a Matter of the Weather; Synthesis of Proteins, of the Soil Fertility

The plant's problem of making the carbohydrate part of its food is not so complex. According to the best knowledge, we believe it a process of the union of carbon dioxide and water brought about by the sun driven chemical process we call photosynthesis. Carbohydrates are the result of uniting these weather-given elements for which but few soil-borne nutrients are required. These are magnesium and iron in the chlorophyl for sugar synthesis; potassium for its conversions into other carbohydrates; and possibly others. But all of these from the soil are required in only very small amounts, and then possibly only in catalytic services with none of them appearing in the carbohydrate itself.

The plant assembles this energy-providing part of itself readily. In fact, the carbohydrate is the basic raw material for constructing the plant mass of cellulose and other major parts of its bulk. This process is the readily recognizable demonstration of increase in size that we call plant growth. It is this carbohydrate synthesis that has long been our measure of agricultural production and of the productivity of the soil. So little of soil fertility is required for mere production of carbohydrates that the deficiencies in the soil seldom impose serious restrictions on this process. Carbohydrates, or energy foods for plants do not represent much of a struggle. They are readily synthesized. They are mainly supra-soil in terms of the raw materials and the energy for their construction.

But for the conversion of the carbohydrates of photosynthetic origin into the proteins of biosynthetic origin, much soil fertility is required. For the growth of the protein-rich legumes, we have long known that the soil must supply considerable calcium. For that reason we have limed the land. We now know that non-legumes, too, require calcium if they are to be more proteinaceous.

Calcium is not only an agent in protein synthesis but is also a potent force in mobilizing other nutrients as well as itself into the plant roots. As a consequence, soils that are not leached by high rainfalls but are still stocked with calcium and other mineral nutrients grow forages, both legume and non-legume, that are rich in proteins and rich in minerals of nutrient values not yet fully understood.

Protein production by our crops, which is recognized more commonly as generous seed production calls for a generous delivery of all the soil-borne nutrient elements by the assembly lines in the soil as well as for a carbohydrate manufacturing activity drawing mainly on carbon, hydrogen and oxygen from the weather. Conditions very commonly permit the plants to produce carbohydrates, but for the conversion of these into proteins the conditions are not so generally favorable. For this conversion some dozen or more nutrients of mineral origin with calcium at the head of the list must be provided. We now know that most plants are potentially producers of much more protein, but that the shortages in the fertility of the soil prohibit their meeting their potentiality and limit them to the delivery mainly of carbohydrates.

Soil fertility comes into decided prominence, then, in the struggle for protein by the plant, by the animal and by us humans. The plant's synthesis of itself as carbonaccous bulk is not seriously stymied by deficiencies of some on the list of nutrient elements we call soil fertility. Nor is it stymied if it reproduces vegetatively. Under such reproduction it maintains the bulk of itself seemingly well. Consequently as long as our observation of the plant as bulk is our only criterion of soil productivity, we are oblivious to the role of soil fertility in making proteins as the important services by plants for higher life forms like animals and man. It is the provision of proteins made up of their many different amino acids that determines the seed yield and the reproduction by plants. It also determines the survival of man and his animals with him. It is via protein production by our crop plants that the pattern of soil fertility gives the ecological pattern of the people in the United States and in the world as a whole.

High Protein Delivery by Plants Occur on the Calcareous Soil Developed Under Moderate Rainfall and Temperature

Since soils are a temporary reststop by rocks on their way to solution and the sea, they vary widely in fertility according to the distance they have been pushed in that direction by the climatic forces of rainfall and temperature. In the early stages of this travel, the soils that are still mainly rock because of low annual rainfall, do not contain enough clay. Nor is that clay sufficiently saturated by a diverse list of nutrient elements through extensive rock breakdown to make productive soils. Very often the clay of such soils is saturated with too much sodium. But under increased amounts of rainfall approaching 30 inches annually, and under moderate temperatures like those of the temperate zone, the soils contain ample clay. This soil separate is well stocked with calcium and other nutrients, to say nothing of there being left also plenty nutrient mineral reserves in the silt separate. These by their continued breakdown serve to maintain a relatively high nutrient saturation of the clay. Such soil areas grow the annual and periodically dormant grass crops we call the prairie grasses. They do not allow forests or other perennials to survive their drought periods. This is the region of the highly proteinaceous vegetation that supports the herbivora today much like it supported the buffalo which the pioneer found so plentiful on the western prairies and plains.

Under annual rainfalls higher than 30 inches the perennial vegetation like the forests is common. With these and still heavier rainfalls but moderate temperatures the leaching effects on the clay result in the removal of its stock of adsorbed fertility. The leaching substitutes hydrogen or acidity on the clay for it. The reserve minerals in the silt are weathered out to leave the silt and sand fractions that consist mainly of quartz and hence of no nutrient values.

Under both higher rainfalls and higher temperatures, the clay as the remnant of rock weathering is no longer the silicate compound with its high exchange capacity for nutrient ions. Instead, it represents the loss of silica and is the red lateritic clay so high in iron and aluminum with almost no exchange capacity. It fails to hold even hydrogen or to be acid. It will therefore hold little or none of the many other cations with nutritional services to plants, animals, and man. Tropical red soils then have little fertility absorbed on their clay. Nor do they contain reserve minerals as potential fertility to be weathered out eventually as is true for soils under moderate rainfall and moderate temperature. They are therefore producers mainly of wood. Animal and other higher life there struggles for proteins. Carnivora rather than herbivora are the rule in their fauna.

Soils that are productive, in terms of delivery of protein, then are those developed under moderate to scanty rainfall in the temperate zone. It is on these where vegetative bulk is not so plentifully produced because, as we so commonly say, "there just isn't enough rainfall". Soils that are highly productive in giving us carbohydrates and much vegetative bulk, occur under higher rainfalls. These larger amounts of water, when under moderate temperatures, leach them to a state of strong acids on a montmorillonitic clay, but to a lateritic clay with almost no acidity under tropical heat. For vegetation as a generous producer of protein there must be both enough rainfall for carbohydrate production and at the same time enough of the fertility of the soil for the biosynthetic conversion of this fuel food into protein as the growth-promoting food. This combination of climate and soil fertility is not so universally found. Hence it is evident that protein production is not so universal an occurrence. Rather it is in limed areas. Outside of these areas it is possible only as we duplicate their fertility conditions by our management of the soil.

Soil Fertility and Protein Production Patterns of the United States are Suggestive

A careful study of the fertility of the soils of the United States formulates a pattern of it that gives helpful suggestions for our struggle with the protein problem. Starting from the arid West and going eastward, there are increasing rainfall and increasing degrees of the development of the rocks into soil. This gives increasing clay content and an increasing stock of fertility on that clay until the rainfall amounts to that of about the mid-continental area. The still higher rainfalls then as one goes eastward from there mean the loss of fertility from the clay and the substitution of acidity for it. This increasing incidence of acidity represents a sharp decline in the supply of the many fertility elements. Unfortunately, however, the calcium supply decreases so much faster than the others on the list of soil-borne essentials. This results then in a narrowing ratio of the calcium to the potassium, for example. This fact represents a decided reduction of the protein-producing power inherent in the calcium, while the carbohydrate-producing power represented by the potassium is much less reduced. Consequently, in this lowered ratio of the exchangeable calcium to the exchangeable potassium, brought on by soil fertility removal either by nature or by man, we have the clue for the lowered protein output by the soils while the output of carbohydrate holds up. Here is the chemical foundation in terms of soil fertility from which we must take our suggestion and work in making protein-production possible through judicious soil management.

Up to this time in our land use we have been putting limestone on our soils under the mistaken belief that the benefits from it rested in the reduction of the acidity of the soil by the carbonate radical. Unwittingly, we have been applying calcium and helping to manufacture more proteins in the legume forages. But, unfortunately also we have gone forward in our soil liming campaign under the belief that lime is all that is needed, and that "if a little is good more will be better". This generous use of lime has mobilized out of our soils and into greater production of our crops many of the other elements among which potassium has been most prominent. We are now coming face to face with the soil's need for potassium. We have credited the lime and its neutralization of acidity with working wonders while unbeknown to us it was helping to exhaust our soil fertility more rapidly in many other respects than calcium.

It is essential to remember that we need potassium to make the carbohydrates first in the plant before it can convert them into protein. Red clover was once said to fail because of acid soils. But this crop as a great livestock feed has not come back on increased acreage now that we have the hordes of trucks covering thousands of acres with limestone. It has not come back because our humid soils need potassium as well as calcium. They possibly need also many other nutrient elements if clover is to grow and to manufacture the collection of amino acids that constitute its proteins and make it such a desirable feed.

We have been fighting soil acidity when we should have been supplying calcium as the foremost help in protein synthesis by our crops. We have been thinking only one element of fertility when we should be thinking several. We have been hunting for new crops instead of restoring the fertility to sustain those that are of higher nutritive values because they require more help from the soil fertility to make themselves so. Instead of undergirding the more nutritious forages in their struggle to synthesize protein we have been juggling crops with their production of tonnage per acre as the only criterion. Sweet clover, bolstered by an application of limestone, replaced red clover because the former has a tremendous tonnage-producing power. This replacement has occurred in spite of the vigorous protest of our cattle against sweet clover as a feed for them, and our appreciation of red clover and alfalfa as so much better feed. Soil acidity has been a mental bayou within which we paddled circuitously about when we should have been rowing down the stream of straighter thinking to reach the conclusion that soil acidity is not a serious trouble per se, but is only the reciprocal of the exhaustion of the soil fertility.

We Have Been Mining Our Soil and Moving Westward Rather Than Maintain Their Fertility

We have now had enough experience in the production of feeds and livestock in the United States to have the problem areas well located. High output of protein as beef and mutton is most efficient on the soils well stocked with calcium and less weathered of their other fertility elements. It occurs on the soils where plants can manufacture themselves more from the soil and less from the weather and make more protein. High output of fat as hogs may be found where starchy feeds dominate and the lower fertility limits us to crops originating more from the weather to give mainly carbohydrate products. That we have been mining our soils and thereby are being driven westward is now becoming evident. The milk-sheds of the East are no longer producing milk by means of the wheat bran, the shorts, and the other concentrates moved eastward so freely from the more fertile soils of the western hard" wheat area. The largest beef cattle market is now Kansas City with other cities located approximately along the same meridian of longitude also handling more sheep and cattle than ever before.

Right here in the Cornbelt we have swelled in our pride of pushing up the yield as bushels of corn per acre, yet during the last ten years the protein concentration in that feed grain has dropped from an approximate average figure of 9.5 to 8.5 percent. The bulk-producing and the fattening powers of our agricultural output have held up. But the power for promoting growth and reproduction, which resides in the protein and not in the starch of the feeds, has gone down. Hybrid corn that disregards its need for reproducing itself, does not report to us the shortages of soil fertility by manifesting its increasing sterility. Here in this feed crop, like in the horticultural crops that are multiplied by cuttings and buddings instead of by seeds, the carbohydrate production holds our attention and generates economic satisfaction while no attention goes to the declining soil fertility that is making seed production — and thereby the plant's reproduction — impossible.

Animal sterility, too, is an increasing trouble. We are not apt to see this as a problem of producing protein in the form of sperm and ova dependent on soil fertility via proteinaceous and mineral-rich feeds. Crop juggling with bulk as the objective has brought more carbonaceous and less proteinaceous forages and feeds into our systems of land use. With them have come the increasing animal deficiencies. We are not very apt to see the declining soil fertility as the cause of these and take to treating our soils for their prevention. Instead we are apt to build a false hope on artificial insemination and other contrivances of the breeding business.

Seemingly only by more disasters will we eventually come to see in the fertility of the soil the ultimate of the synthetic performances that give us protein, which not only represents the power of reproduction but the power of growth itself. When only 60 percent of our annual pig crop survives to be marketed, and when "shy-breeders" cause much of our animal reproducing power to stay idle annually, we need to see that these troubles in their pattern of severity superimpose themselves on the soil. We cannot continually move westward to fertile virgin soils. We must face the problem that we can no longer run away from it.

The Protein Problem is a World Food Problem According to Soil Fertility

Two world wars that were fought under the slogan that "Food Will Win the War and Write the Peace", ought to encourage our inventory of the soil resources that were the food resources by which one group of the fighting nations became the victors while another became the vanquished. We may well look to the soil fertility supplies by which the Three Great Powers emerged in the category of that distinction and only by which they will stay there.

One needs to look at the soil map of the world and to remember that proteins of high food value as found in hard wheat, beef, and mutton, for example, are the products of soils that are only moderately weathered. Such soils and such protein products, then, must occur under moderate rainfalls and in the temperate zone. Such soils with extensive areas of hard wheat and animal herds in large numbers occur in the mid-continental United States. Likewise there are similar extensive areas in the Soviet Republic. It is these soil fertility resources in terms of protein production that give strong suggestions why these two nations are listed among the Great Powers. As for England in this category with them, the British Isles do not have extensive areas of soils that produce hard wheat. But when Canadian soils represent high protein-producing powers, and corresponding soils are extensive in Australia and South Africa — all parts of the British Empire — there is ample suggestion that ships on the sea represent the strength of this third one of the Three Great Powers.

The strength of any nation — in what is too readily considered as a political strength — depends on high levels of fertility of the soils that represent protein production as food. The weak powers, under the analysis for their soil resources, all reflect very clearly their insufficiency as producers of food proteins. It is in terms of soil fertility resources and not of international politics that the world must be inventoried if we are to understand and solve the international food problem. We must realize that it is very acutely a protein problem rather than one of only calories.

Conservation of Fertility Must Become the Major Effort of Soil Conservation

Seemingly we are still nomadic in our hopes and in our thinking about our future food supplies. We are delayed in realizing that about all the land areas of significant protein power have been taken over and put into production. We are still more delayed in appreciating the problem of maintaining in the future the capacity to produce protein where such was a simple matter in the past. We need careful inventories of the fertility resources in our soils, and of the supplies of minerals that can serve as fertilizers in soil fertility restoration. Those of us living in cities, those managing big industries, and all in the congested food-consuming rather than food-producing centers need to understand and appreciate the rate at which our soils are being exploited and not rebuilt. All of us need to aid and encourage soil restoration in terms of those nutrient elements serving in the struggle for protein (a) in the life of the microbe in the soil, (b) in the life of the crops in the field, (c) in the life of the animals, and (d) in our own human lives. We need to realize that T-bone steaks are not grown on city pavements, but only where the fertility of the soil keeps the assembly lines filled with the raw materials on which all agricultural production, and thereby food production, depends.

As fast as that realization comes to us, we shall become soil conservationists aiming not only to stop the damages to the soil by running water, but also to rebuild the fertility strength in the body of the soil. It was by that kind of strength that the soil originally saved itself and that it can do so again under our realization of the fertility facts and by our action accordingly. Only as we build back according to the pattern of the soil fertility can we solve the problem of producing plenty of protein, which as a food product is not the particular concern of the meat industry alone, but of us individuals, of the nation, and of the whole world itself.

CHAPTER 9

As Animals Judge Your Crops & Feed Values Are Soil Values

IN CALCULATING THE VALUE of fertilizer treatments or of manure spread on the soil, we have been inclined to charge the cost of the application against the first crop following it. Just how many successive crops on the land are benefited by a single fertility treatment and how long it continues to render returns is a question that has often been raised, but not answered specifically.

By comparing the weights of the crop from the soil once fertilized with those from soils not so treated, one commonly finds that crop increases so measured are not carried forward over many years. However — when the crop's improved feeding values for livestock and the discriminating selections by animals are brought in to evaluate the effects of putting some fertility back on the soil — then, the effects appear to be much more lasting.

The testimony of the dumb beast points out that we have not appreciated the long-time effects given by barnyard manures, fertilizers, green manures and other restorative additions to the soil.

A Missouri Demonstration

For just how many years the cattle can recognize the effects on the hay from fertilizer put on the surface of a meadow was effectively demonstrated by the herds of some 200-300 head of cattle on the farm of E. M. Poirot, Lawrence county, Missouri. In the spring of 1936, he top-dressed a small part of a virgin prairie meadow by drilling fertilizers of various

The haystack (left) containing some hay from fertilized soil mixed through part of it, as the cattle were cutting it in two, to leave one end (stack at the right) made from "unfertilized" hay. After eight years, livestock cleaned up the "fertilized" hay entirely before consuming the other stacks from unfertilized soil.

kinds. This was done in the hope of improving the natural grasses and legumes by this simple method. No rates of any one application exceeded 300 pounds per acre. Not more than two treatments were combined.

The soil treatments were mad across one end of the meadow and covered scarcely more than four of the 100 acres in the field. Because lime was so badly needed on his soil, the fertilizer nitrogen was used as calcium cyanamid.

Examinations of the grasses were made during the early summer following the soil treatment. Later in the season the prairie grass was cut for hay. That from the four acres given fertilizer was a part of 25 acres that went into the first stack. Three additional stacks, each of hay from an area of 25 acres without soil treatment, were the balance of the winter hay supply in this field.

In late October, the cattle were turned into this 100-acre field with the four haystacks. They entered from the end opposite the one where the fertilizer treatments were made. Surprisingly, the cattle soon were gathered about the one stack consisting in part of the hay from the fertilized soil area. The other three stacks were disregarded daily, as the cattle went by them — back and forth between this chosen feed and the water and salt in the lot adjoining. This stack of their first choice was consumed before the cattle took the three remaining stacks from soil without treatment.

After 1936 no more fertilizer applications were made. But each year and on through 1943 the hay was made and stacked in the usual manner. Likewise the large herd of cattle was turned in to consume the hay as winter feed. Year after year, they took first this one stack into which there was mixed less than one-fifth of its bulk of hay from soil given fertilizers back in 1936. For eight successive hay crops, the cattle recognized in the hay mixture the effects of the soil treatment on only a small part of it.

Still Strong After Eight Years

During 1943, the eight time of this manifestation of choice by the cattle, their discrimination was particularly keen. In making the hay that year the stack bottom initially laid down was not large enough to include all the hay from the 25 acres which usually went into the first stack. Consequently, after the hay from the treated soil had already been swept in, with considerable from soil given no fertilizer, the stack was extended at one end. Into the extension went the hay that came from untreated land.

When the cattle were turned in that winter they again went to this stack in preference to the other three from soil that had never been fertilized. But they did not take the entire stack. They ate first only that part in which there was mixed the hay from soil fertilized eight years before. They literally cut the stack in two. They left the end made up only of hay from soil never fertilized. Then when this hay was all that remained, the herd no longer crowded about the one stack. In stead, they distributed themselves about the other three stacks are readily as about this remnant.

Dividends Over Long Period

Here was evidence given by the cattle that after eight years there were still in the hay crop some recognizable qualities produced by putting back on the soil some of the fertility that it gives up in crop production. Here the cattle were reporting that, for eight years after one application of small amounts of plant nutrients, there were still returns to be had in better crops, as the animals judge them. The better crops represented better feed consumption and, therefore, doubtlessly better animal gains.

Such discriminations by livestock are pointing out that when we put manures, fertilizers, and other contributions of fertility back into the soil we gather dividends over a much longer period than we have commonly believed.

Feed Values Are Soil Values

Recently a farmer friend of mine told me, "I've moved to another farm where I get bigger yields in all my feed crops. But even though I shovel much more corn and pitch a lot more hay, I can't get my calves to market as early. I'm just not growing as much meat per acre."

This man doesn't realize that feed bulk is no indication of feed value. Livestock will not gain more on larger rations unless the feed value of any crop is derived from the basic plant food elements found in the soil. The crop must first build up the woody structure that makes up its bulk. Then, if soil conditions are right, the plant will store up a supply of the raw materials of protein, vitamine, and mineral compounds. Thus, whether a crop offers anything more than bulk and fattening power depends on the condition of the soil on which it grew. *Live stock may be fed great quantities of feedstuffs produced on poor soils and still fail to gain weight.* It is soil that has been guarded against erosion, fertilized properly, and carefully managed, that grows nutritious crops. Such soil will produce crops that give better feeding results and make more meat per acre.

CHAPTER 10

In Defense of the Cow

NOW THAT WE ARE beginning to be more conservation-minded nationally, it was recently well said by Bernard Frank, "Wherever man seeks to improve upon his environment — to increase the productivity of his land and water resources — without adequate knowledge of the ecological mechanisms thereof, his ignorance — even though innocent — is more likely to upset the balance of nature. And whenever man carries this process of improvement to the point of exhaustion of the resources, he must look around for something on which to put the blame for his folly."

Because man is above the animals and other life forms in the biotic pyramid between him and the soil serving as the foundation of all of them, his failure to fit himself into nature makes him pick on his scapegoats. We are taking the cow as a case in question for this discussion, and are rising as her defense attorney to plead her case.

In view of the above quotation, which summarizes so well our failure to practice conservation of our natural resources, one can see in those remarks the outline for this discussion which divides itself nicely into five sections.

1. *Man's assumption of the natural resources for his exploitation and use while oblivious of their contribution to him through other life forms.*
2. *His inadequate knowledge of ecological arrays, or patterns, of life according as the soils create and nourish them.*
3. *The upset of the balance of nature, by his technologies used according to his economic criteria for improved environment.*
4. *The impending exhaustion of our neglected but vital resources, especially the soil fertility.*
5. *Other life forms paying with their death penalty by taking the blame, as illustrated by our foster mother, the cow.*

The cow, as one of our livestock forms, may well serve in this discussion as the scapegoat for man's folly in aiming to increase the productivity of his land resources without giving consideration to how she and all the other life forms, including man himself, are paying for his folly in not fitting into nature when he believes he is managing and controlling all.

Man Today Assumes the Natural Resources for his Exploitation and Use; But Forgets Their Contributions Through Other Life Forms

Man is of necessity the apex of evolutionary forces. He is also the most complex physiological unit of different life processes. Consequently, he makes the most demands for, and covers most land area in finding the means of satisfying his nutritional requirements. The cow, only one step lower in the evolutionary scale, must also cover much land area in collecting her feed essentials.

Primitive man, living closer to nature, and in fuller respect of the cow's instincts for wisely selecting her necessary nourishment, put the cow ahead of the plow. She went ahead and he followed. By her choice of grazing, she was assaying the fertility of the soil according as this grew vegetation which was truly building her a healthy body, reproducing her offspring and thereby multiplying her species. Primitive man followed the cow to outline the agricultural areas of the early world. He was not oblivious to her contribution of essentials for herself in the contributions by plants. She was synthesizing them into still more complicated organic compounds. All of these were supporting primitive man and making possible the many intricate and unknown physiological processes by which he, as a reasoning animal, may have dominion over the rest of them. Primitive man was fitting himself into nature rather than fighting her as his ruler.

Modern man stepped out of the confines of territory outlined by the cow. He disregarded her ability as an assayer of the soil fertility creating her nutrition in terms of proteins, vitamins and mineral elements, all combined into high-quality feed along with carbohydrate bulk. He put the plow ahead of the cow on more lands to conquer. Equipped with newer tools and more power in his command, he moved out of the semi-arid lands. He moved away from the sea shores, out of the cow pastures, and into regions of high rainfall, and high yields of bulk of vegetation.

But he moved into regions of less proteins, where no life forms duplicating his complex physiology, or that of the cow, had ever been known to survive. Did the Pilgrim fathers find any human life form surviving in New England, unless a fish as fertilizer under each hill of corn was used to grow this starchy crop? Did they find cows or other herbivorous feeders scattered in good numbers throughout Virginia and the south to suggest that the soils were growing forage crops giving much of the proteins and these complete enough for fecund animal reproduction? Modern man overran large territories. He expanded his domain. He gloated in the control of it and in his new-won freedom, but he was dragging the cow along in spite of her protest.

The cow, transplanted under such circumstances to the eastern United States, has been in extensive revolt there. She refuses to subscribe to the economics of cheap gains and cheap gallons. She objects to being confined by fences, in spite of tortures by the yokes and barbed wires on going thru them. She goes out on the railroad right of way or highways to be killed by speeding trains, autos, and other death-dealing transports.

In the south, she insists on coming out of the Piney Woods to graze along the very edges of the pavement so persistently that her mangled carcasses on the highway shoulders are not an unusual sight for the motor traveler in the Coastal Plains areas. She is refusing to conceive and to freshen according to our planned schedules. She takes to mastitis on slightest provocation. She is putting bacteria into her milk more commonly. She is not nursing her own calves successfully enough to escape calling in foreign nurse cows. She is taking all kinds of baffling "diseases," ailments and irregularities in her health. She is moving in that direction so badly that killing her to save other cows, and even humans, is threatening her own bovine species with extinction.

The cow, too, enjoyed expansion of her domain and of her freedom on being taken west. That was her bonanza when she arrived in the mid-continent. There the bison had mapped out the soils in his assay of them according as they were regularly helping little buffaloes become big ones and big ones make many more little ones every spring.

But from there she was soon pushed farther west. A grain agriculture replaced her. Suitcase farming, like all extensive, highly mechanical cultures, has always disregarded the cow for her contributions to the good food and good health of man, readily forgetting her as his foster mother. That disregard was provoked by the rush to collect (rather than earn) the most possible from the natural resources. That rush for the resources comes at the cost of their speedy exploitation and not their conservation. While modern man's technologies have lengthened his life lines and lifted his living standards far above those of the primitive, they have shortened and lowered, most seriously, those of the cow.

Moved to the urban pavements now to the extent of more than 90% of our population while but 10% and less of it retains contact with the soil, according to a late census, it is difficult to appreciate the dangerous length to which man's life lines are stretched. Many of them are breaking. Many are being shortened and even cut off. Are we surprised that man, so far removed from the source of his food, and from the experience of his hands working directly in the creation of it, should be a ready victim of crowd psychology, or of communistic promises for collecting a living rather than earning it?

Do the violent swings in election results and the mounting numbers of such swingers not suggest that we are no longer living by democratic principles which classify each of us as independent in our political philosophy, but rather, as we are running hither and yon, take to any kind of belief offering more for less? Can our dwindling natural resources per person as a result of exploitation and increasing population be lessening our faiths in our individual future securities?

Insufficient is Our Knowledge of the Physiology of Different Agricultural Plants and Livestock Dominating the Location According as the Soil Fertility Supports Them and Their Output of Created Values

When the cow went west, where she has been doing so well by "rustling" for herself on the range, she was merely reporting that it is the soil and not the particular grass species that supports her in making her calf crops. She is telling us that agriculture will not give an abundant production by our animals merely because of what species of crops we choose. Rather she is telling us that most abundant production by our animals will be possible only when the soils anywhere offer to any plants the protein-producing, the life-creating potential they offer in the semi-humid soils along the 97th meridian. The cow is revolting against our ignorance of her choice of crops grown on fertile soils delivering body-building rather than fattening values. She is pointing to the soil fertility pattern in control of the different ecological array of plant species, and thereby of all animal species, including even the human.

That any and every soil should provide balanced fertility for any plant which we might choose seems to be taken for granted. Shall we expect alfalfa, which is famous as a protein supplement, to make its excellent feed values on the same soil where Korean lespedeza accepts broom sedge (*Andropogon virginicus*) as its nurse crop? We turn our crops out in a seeding operation in the spring time and expect them to "rustle" for themselves. At harvest time we go out with combine or picker to round them up and measure the yield, much as the pioneer Ozarker turned the sow out into the woods in the spring and then in the colder fall weather, when sow-belly as supplement to cornpone was needed, took his gun to round up the sow and litter to see the size of the pig crop.

Our knowledge of plant requirements as soil fertility is insufficient to know on what soil to put each crop for the highest yields in both *quantity* and *quality*. Nor do we know just how to feed each crop to make it good feed for the cow, even if with the use of nitrogen we are making hundred bushel corn crops very common occurrences. We call it a crop rotation when we have in succession on the same soil even a 50-bushel corn crop creating 225 pounds of incomplete protein in the grain and then a red clover crop that fails in yielding two tons of forage representing nearly 500 pounds of much more complete protein, and equal to making up the protein deficiencies in corn by serving as a protein supplement for it.

If we haven't yet learned how to keep the same crop growing continuously and successfully on the same soil, why should we believe a collection of four or more crops juggled into a rotation on the same soil should be more wisely, or suitably, nourished to create the collections of widely different nutrient compounds by which each of them grows? Why should there be nutritional virtues in crop juggling because there are more virtues in the rotation in relation to the labor program, or other economic aspects of farm management? Isn't it high time that we learn just what each crop must be given, via the soil, to feed it for the creative (not just filling) functions it performs? When we discard certain small grain varieties in favor of new ones because as we say "The old varieties are running out" can't we believe they are running out in search of nourishment just as the cow is doing when she breaks through the pasture fence? Is the case for the hungry crops which are confined to the soils of declining fertility any different from the case of the hungry cow breaking out of the much-farmed, fertility exhausted pasture to get to the unfarmed and unexploited soil on the highway or railroad right of way?

Crop juggling to get various rotations and juggling out the "tried and true" while juggling in the "new," have been popular agronomic pastimes. We have juggled in the substitutes with no thought of their fertility demands on the soil. Yet we claim high feeding values for the cow from certain crops as if these qualities in the harvest were guaranteed by the pedigree, regardless of what the plant might find in the soil to live up to the claims for it by the seedsman. When reputable crops failed, we searched the world for substitutes. When the substitutes made equal or more bulk they were accepted as of equal value to the cow, compelled to consume them in her struggle to survive. In spite of the deaths from bleeding disasters by cows fed on sweet clover substituting as a legume for red clover, and many other sad disasters for her, our juggling of crops continues to bring in those of less and less feed values on soils under declining fertility levels. Shall we not defend the cow against such ignorance of crop differences in their values as feeds when we do not realize that much crop bulk per acre is no guarantee of correspondingly much true feed value for the dumb beasts unless the fertility of the soil guarantees it?

More recently we have heard much about juggling the cow from one pasture to another through the season in so called "pasture-systems," assuming the cow to be little more than a mowing machine. Can it be good nutrition if she is compelled to take nothing but a non-legume on one soil for two or three months; then nothing but a protein-rich legume in the next phase of this system; and then some other crop, and so on, with no chance to balance her diet daily as she does remarkably skillfully to make more cow, more calf, more milk, and more money for her owner in pastures of mixed herbages on fertile soils? Should we not defend the cow against systems placing her as a live, physiological unit on the level as low as a mechanical grass cutter?

Just as the cow is struggling to find what she requires to grow in her body, so plants are struggling to find in the soil what is required to grow their plant tissues. The problem of protein supplements for the cow points out that she is struggling to find not just "crude proteins" or any organic substance containing nitrogen. Instead she is searching to find the required array of amino acid components of complete proteins to grow her body, to protect her against disease, and to reproduce her kind.

For man, the truly complete proteins must supply him with at least eight specific amino acids. For the white rat of common experimental use, the completeness of the proteins demands ten different amino acids. For the pig and the chicken these specific requirements have not yet been so completely worked out, but for them the proteins and amino acids of animal origin are still a major safety factor. For the cow the requirements are simpler. She solves her own protein problem if given ample range over young herbage of variety and the cooperative, synthetic helps of the microbial flora in her paunch and intestinal tract. That the synthetic services of the latter transcend those in the intestines of the pig and chicken, is suggested when these last two animals have always taken to the cow's droppings long before the nutritionists believed some vitamin B12, or the so-called "dung factor" (cobalt), passed from the cow for the benefits recognized by the pig or the chicken following her. Our knowledge of just what the soil pattern is by which our livestock is well fed, especially in respect to the proteins, is still much of an unknown. It leaves much to the cow's own selection if she is to be healthy and reproduce readily and regularly.

Our Industrial Rather Than Biological Direction of Agriculture Under Technologies Upset the Balance of Nature

While we commonly boast of our technological knowledge and skills in manufacturing implements, machines, and household gadgets, contributing much to our high standard of living; while that high standard is now about as common out in the country, where things grow, as it is on paved streets, where as the Indian pointed out "Nothing will grow"; and while one man in agriculture can now produce many times more bushels of corn, wheat, oats, etc. than one man produced a quarter century ago; nevertheless, agriculture cannot be viewed wholly as if it were an industry. It may apply industrial principles to the transformation of the products it grows. But the creation of those agricultural products is *not man's, but nature's production*. Life processes in their complexity and their interdependencies are not yet extensively comprehended, much less, are they submitting themselves to man's complete control.

The growing of calves does not lend itself to mass production and assembly line procedures as does, for example, the manufacture of washing machines. Mass production for lowered cost per washing machine is a sound business, economic and industrial principle in case of the latter, but not in the former. Quite contrary to the common concept, the cow herself, and not her owner, or herdsman, is the major director and manger of the calf-producing industry. Materials and machines have let us tabulate their limited properties and behaviors for use in an industry. But even then, our initial design of the washing machine soon revealed its many weaknesses and found so many of its parts out of proportion and out of balance to call for modifications of design about as quickly as the costs of tooling up had been covered.

While some phases of agriculture may be guided by principles used in industry, nevertheless agriculture cannot take its necessary raw materials for granted as available in ordered quantities and at regular costs. Agriculture deals with living, perishable things. These are involved in numerous and uncontrollable interrelations with other living and perishable matters. The growing of calves calls for living cows, and living bulls to create them; healthy milk from healthy cows to nurse them; grass, hay, grains, carbohydrates, proteins, vitamins, trace elements, antibiotics, and a host of possible unknowns to feed and grow them. Calf production is not a case of control of this process by the herdsman. Instead he soon realizes that he is merely an observer and attendant of a business the cow herself is managing and controlling. It is not an industry on her part. She seldom indulges in what even suggests mass production. Quite otherwise, it is biology first. Living cows and calves are always biological processes first and foremost. They may eventually become the raw materials, on their death, for industrial processing in the slaughter house. From that point onward the cow ceases to manage the meat-producing business, and contributes the raw materials for the meat-packaging industry.

Up to this moment much of agriculture, emphasizing the industrial viewpoint and the economics of it, has been slowly upsetting the balance of nature. While those imbalances in many cases represent deficiencies initially unrecognized, they eventually magnify themselves into disasters. Under so much emphasis on industry, with increased output and consumption of resources at a greater rate, the balance of nature is also moving into serious threatening upsets.

Many cases may be cited. Students in wildlife pointing to our exploitation of game have given us many of them. The fox-prairie dog balance is commonly cited. For our discussion here, the imbalances of soil fertility and plant species bringing on the plant species — animal imbalances and the whole series of balances upset by soil exploitation and attempted remedy by fertilizer treatment may well be called up in defending the cow compelled to live under these many former balances of nature we have upset.

Our criterion of agricultural production has been that of weight or volume per acre, per cow or per other producing unit. More weight or volume delivered per animal per unit of time has been considered the economic requisite in animal production. More bushels or tons per acre are praised as agronomic accomplishments. In searching for crops for maximum mass output per acre while taking our soil fertility for granted and exploiting it, we have brought in those crop plants producing mainly carbohydrates, or photosynthetic bulk, but a lowered concentration within that vegetative mass of the proteins, vitamins, inorganic requisites and other nutrient essentials. Production of much vegetative mass, but less of seed per unit of that weight, encouraged the belief that a grain-producing agriculture is poor economy and a grass agriculture should be substituted for it.

Hybrid corn has been an excellent illustration when the crude protein concentration of that pre-hybrid grain as a mean of 10.3% some 30 years ago, has dropped to a low of half that during the last three or four decades in the United States. These figures tell us nothing about the nutritional quality of the protein, particularly the deficiency of certain amino acids to the point of demanding protein supplements to corn even for fattening services by this grain. Here, literally, a new plant species was brought in, pushing out an older one as either the vegetative production went up or the soil fertility went down. Nature's balance is being upset slowly but decisively.

In our increasing carbohydrate production — which is also a case of decreasing protein synthesis — naturally the animal-plant balance is upset. Animal fattening and all the speculation connected with buying low and selling high has become the major phase of what we call animal husbandry. Hybrid corn and the soils under it, even if put to other crops, have not been the regions for growing calves even though they are the areas for fattening them. They are the regions for hogs, made up as their bodies are largely of fats, or of converted carbohydrates. They are the regions where animal diseases prevail, and those diseases apt to be considered contagious rather than degenerative or deficiency ailments, because so many animals are so often in contact.

The introduction of the high-yielding fescues for lush, late-season grazing and hay is too much bulk and so little nutrition for health that it often invited the lameness of a swollen rear ankle, called "fescue foot," curiously, it strikes the left hind foot first and the animal's extended lameness offers little hope for profitable recovery, much like the once-considered highly contagious "hoof and mouth" disease.

The cow-plant species balance of nature is so badly upset that we are now pushing animal populations to smaller figures, even if the cow population is at this moment relatively high. It is slowly dawning on us that fattened animals are not healthy animals, at least not in a condition which is healthy for the species. One needs only see the fattening geese in Strasburg, France, where American corn is fed them until fatty degeneration of the liver makes that organ the desired delicacy of the slaughtered goose while the rest of her body is scarcely considered for food purposes, to make us realize that fattening our castrated cattle does not improve their health or the chances for survival of the species. Can agriculture as a biological procedure, long maintain itself when nature's balances are so seriously upset that they eliminate the animals that give us our major foods in the proteins?

Other illustrations of imbalance may be cited, like our campaign on what we call "weeds" coming in as competitors to other crops. Are we not "fighting" weeds because we fail to have enough fertility by which the desired crop would dominate the area so thoroughly that the weeds would not be competitors? Shall we not consider weeds as plants making so much woody bulk on so little fertility that they survive where crops demanding much fertility for little but highly nutritious bulk cannot dominate them? In our fight on weeds with herbicides, we are scattering the deadly carbon-ring compounds in chlorinated and sulfonated arrangements so profusely that not only plants, but microbes, animals and even man are confronted with dangers to health and even with death. Such upsets in Nature's balances are the result of the changed combinations of fertility of the soil not generally considered as the determiner of agriculture itself. Once we upset them, then, like Humpty Dumpty, they cannot be put back together again.

The Gradual Exhaustion of Our Resource, Namely, the Fertility of the Soil, Goes Unheeded While Our Livestock Suffers

Our efforts to increase productivity of the land have slowly come to consider the soil as the point where the major effort must be applied to serve. Unfortunately, so much soil has already been exhausted before we come to the realization of the soil as the starting point of the assembly lines of agricultural production. National propaganda for soil conservation that started with gullies has finally arrived at consideration of conservation and restoration of soil fertility where gullies start.

The need to put fertility back into the soil was first appreciated in the south, where bird guano from South America was one of the early fertilizers. Clearing of piney woods by the colonial pioneer in the south gave rainfall, fresh air, blue sky, and sunshine, but no significant fertility for extended crop production. There was soil organic matter originating in pine needles, but this didn't release much fertility on cultivation. Nor did the soils of the south have much mineral reserves of fertility to improve the land by "resting" it. No unweathered minerals are washed in by the rivers, if the delta is excluded. No windblown additions of high fertility come in as is true for Missouri, Iowa, Nebraska, Kansas, and other states with "loessial" soils. No unweathered subsoils are turned up by the plow or are within root-reach. The soil fertility was already seriously exhausted from the soils of the south when the Creator managed the place and could do no better than create pine wood, and little or no protein to support even a timber squirrel.

Because of that climatic setting, attention went to feeding the crop plants with fertilizer intensively and extensively. That was necessary on those nearly lateritic soils, which are not only low in fertility but so low also in their adsorption and exchange capacities that they would not even become seriously sour or acid. They will not hold much applied, soluble fertilizers, and let much go out in drainage waters for loss of economic returns from this salvage effort. With no serious acidity, the needs by the crops for calcium and magnesium were neglected, save for the calcium applied in ordinary super phosphate and possibly some magnesium used unwittingly for the correction of fertilizer acidity.

Sulfur too was highly exhausted from the soils of the south but applied unwittingly with benefit through mixed fertilizers made up mainly of super phosphate, carrying about half as calcium sulfate. This element suggests its serious exhaustion from, or serious deficiency in, the soils of the South if one dares to conclude from the fact that peanuts, a significant food legume of the south, provide protein but one so low in the sulfur-containing amino acid, methionine, to require protein supplements of it when fed. Might we not see other legumes also deficient in feeding potential for the same reason?

Other elements, particularly the trace elements, may also be highly exhausted in the soils. Their use for citrus crop improvement, and on peat soils, raises the point seriously whether we must not view our soils more and more as being feedlots for our crops if these plants are to synthesize feed values rising above those represented by pine needles. Must we not see more and more soil fertility exhaustion giving us crops that may be supplying only bulk but not necessarily proteins, vitamins, mineral elements and all that is truly animal feed?

Can this vision of the soil help us believe that carbohydrate crops of starch, oils, and cellulosic fiber dominate the ecological pattern, because of these deficiencies in soils highly weathered under much rainfall and high temperatures? Even cotton seed protein will not supplement corn for pigs or chickens, but will for the cow where the paunch seems to overcome the handicap of this protein supplement for animals not symbiotically propagating a similar internal bacterial flora.

Now that we have taken thirty million acres out of growing horse feed and turned them over to cattle; that sheep at the maximum of numbers in 1942 are now at the lowest since we began counting them; and that hogs are also less now than formerly but yet cattle have not increased to the extent that decrease of horses would suggest; isn't it time for someone to rise in defense of the cow as the symbol of our livestock on the decline? Is not the declining soil as declining feed quality possibly causally connected with livestock troubles? Cannot increasing livestock troubles and failing health be due to failing quality of feed and that due to failing soils? Can our crop juggling and disregard of exhaustion of fertility have finally brought the nutritional values of forages and feeds so low that what we call cattle "diseases" is no more than failing cow physiology because she can stand up under those deficiencies no longer?

Our Livestock is Taking the Blame and Paying the Penalty While We Fail to Defend the Cow

One needs only to take a long range view of what is happening at the marketplace and in commerce to see signs and suggestions over the long range. Beef has risen in price to tell us that the supply is short in relation to demand, but is taken even at the unusually high prices. Producers of hogs are talking about shifting this former mortgage lifter by means of fat to more of a protein producer by means of its lean muscle.

Can beef that once grew itself in the western U.S. now be dwindling there where high protein wheat is rapidly becoming soft, starchy wheat because of soil fertility exhaustion? Why are hogs being pushed westward and away from grain to more grazing on alfalfa in the plan for their growing more muscle cheaply in place of excessive fat? Have not beef cattle markets travelled westward so rapidly across the United States to locate themselves in Kansas City, St. Joseph, and Springfield, Missouri, and Omaha, Nebraska, because that is where the beef was making itself as the cow selecting the soils determined it more than any diversified farming plans of ours would have it? Isn't it out on the range where the less weathered soils and high protein forage really *grow* the cattle while on the highly weathered soils of the East we only *fatten* them?

When our pastures fail in their fertility required for the nutritious forages they still produce many plants we call "weeds." We say "The weeds took the pasture" and then start a "war on weeds." We fail to realize that the plants we call "weeds" are merely those which can make much bulk on the low fertility where the desired forage could not. Weeds grow prominently in the pasture because they are not making enough feed values to tempt a cow to eat them. In place of defending the cow's judgment of the low nutritional value of the so-called "weeds" and her report thereby of the soil fertility in the pasture that needs rejuvenation, we fight the weeds with mowing machinery and more recently with the dangerous and deadly poisons. Isn't it time that such judgment of the forage and of the soil fertility by the cow that transcends our own be defended?

Now that drugs and poisons not only for fighting weeds, but for fighting insects and microbes are demonstrating their dangerous side reactions as well as supposedly beneficial main reactions, it is essential that we consider the animal as a complex physiology more than as a piece of property. With chlorinated naphthalene's finally connected casually with Keratosis, virus X or other baffling ailments, it seems well that we see our failure to protect and to nourish our cows as responsible for many of the troubles for which we blame and even kill the dumb beast.

When in the state of Missouri the calf crop at weaning time was only 60% of the conceptions before artificial insemination was used, and now is of no larger percentage figure when artificial insemination is such a common practice, has the scattering of noble pedigrees by this artificial technique done anything to increase the species? Is the increasing legislation against disease, and are the increasing indictments of sales barns not suggesting that the animals are not protecting themselves as they once did? If we keep on killing sick cows to protect those we have not yet examined or detected, will our cow population increase, and can the producer take the shock of the loss of his herd that suddenly shows positive to some possibly questionable test when on the proceeding inspection a clean bill of health was given?

Now that our once-specialized barn-feeding technique of such high repute not so long ago is failing to serve, we are suddenly going to a grass agriculture. Is this because out of desperation from our failure in feeding the cow, we are turning that responsibility over to the cow herself? If so, it is relatively late in the experience, now that our soils are so low in fertility that they must be kept in grass cover to keep them from eroding, for us to expect the cow to give us a market for the quality of grass that is no more than just soil cover. If we are finding the soil fertility too low to create other crops than grass with economic returns, isn't it foolhardy to believe the shift to grass a way of getting more creative services via an animal on such a high physiological level as that of our foster mother? Shall we not look at the grass agriculture as the last desperate crop juggling act, when grass by its dense root system has more soil fertility extracting power than other crops, and thereby a maximum of survival under direct circumstances? Will we not finally turn to putting fertility into the soil to feed our crops with some measure of what is needed for plant nutrition just as we try to feed ourselves according to standards of good nutrition? Only when we feed our crops properly by correctly treating the soil with applied soil fertility and restored soil organic matter, will we initiate the processes which can carry the synthesis of feeds and nutritional values from the soil up through the plants to the animals and to man for the benefit of all these life forms in good nutrition, in good health and in fecund reproduction. Only by such condition will creation work in the fullest sense.

Only by considering all life forms in balance, and by viewing the ecological patterns of microbes, plants and animals in relation to the soil fertility that creates them, can we wisely direct our agriculture, and modify our environment or improve upon it for greater productivity. The cow as man's foster mother has brought him out of his primitivity and helped him design his technologies for his high standards of living. By means of those he has taken to exploiting his environment with the disregard of the cow, and against her continued protests. She has outlined the ecological patterns for herself and delineated the soils on which she and man could primitively survive. Displaced as she is, she is no longer able to defend herself and is slowly going down in defeat. She is being killed because she gets sick, and is being turned upon by man for whom she has been foster mother. Are you as a jury going to decide against her, or are you not going to vote for her acquittal and for fertile soils under her and thereby under you and the generations you procreate? You as the jury must decide.

CHAPTER 11

Feed Efficiency in Terms of Biological Assays of Soil Treatments

RESULTS OF MOST AGRONOMIC researches are measured in terms of increased yields as bushels or tonnage of crops per acre. Biological assays now point out that these measures may not be accurate when agronomic products are to render their service in sustenance for animals. The values of improved varieties, of fertilizer treatments, of rotations, or soil management practices are based primarily on the number of bushels or pounds as increase over others that will be produced during a period of years by a new variety or practice. Other visible factors, such as quality, resistance to disease, and drought resistance, have been considered of secondary importance. Little or no attention has been given to chemical differences in the feeds or foods caused by different agronomic changes that could profoundly influence the animals and humans that consume these plant products.

The data of animal gains presented herewith demonstrate that forages and grains from the same soil given different treatments have varied widely in their capacities to produce animal gain. When the chemical composition of the feeds was changed by the different soil treatments, the animal response was not correlated closely enough to warrant the acceptance of the chemical analyses as an index of nutritive value. There is the strong suggestion that differences in feeds are brought about by soil treatments other than those commonly measured by standard methods of feed analyses. Only through assays with animals can these differences be determined.

On a soil low in lime and phosphorus, addition of phosphorus alone increased the efficiency of forage when fed to lambs. When limestone was added in addition to the phosphate, the nutritive value of the hays was further improved. Differences in the amount of improvement due to the different soil treatments varied from year to year. However, the relationship with reference to soil treatment held true in all trials. It appears that nutritional differences were greatest in seasons unfavorable for plant growth. The protein and mineral contents of these hays did not differ as widely as their efficiencies in producing animal gain. This would indicate that the soil treatments brought about other composition changes not commonly measured. The animals made more gain from each unit of grain consumed as a supplement to the phosphated hay than to the untreated hays, and those fed hay from the soil receiving lime and phosphate made more gain on the grain consumed than did those receiving hay from the land where only phosphate had been applied. All animals fed on the hay from the soil receiving both lime and phosphate had a higher oil and yolk content. There was a significant difference in the nitrogen, sulfur, and phosphorus contents of the wool. Further differences were obtained when the wool was scoured by means of alkali. In the alkali solution the wool from the lambs fed the phosphated hay decomposed while that from the soil receiving both lime and phosphate retained its luster and carded out to give customary fluffiness. It is significant that a simple treatment applied to the soil changed the composition of plants, altered the physiology of animals consuming the hay, and affected the appearance and properties of the wool. Since the wool qualities were changed by soil treatments, it is not unreasonable to assume that other body processes could have been altered so as to affect profoundly the metabolic and reproductive processes in the animals.

The addition of any plant nutrient to a soil without regard to the amount applied as related to the kind and supply of the nutrients in the soil may not always give feed of improved nutritive value. Evidence is presented where the addition of fertilizer or lime brought about an unbalanced nutrient condition in the soil which actually resulted in crops of lower efficiency than where no nutrient additions were made.

Timothy hay grown on soil having an excess of nitrogen, alfalfa with an excess of lime or phosphorus, and soybeans grown on a soil made deficient in potash through excessive applications of lime have all been lower in nutritive value than where no soil treatments were added. However, when these treatments were balanced by the addition of other plant nutrients, the quality of the feed was improved over that from the untreated soil. These results would indicate that tonnage yields are not a complete measure of the value of soil treatment and that maximum feeding value of forages can be obtained only when all soil nutrients are present in the proper ratios.

Since grains are only produced by crops after vegetative growth has been completed, the composition can not be altered as much by soil treatments as can that of forages (8). Nevertheless, the effect of soil treatments on the nutritive quality of grains was demonstrated. Trails with kafir and corn showed that the nutritive values of these grains produced on poor soils may be improved by addition of moderate amounts of the deficient elements. However, when some elements are added in excessive quantities, the nutritive value may be reduced below that of the untreated grains. Pressure tests have shown that the hardness of corn may be markedly influenced by soil treatment. It is not unreasonable to assume that grains varying in hardness will contain different organic compounds that may have a different effect on animal metabolism.

When animals were given a chance to show preference for grains from differently treated soil, wide variations in choice were found. In corn, hardness is one of the principal factors observed to influence choice. However, with such grains as oats and wheat the preference of animals for the grain from a particular soil treatment can only be attributed to chemical properties.

These results all point to differences in the value of plants as animal feed brought about by soil treatments, and that there are other differences in these plant products than are commonly determined by standard feed analyses. It has been well established that lignin accumulates within the plant when some growth factor, such as climate, or lack of fertility produces slow growth of plants. It is possible that this material could prevent the animal's digestive juices from attacking the cell contents and that the feed would pass through the animals undigested.

The functions of the different nutrients in plant metabolism are not well known. Where deficiencies exist, it is possible that some organic compounds, highly essential in animal growth, might not be synthesized within the plant and thus result in a feed of lower nutritive value. Since all results indicate that feeds produced under well-balanced fertility conditions are usually most effectively utilized by animals, it is not unreasonable to believe that an excess of some element might also prevent the synthesis of these compounds essential for animal growth, or that it might cause compounds to be formed that would be injurious.

All of these results point to the necessity of knowing the fertility properties of individual soils. If nutritious feeds are to be produced for animal and human consumption, then the soil on which they are grown must contain not only all the proper elements for plant growth, but these must be presented by the soil in proper ratios. It is only through proper and intelligent management that farm acres can be made to produce high yields of quality products. On soils of low productive capacity, the soil treatment can be expected to give benefits in addition to those of merely increasing the tonnage yields. The full value of these treatments, however, cannot be measured as yet without the use of animal assay.

CHAPTER 12

Are We Poisoning Our Sheep?

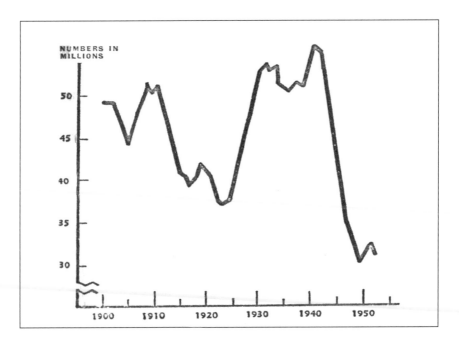

IN 1942 THE SHEEP population of the United States started on a decline which reached the lowest figure by 1950 for our history of the recorded numbers of sheep. Also in 1942, the drug, phenothiazine, a carbon ring — sulfur compound, was introduced and subsequently put into extensive use as a vermifuge (worm and parasite killer). The use of this drug resulted in the discontinuation of the practice of regularly giving the sheep copper sulfate, or bluestone, formerly used for that treatment.

Now that we are appreciating the significance of many of the trace elements, including cobalt and copper, in the biochemical activities of microbes, plants, animals, and man, and since we are also recognizing the slowly accumulating lethal effects on man and animals by the many sulphonated and chlorinated carbon ring compounds, the phenothiazine as one of them should be coming under question.

Might not the introduction of this drug into regular use as a worm remedy for sheep have some casual connection with the serious decline in the sheep population? These three simultaneous phenomena, namely, (a) the cessation in the use of copper sulfate, (b) the extensive use of phenothiazine, and (c) the sudden decline in sheep population ought to prompt every sheep owner to consider the hypothesis — or to ask the question — namely, "Might the change in worming procedure in 1942 have been the cause of the decline in the sheep population?"

One may well raise the question whether the discontinuation of the use of bluestone was not the cause, or at least a contribution, since it meant failure to feed copper as a possibly necessary trace element or its accompanying sulfur as a requisite in making wool fiber which is so high in cystine, the sulfur-carrying protein constituent.

When in Australia scientists have demonstrated the shortage of copper in the soil and the forage as the reason for black wool turning to a gray color, and when in Missouri the sheep born of black wool turn to gray, the withholding after 1942 of the formerly administered copper sulfate may theoretically be considered a reason for the decline in our sheep numbers since that date.

Perhaps our regular dosing with copper was not so much a case of giving medicine to kill worms, as it was a help toward improved nutrition for healthy sheep in which the worms found no place. Copper and sulfur may have been supplementary feed requirements since we are expecting sheep to do well on soils today where nature had never grown any animals of a physiological performance similar to that of the sheep. Have we not probably pushed the sheep off the very fringes of the soil fertility areas on which they can survive or be really healthy? With a sheep population of less than 32,000,000 now when but ten years ago we had 56,000,000, should we not be asking a whole series of questions?

Trace Element Deficiency

The question of the deficiency of trace elements in the soil was brought up some years ago. At first it met with little concern and much less reaction. But trace elements have now come to be used more extensively both as feed supplements and as fertilizer treatments on the soil. Much more suggestive for consideration as the cause behind the sudden decline in the sheep population since phenothiazine was introduced, is the accidental discovery this year, through some experiments with rats, that this drug prohibits the thyroid gland from taking up iodine and from exercising its normal function of encouraging regular growth or normal body metabolism.

Test Shows Thyroid Damage

This report comes from the work of Roy V. Talmade, H. Nachimson, L. Kraintz, and J. A. Green in the Department of Biology, Rice Institute, at Houston, Texas. They were observing the regular movement and concentration of radio-active iodine into the thyroid glands of rats when a supposedly regular batch of the usual feed suddenly prohibited that normal process. It resulted from the mistake in getting a feed carrying some phenothiazine. Then tests of the phenothiazine in separate trials revealed its

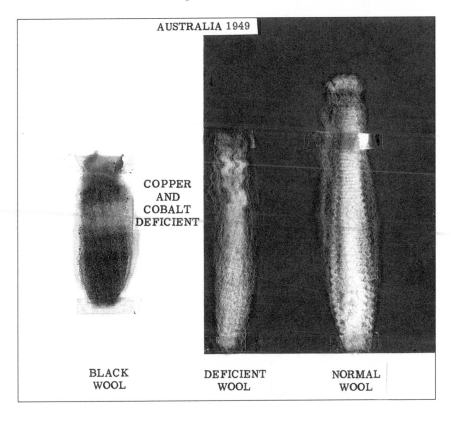

AUSTRALIA 1949

COPPER
AND
COBALT
DEFICIENT

BLACK
WOOL

DEFICIENT
WOOL

NORMAL
WOOL

damage to the function of the thyroid gland of the rat with a severity in the same range of that when thiouracil was administered as 0.1 percent of the same diet for but 16 days.

The gray band of wool in the staple of a black sheep (A) resulted when the sheep grazed on fields deficient in copper and cobalt. The harsh "steely" top portion of the white staple (B) was grown by sheep in similar soil. This is in sharp contrast to the regular crimp in the staple of normal wool (C).

Question Drug

With this fact coming out of the rat laboratory, phenothiazine certainly comes under question. That discovery makes us ask ourselves whether we should not run some metabolic tests or other diagnostic procedures on our sheep fed this drug to learn whether we are not making cretins of them as we see this deficiency among humans suffering from iodine deficiency or from the reduced rate of growth due to the irregularity in metabolism of the mineral iodine.

A news item from Cedar City, Utah, June 6 (*Kansas City Star*) under the headline, "Utah sheep men are stricken," told us that "Lambs have been abnormally small this spring and many have died. Some ewes have bare faces and scabby noses as though they have been burned. Some sheep also were reported losing their wool. Dr. John Curtis, State Veterinarian, made the first investigation May 24. He said 500 to 700 lambs and about 100 two-year old ewes died in one herd. He could not diagnose the malady." The question was raised whether the atomic bomb could be blamed.

Reports from an able veterinarian and a capable student of animal nutrition in Iowa serving the western states, tell us that "Sheep are not growing as they should, and in spite of all the feed supplements we try. The fatalities during the lamb feeding periods are decorating the fences of the feed lots with too many pelts pulled off the dead ones. Such happenings fail to keep up a man's interest in the sheep business." It was those observations that prompted him to put the query "We can't find the trouble in the feed. Could the trouble possibly be in the soil growing the feeds?"

Declining Soil Fertility

In answer to his question, coming likewise from many other livestock folks, one must reply that our declining soil fertility is cutting down the ratio of the proteins to carbohydrates and is giving us "fattening" feeds rather than "growing" feeds. Failure to improve the soils has also suggested the mounting deficiencies in the nutritional qualities of the proteins we grow. They are still only "crude" proteins.

But when these reported troubles are so severe where sheep have been on the range and where they have been doing what they could by their own instinct, it looks as if these troubles fall back on us rather than on the sheep. It is all the more significant that we examine critically in this case, not the *sheep nature,* but *human nature* when we use these chemicals carrying the sulphonated carbon ring compounds, or the chlorinated rings. Many of these have always been considered as poisons even if they were not so highly lethal.

The carbon ring structure is not readily broken down by digestion. Nor do the microbes of the soil break it down as they do most other substances which we bury for their disposal through microbial help. Shall we not connect our troubles in growing sheep possibly with our own inclination to use drugs to fight worms, microbes, and diseases when we ought to be looking to better feed and normal nutrition for good health of our animals via more fertile soils?

Reaching Conclusions

Of course, there is always the possible fallacy in drawing the conclusion that when two things happen at the same time, the one must be the cause of the other. In like manner the terrific decrease in sheep numbers, happening just after we quit feeding sheep copper sulfate and began dosing them with phenothiazine may be just a coincidence rather than a cause in the latter for the former. Nevertheless, when the drug has now shown its damage to the health and to the physiological functions of the laboratory rat, no flock owner is going to be kept from putting under question the phenothiazine in sheep feed.

A theory will get attention apparently only when disaster of terrific magnitude befalls one. It would seem well then to put under test the theory which has now become a serious likelihood. Perhaps if properly tested, the sheep themselves will come up with the answer later. Only after the many sheep flock owners attack the problem can the falling curve of our sheep population be reversed and result in restored profit in the form of more lamb and more wool as we learn — from a possibly sad experience — to feed sheep better and to drug them less.

CHAPTER 13

Better Soils Make Better Hogs

Hogs Discriminate Feed Differences as Delicate as Kinds of Green Manures Used

WHEN PROFESSOR EVVARD of Iowa once said "If you will give the pig a chance, it will make a hog of itself in less time than you will," he was the first to point to the hog as a capable assayer of the nutritional values of the components of its ration. As a feed chemist the hog is demonstrating a much more refined technique than we might believe when just watching it as it balances its carbohydrates against proteins and minerals from the supplies of these we have put into the self-feeder. In fact the hog, like many other animals both wild and domestic, is capable of selecting its feeds according as these reflect the higher fertility of the soil growing them. Have you ever thought that better soils make better hogs because of the higher nutritive value per unit in the feeds through higher fertility in the soils growing them?

"Yes," you may say "the hog is closer to the soil than most other animals, since it wallows in the mud puddle in the warmer summer and usually roots up the sod during the spring. It eats so much of its feed right off the ground too, so of necessity it is ingesting much soil and gets much that is purely mineral." However, the question may well be raised as to just why the hog roots; when it does so mainly in the spring after a winter on low-protein and mineral-deficient feeds; then, too, when it doesn't root later in the season after it has gotten green feeds; and when it seldom roots if it has access to good green alfalfa. We are slow to believe that the hog — once a roamer but now confined by fences — is trying to report the poorer quality of feed because of the declining fertility of the land also enclosed inside of them. What we might be prone to consider just plain "cussedness" in the hogs' breaking through the fence to the highway and their insistence on rooting, may be our failure to appreciate (a) what all is demanded to give most efficient feeding of them, and (b) their behavior as indicators, or helps to tell us what in the way of extra nutrients they need.

The Hampshire, which in its domestication has not yet been turned so completely to "slothfulness and gluttony" as possibly some other breeds, is credited with being "a good rustler." Might this not be merely a good ability to search out the essentials for making up its own well balanced ration. Along with this ability as a rustler goes the reward for it, namely, the larger number of pigs per litter for which this breed has the claimed and granted reputation. All this suggests that if we will give the pig a chance to meet up with better soil fertility over which it feeds, it will not only make a hog of itself quickly, but will make more hogs as offspring as well.

The part of the forty-acre field where Mr. Cliff Long of Johnson County, Missouri, once used lime and other fertilizers was taken first by the hogs. They "cut corn" to the very exact border. (Photo by Virgil Burk, Columbia, Missouri.)

Corn on More Fertile Soil
"Hogged Down" First in Search
for More Than Only Minerals

That the hog will select its feed according to the fertility of the soil growing it was forcibly demonstrated in Missouri some years ago on the farm of Mr. Cliff Long in Johnson county. In attempting to "hog down" some corn, the tankage and water were kept at the gate of the forty acre field. The hogs came out for water daily and went back and disappeared. The absence of indication of their activity caught Mr. Long's attention. He was becoming concerned at about the same time that his neighbor, across the road along the opposite side of the field, reported to him about the clean job of corn harvesting the hogs were doing.

On examination of the area hogged down, Mr. Long found that the hogs were carefully working to the very border lines of the small part of the field where several years before he had limed and fertilized the soil to grow some alfalfa. The hogs had roamed the forty acre field; they had selected this more fertile area; and they had taken first the grain grown on it. *They had mapped the soils of this field according to the differences in their fertility, and with an accuracy no soil surveyor could even imitate.*

"Just what is the characteristic of the corn that is being searched out and recognized by the hogs?" you are already asking. Much has been said about it being the minerals, because hogs eat soil, coal and other minerals, and too it was mineral fertilizers that were added as the original soil treatments for the alfalfa. There could be nothing else but minerals, though not necessarily directly, responsible for making this particular soil area in the forty acre field different from the rest of it. Of course if the chemist should analyze the grain he would burn it down to ash for his determinations in search of differences. Consequently, any difference would be reported as one of the minerals.

There is doubt, however, whether the hog is assaying its feed wholly according to deficiencies or differences in the ash or mineral constituents. The hog is taking part of its foods as carbohydrates for energy more than these for their ash. It takes food for its protein content more than for the ash associated with this dietary constituent. Doesn't the plant do more for the hog than just haul minerals to the trough and the self-feeder? Certainly it is within the plants — and only by the processes there — that synthesis occurs of the amino acids out of which proteins are constructed by the animal body. It is of proteins that muscle is built. It is the plants that construct carbohydrates through photosynthesis. It is the carbohydrates that help the hog to lay on its fat and that give energy to its body. These services performed for the animal by carbohydrates and proteins result from them as complex compounds synthesized by the plant's life processes and can not be performed by the mere presence of the plant's ash-comprising minerals. The hog is not assaying for the mineral contents of its feeds. It is assaying for the degree of balance which its feed contains of the many complex nutritional substances — carbohydrates, proteins, fats, minerals, vitamins, etc. — that only the plant can put together and then most effectively only by the help of a good store in the soil of all the elements of mineral fertility.

Crops Requiring More Fertile Soil Grow More Protein and More Pork per Acre

It was Professor L.A. Weaver of the Missouri College of Agriculture, who demonstrated the significance, and good performance of high soil fertility in terms of pasture for hogs. He used a series of different crops as grazing for them and used corn as the supplement. If this series of crops is arranged as they require less fertility from the soil for their growth — or as "they can be grown more easily" as it is more often said — his results show that they also make less pork per acre. Alfalfa, which is considered the hardest to grow is at the top of the list of the crops with its recognized high pork production per acre of 591 pounds. Then the other crops follow in this order, namely, red clover 449; rape 394; sorghum 275; bluegrass 274; soybeans 174; and cowpeas 149 pounds of pork per acre. These are their capacities to support the hog in its inclination to become pork when corn was a supplement. In respect to the amount of corn, as bushels, required to make a hundred weight of pork, these hog pasture crops listed themselves with the following figures: Alfalfa 5.5; red clover 5.2; rape 5.3; sorghum 7.1; blugrass 7.8; soybeans 4.6; and cowpeas 5.2 bushels.

When we say a crop is "hard to grow" because it requires fertilizers like lime, phosphate, magnesium, potash, boron and other nutrient elements, we forget that it is just those "hard-to-grow" crops that are more nearly manufacturing all that it takes to convert a pig into a hog quickly. Alfalfa, for example, grows naturally today on the soils that made buffaloes as big and numerous as the Forty-niners found them. No one ever reported the buffalo as having a separate source of protein supplements. He found his protein synthesized by the short grass that bears his name. But that grass was undergirded in its protein manufacture and its mineral delivery by an ample fertility supply in the soil that had not been leached out by heavy annual rainfalls. It had not been weathered out to the degree where forests or wood was about all that the plants could synthesize.

The hog as producer of a higher percentage of its body as fat, than is the case with the buffalo, or cattle and sheep, is able to do better than these on soils that grow carbohydrates, like corn, more commonly and more easily than they grow protein, like hard wheat. Nevertheless, the hog must also have its proteins. Unfortunately, for the better upkeep of our soils, proteins are too commonly considered as something that must be purchased in a bag rather than grown right on the farm in our non-legume crops by giving the soil some lime, phosphates, and legumes or other nitrogenous fertilizers, which increasingly greater areas of the soils now require to produce it.

Hogs Discriminate Feed Differences as Delicate As Kinds Of Green Manures Used, and as Kinds of Minerals Applied on Soils Growing the Feed

That the hog discriminates between the corn or the wheat, for example, according as it was grown on soils with the different fertility levels or different fertilizer treatments has been demonstrated very positively. The hog has been recognized, under experimental tests, as a very good assayer of differences in the soil fertility growing its feeds. The same hybrid corn or the same variety of wheat was grown, for example, on three plots of soil given (a) lime, phosphate and potash, (b) lime and phosphate, and (c) lime only. One hundred pounds of the grain harvested from each of these plots is put into separate compartments of the self-feeder and the hogs allowed to consume these according to their choice. Regularly the remnant amounts are weighed, and the compartments refilled with weighed quantities but not in the same order or position of the different grains in the self-feeder. This is the procedure used to test other kinds of soil treatments. This method of asking the hog to assay the values of different soil fertility treatments does not report them as increases in bulk, such as bushels or tons per acre. Rather, it is the pig's report on the nutritional quality of this part of its feed and the pig's suggestion on what we can do in helping it to make a hog of itself most efficiently.

When turning under a green manure like sweet clover to make more bushels of corn, we must also ask the hog whether the corn resulting would be taken first among other kinds.

What then are some of the reports by these pigs as endorsers of our efforts to improve the feed at the source of its production? When the three soil treatments listed above were used under a rotation with *red clover* turned under ahead of the corn which was followed the next year by wheat and this latter grain was fed, it was consumed (a) 100 percent; (b) 95 percent; and (c) 85 percent, respectively, for the order of fertilizer combinations given. The complete treatment of lime, phosphate and potash was the hog's first choice in terms of the wheat grain so grown. But when *sweet clover* was the green manure ahead of the corn to be followed by the wheat, this second grain was chosen first when only lime and phosphate were used. The second choice was the more complete fertilizers, namely lime, phosphate and potash; and their third choice was lime only.

When a variety of different green manures was tested, each used separately, and with the same complete mineral addition given above; and when the corn grown immediately after the green manure had been turned under, was offered to the hogs; their choice of the corn grown immediately after these green manures ranked the soil treatments as follows: lespedeza 100 percent; red clover 90 percent; sweet clover 81 percent; and timothy 66 percent.

In both of these citations given, the hogs were seemingly "turning thumbs down" on the wheat and on the corn grains when sweet clover was used as a leguminous green manure either immediately ahead or one year ahead of the grain crop offered them. This was a case of the hogs seemingly voting against the sweet clover when it was used distinctly as a green manure.

Such was not the vote of the hogs, however, when the corn followed a crop of sweet clover grown to maturity for the harvest of sweet clover seed. Corn was grown on a set of plots with corn, oats and sweet clover as the crop rotation. On one plot the sweet clover was turned under ahead of the corn as a green manure to make this a 2-year rotation. On the other the sweet clover was allowed to mature and its seed was harvested. This left the sweet clover trash on the land during the third year in the rotation ahead of the corn.

With sweet clover as green manure and with (a) lime, (b) lime and phosphate, and (c) lime, phosphate and potash, to give increasing amounts of sweet clover to be turned under with the resulting more bushels of corn per acre as more fertilizers were put on the land, the hogs recorded their choices as follows: (a) 100 percent; (b) 80 percent; and (c) 67 percent, respectively for the above order of the fertilizers. They were not voting in favor of putting more sweet clover under by the help of more kinds of fertilizers, nor were they voting for more bushels of corn yield per acre. In fact they were "again" all of it. But with the sweet clover as a seed crop using the entire crop year ahead of the corn, and with these same soil treatments the hog's vote was for the exactly reversed order of these soil treatments with the figures (a) 62 percent; (b) 85 percent; and (c) 100 percent, respectively.

In the case of this hog choice it was not the minerals added to the soil that corresponded with the particular selection of the grain by the hogs. Surely, then, it was not an increased ash content of the corn or of the wheat as a result of putting mineral fertilizers on the soil ahead of that particular crop that guided their selections. Rather it was some effects prompted by the nature of the organic material turned under as a green manure. When the hog, by its choice of the corn, votes against more kinds of fertilizer elements applied to the soil for sweet clover used as a green manure under that corn, and then votes in the very reverse order when the sweet clover matures as a crop ahead of the same kind of corn under test, surely it is not the simple aspect of the mineral fertilizers as deliverers of such elements that exercises the effects recognized by the hog. Surely mineral fertilizers are not of influence only as minerals. Rather they are in control of what products the plants manufacture in consequence of the minerals' presence in the soil. Here by their most discriminating selections from amongst these different soil treatments, the hogs were demonstrating the same uncanny capacity as able compounders of their rations that they demonstrate before the self-feeder.

Hogs May Well Help Us Find the Better Feeds for Them

Now that we have been farming long enough in this country to have seen soft or starchy wheat follow the hard or protein-rich wheat going westward; and when the pork market centers have been following the beef market centers also moving in that direction, are we not about ready to believe that the exhaustion of the soil fertility is compelling the production of less protein in both the plant and animal crops and is limiting animal output more to mainly fat? When the wild animals roamed so widely and searched out the feed so carefully according to the soils growing it, can't we see that the fence that encloses the hog throws on us as husbandmen the responsibility of selecting the nutrients for the hog's ration with somewhat near the accuracy and delicacy with which the hog could do it herself? Have you ever thought that you might use the hog to test the corn lots from different parts of your farm for their differences in feed value? Are we not now approaching the time when perhaps an animal assay may be a good basis for discriminating against the use of one lot of corn from soil of neglected fertility and for acceptance of another lot of feed according to the hog's approval of the better fertility of the soil growing it? If your skepticism about this flares up why not let the hog demonstrate for you before the self-feeder in your own hog lot where you can try a few hundred pounds of each different grain and have the hog's judgment support you in the decision? When more hogs can speak to us by this method we shall not delay long our increased attention to the fertility of our soils for higher feed values. The conviction will soon become universal that more efficient hog production can well be founded on the fact that better soils make more and better hogs.

CHAPTER 14

Hogs Benefit From Crops
Grown on Fertile Soils

ECONOMY IN CORN USE, or more pork per barrel, is the constant watchword of the corn belt hog feeder. The continued search for less costly, but yet effective, supplements to the corn grain involves the desire to make the combination a completely "home grown" ration as far as possible.

Forage farming is coming in as a desirable shift in land use and we are going away from excessive corn acreage to put erodible soils under more continuous and compact crop covers which will reduce erosive effects of heavy rainfall. These changes naturally raise this question in the minds of hog men, "How effectively can the different forage crops be used as corn supplements?" Such a question is perfectly natural when we remember that the wild hog as progenitor of our domestic one was an herbaceous feeder and certainly not accustomed to living on much corn.

The hog carcass with its high percentage of fat makes us appreciate this animal's consumption of carbohydrates as fattening foods. It makes us classify it as a "starch burner" more than a "straw burner." For consumption of roughages we scarcely think of the hog, but rather of the cow and sheep.

Satisfied on Grass

It is well to remember, however, that the cow and the sheep must be solving their protein and mineral problems when they are stoking their paunches with grass and converting it into protein-rich meat and milk. That pork production can move the hog to no small degree into the animal group of forage consumers was shown by the work of Prof. L.A. Weaver of the Missouri College of Agriculture, when an acre of alfalfa with corn as its supplement gave almost 600 pounds of pork. This forage use turned out 100 pounds of pork for each five and one-half bushels of corn. This small amount of grain catches our attention immediately in contrast to much larger figures commonly quoted in speaking of corn-hog ratios. It is deserving of more attention when we note that no concentrates or purchased protein supplements were used.

The experimental trials of growing hogs on forages under Professor Weaver's direction, as reported in bulletin 247 of the experiment station, show wide differences in pork output to the acre of the different forage crops. These differences are better shown in the tabular form where there are given also (a) the pounds of corn required per pound of pork, and (b) the bushels of corn per hundred pounds of pork. As another help in our appreciation of the differences, the tables gives the pounds of pork per acre on a constant amount of corn, which is a figure obtained by dividing the pounds of pork per acre by the pounds of corn per pound of pork on a particular forage.

Most Pork From Alfalfa

The outstanding amount of pork delivered by the alfalfa crop catches the eye immediately. This crop produced the most pork an acre in total and as related to the corn constant. Another legume crop, red clover, is also very efficient when used alone. But one cannot say that it is the legume aspect alone of the forage crop that speaks for efficiency in pork making, when the red clover mixed with rape (rapeseed) and oats as their nurse crop is second only to alfalfa on the acre basis in either way of using the figures.

The difference in total pork to the acre are in no small way connected with the differences in the length of the season the crops supply grazing feed for hogs. But even then the different pork values to the acre cannot be arranged in true order on this basis either. Bluegrass, which is commonly a pasture throughout a relatively long season, gave much less pork to the acre than oats and rape as a forage of similar length of season, and 30 percent less than rape, the nonlegume crop, used alone for a shorter season. Quite disappointing would be the figures for soybean or cowpeas alone, if it is not recognized that these crops are limited to the warmer season of the year, to a short growth period of service as feed, and to a rapid shift from a palatable leafy herbage to one of woodiness or mainly of proteinaceousness in the seeds of which a large portion is apt to be wasted.

Certainly, then, the different forage crops differ widely in their total amounts of pork to the acre when a perennial legume like alfalfa will make 591 pounds and cowpeas, an annual legume, just about one-fourth

Pork Production per Acre of Forage and per Amounts of Grain

Forages Used	Pounds of Pork (per acre)	Pounds of Grain (per pound of pork)	Bushels of Grain (per 100 lbs. pork)	Pork per Acre (corn constant)
		Grain Required		
Alfalfa	591	3.07	5.5	192
Red clover, rape, oats	470	2.74	4.9	175
Red clover	449	2.93	5.2	153
Rape, oats	398	3.16	5.6	126
Rape	394	2.98	5.3	132
Sorghum	275	4.00	7.1	68
Bluegrass	274	4.41	7.8	62
Soybeans	174	2.59	4.6	67
Cowpeas	149	2.91	5.2	51

as much or 149 pounds an acre. Such differences in efficiency of forages blot out the differences in length of grazing season as their possible causes. Their tonnage yields per acre are also pushed out of the way as significant causes of differences in efficiency.

Wide Differences in Corn Needed

Their contrasts are even more significant when for bluegrass, a non-legume of long grazing season, the corn requirements as supplement per 100 pounds of pig growth was 7.8 bushels, but for rape, another nonlegume, it was 5.3 bushels. For the soybeans, which is a legume, the corn requirement dropped to the startling low figure of 4.6 bushels. With such figures for the amount of pork that can be made on an acre of land, and such figures for pork per bushel of corn, there is every reason for any pork producer to begin figuring and planning how he can use either legume or nonlegume forage crops, more extensively, and to struggle for an understanding of what underlying causes make some of these crops so much more efficient in the pork per acre or per bushel of corn.

Perhaps you have been thinking that these forage crops differ in efficiencies because they are different in their contents of protein, carbohydrates, fats, nutritive ratios and other similar chemical properties usually listed in the common feed analysis. Unfortunately, these chemical differences are not as wide as the pork production differences per acre. Alfalfa isn't twice as high in carbohydrates, fats, or even proteins as is bluegrass: nor is it four times as concentrated in these respects as is cowpea forage, which are their differences in the pork they give per acre.

Soil Fertility Counts

It will be more helpful in understanding these differences in feeding efficiencies of forages for hogs if we will begin to think, and to believe that the delivery of fertility by the soil through the crop enters into the picture. Making the growth of an animal is a natural manufacturing business that is much more complicated than simply burning starch to convert some of it into fat, or than merely packing plant protein into animal muscular tissues. The better feed plants are grown on the more fertile soils. Back of these different values of forages combined with corn as hog feed are the different levels of soil fertility required to grow the forage crops.

Making the growth of a plant is another natural manufacturing business that is much more complicated than merely having plenty of acres and getting plenty of rainfall and good weather. It is one of providing a list of a dozen or more chemical elements in the soil. It is one of delivering these to the plant roots at rates sufficiently high to match the needs of the synthetic performances in the plant top that is giving off water and taking in sunshine energy and carbonic acid gas from the air. It is the internal manufacturing business of the plant that covers some of the secrets of these differences in feeding values of forages whether considered as pork per acre or per bushel of corn. These differences of forages as a combination with corn for a hog feed come "from the ground up" as internal performances first by the plant and second by the animal, that are not so easily detected as differences in feed analysis, in growing season, or in tonnage yields per acre.

Soil Minerals Best

Feeding our animals mineral mixtures as supplements or substitutes is a new phase in the thinking about feeding by many men. Ground limestone as a means of providing calcium, and bonemeal as a help to make up the shortage of phosphorus in the feeds were not given to the hogs by the generation of husbandmen just ahead. Have you ever thought that this increasing practice of dosing animals with mineral mixtures is a finger pointing to the declining supplies of soil fertility and decreasing amounts of calcium and phosphorus coming in the deficient crops from the deficient soil?

We need to remind ourselves that the crops at the head of the list of better forages for pork production are the crops which like the animals, are also suffering shortages of lime and phosphate in their diet delivered by the soil. Any crop grown on the less fertile soil is delivering less of the essentials for the animals. The animal denied calcium and phosphorus cannot build bone or carry on the blood-making business within the bone. The plant, too, cannot carry on its internal creative performance without these fertility elements, calcium, phosphorus, and about ten others coming from the soil. Here are common shortages in the soil that are disturbing the secret internal workings of the plants, which, as a consequence, are disturbing the profitable internal workings of the animal. Forages are more efficient in making pork according as the higher level of soil fertility makes them more efficient manufacturers of the many compounds and complexes that combine with corn to help the pig make a hog of itself in the shortest time.

It is true that the better forages give to the animal more of calcium and phosphorus, the two elements in the components of the common mineral mixtures. But even in the simple service of hauling limestone and phosphate from the field to the feed lot the forage crops are widely different. Rape, a nonlegume, and red clover, a legume, both give large pork yields per acre. These crops are also rich in lime and must have plenty of it in the soil to grow well. Because rape has not been so universally tried as red clover, we do not appreciate so highly the demand for lime in the soil by it and by its close relatives in the cabbage family for good crop growth.

Lime Aids Other Elements

These more efficient pork making forages, with which lime and phosphate associate themselves as responsible for both the plant and the pork, do more with these fertility elements or nutrients than pack them into their tissues as a means of hitchhiking to the animal's stomach. Lime in the soil pays for its transportation costs to this animal destination. It may be instrumental in mobilizing from the soil into the roots of the crop larger quantities of phosphorus and many other nutrient essentials less abundantly delivered from lime-deficient soils. Lime serves within the plant in the manufacture of protein, the one particular feed essentially credited to lime-loving legumes and a big help toward solving the problem of the "home-grown" supplement.

Such differences in the plant as a feed that are brought on by greater intake of calcium alone leave suggestions of many other improvements in the plant's delivery and manufacturing businesses that may be encouraged by more phosphorus, magnesium, potassium, and other fertility items provided by the soil. It is through these minute betterments in the soil's contribution that all the plant activities may record their more efficient services in the better animal growth. Pork production and crop production are performances that are both premised on the fertility of the soil.

Already you have been asking yourself these questions. Can't we expect better pork or better animal production in general from such soil treatments as phosphate and limestone? This question can be answered in the affirmative as experiments and increasing farmer experience testify. Trials with sheep have shown better gains from the same grain combined with soybean hays and lespedeza hays grown on adjoining plots but given different soil treatments. Even the qualities of the fleeces of wool were different.

Forage crops can go into pork production more extensively but not merely as a shift in land use by juggling the crops as to different kinds or as to different successions in their coming on the field. Soil conservation is more than keeping the same fertility-deficient soil at home by putting it under forage crop cover, and expecting greater farm economy by sending the animal out to harvest it rather than doing so ourselves. Soil erosion has come upon us, in no small measure, because the soil fertility was too low for nature to grow its crop cover quickly enough. With soil erosion came the less efficient feeds and the higher costs of animal production. Hope lies ahead only in remedying the troubles at their basis, which is the fertility of the soil. Farmer experience with the extensive use of limestone, phosphate, and fertilizers going above any amounts ever used in the state is ample evidence that soil conservation is going forward on a basis that is making more efficient use of the soil, and of the crops in the services for which land is intended, namely the production of food. Soil fertility is at the basis of Missouri's farming, and pork production as one phase is no exception.

Section 3

Soil Fertility
and Human Health

CHAPTER 15

Healthy Soils
Mean Healthy Humans

THE INTENSE PUBLIC CONCERN focused on the dangers from poisonous — even carcinogenic — chemicals sprayed on the landscape, makes appropriate the home-spun remark by George Washington Carver who said, "When the manger is empty, the horses bite each other."

For us to see the analogy between his last five words and the chemical warfare on pests and diseases, calls for no unusual stretch of the imagination, which pictures man as the top stratum in the biotic pyramid "biting" all the other strata beneath — but supporting him.

It may, however, be going beyond the elastic limit of your imagination to see another analogy between Carver's first five words, and the declining or exploited fertility of the living soil now failing to serve, via nutrition, as the foundation stratum for all others, viz. microbes, plants, animals and man.

That this changing lower stratum should cause the "biting" of each other by the upper ones may not be so self-evident.

But that pyramidal construction of the many life forms, from the soil upward, represents the evolutionary succession which arrived at man as the apex; all via their individual healthy survival.

The latter was possible only by fitness of each in the climatic soil setting growing suitable nourishment. Only by that combination could all of them have been available to feed man on his very late arrival.

Accordingly, the healthy human survival calls for consideration of that struggle also from the soil upwards, through nutrition for self-protection against so-called 'diseases'.

That call seems more logical than one for more powerful drugs, of which each is catalogued against a specific ailment for its cure, through man's ministrations from his uppermost stratum downwards.

In support of the importance of the soil as nutrition for healthy self-protection and prevention of diseases and pests, observations and research studies at the Missouri Agricultural Experiment Station in the U.S.A. deserve citation here in connection with plants, the only producers of food through their collection and storage of the sun's energy.

Those bits of knowledge are particularly appropriate as ecological approaches in the broader scope of the interrelations and interdependencies of man and other forms of life. We need, especially, to see the interdependence between ourselves and the more lowly ones, including the living soil and its microbes by which, in the ultimate analysis, we must be fed.

As far back as the 1920's, there came suggestions from Missouri's agricultural research that plant diseases may be caused by deficiencies of some of the inorganic elements required from the soil as nourishment.

Those suggestions turned up in connection with the early application of the technique in which purified acid, colloidal clay, with calcium adsorbed in it, was used as increasing amounts in quartz sand to study the growths and their bacterial nodulation of soybean plants.

This method served as the tool to control, in refined detail, the plant's diet of fertility elements offered, and to measure the resulting chemical contents of healthy plants proving themselves users of atmospheric nitrogen and producers of satisfactory yields of forage.

This discovery of a case of plant "disease" caused by deficient nutrition was an accident when the plants were suddenly — and some very severely — attacked by a fungus. The symptoms suggested a "damping-off" disease.

That accident, in the plans of the research programme, brought to mind a scientist's statement, namely: "Many discoveries are accidents for the minds prepared to recognise them."

Consequently, those irregularities prompted more careful examinations, which revealed that the differences in percentages of healthy and diseased plants were a clear-cut case of the numbers invaded by the fungus as a reciprocal of:

(a) the increasing amounts of exchangeable calcium offered as nutrition; (b) the better plant growth shown by more height and heavier weights; (c) the greater uptake of calcium; (d) the more and larger nodules on the roots; and (e) more nitrogen fixed from the atmosphere through synthesis of more protein and thereby the autoimmunity through physiological defences, often viewed as antibodies and other such mechanisms.

Since each of those several factors could suggest by its increase that it was the cause of the highly correlated decrease in the numbers of sick plants, there is much danger of erroneously concluding that such causal connection holds true.

But correlations are perfect when both phenomena have a common cause, as was true here. The larger plants, the less of disease, and the more self-protection resulted because of the several increased effects via nutrition which was improved through the increases of calcium available in the soil.

Other research on the variable composition of plants, grown by similar techniques of feeding them, showed that by narrowing the ratio of calcium to potassium, offered by the clay of the soil, one could grow large yields of legume-plant bulk carrying increased carbohydrates but reduced concentrations of amino acids or proteins, and reduced nitrogen fixation from the atmosphere.

By using a wider ratio of calcium to potassium going to the plant roots from the clay, the plant's yield as bulk was decreased, but the amino acid contents in protein and the fixation of atmospheric nitrogen were both increased.

Accordingly, in some of our crop production which disregards balanced soil fertility, we can see plants being literally "fattened" under their protein-deficiency, but their larger carbohydrate output, with a "sickening" effect on the plants — much in the same manner as humans develop obesity — and our fattening of livestock, brings on increased susceptibility to diseases.

In the self-protection by plants, the significant factors suggest themselves as causes according as they favour nutrition, including more complete protein synthesis.

That nature projects self-protection (against insects) into the next generation, according as the soil grows it, was also demonstrated by some research studies by the Missouri Agricultural Experiment Station.

One readily accepts the theory that any seed, as a dormancy or with life processes at a very low rate, must preserve those processes in their health between their very high rates of the crop making the seed and of the succeeding generation started by the planting of it.

If such were not true the species extinction would result.

For demonstration of the theory as fact, ears of hybrid maize, grown on soil given nitrogen fertiliser only and on soil given both nitrogen and phosphorus, were wrapped and bound as pairs within cellophane sheets with the ends of the ears exposed to permit entrance of insects, common to stored grain.

The grain grown from soil given nitrogen only was taken by the lesser grain borer first. The inside of almost every grain per ear was bored out to leave the shell and the waste meal resulting.

In contrast, there were but a few borer holes in the grain grown on soil given both nitrogen and phosphorus. That damage was only at points of close contact of the two different grains.

The damage had occurred during about two and a half years of storage. During the early part of that time, the absence of insects prompted neglect of observation, hence the date of the first attack is unknown.

After the two and a half years, some open-pollinated corn, grown on soil fertilised with barnyard manure, was added to the pairs, with their active insect fauna, and the storage period extended for about six months.

During that period there were some few additional insect attacks on the second hybrid but the open-pollinated grain, grown by the soil treatment of barnyard manure only, had but one hole suggesting borer damage.

Such observations of nature in action on stored grains, raise the question whether we exhibit much wisdom in our designing of chemical poisons to fight the disease and pests, when by evolution nature grew the species of our diseased and insect-ridden crops which were not so attacked and destroyed.

That fact was shown by their healthy presence when we came along so late for domestication of them. Plants had their self-protection grown in them. They passed that attribute to their seeds in storage and even, apparently, on to the next generation to continue the ingrown capacity its predecessors demonstrated.

That farm animals (and wildlife) grow better health or more autoimmunity on better soils has been a continuing farmer demonstration, more particularly by a herd of 200 beef cattle, by the Poirot Farms of Golden City, Missouri.

During the past forty years their exhausted soil of the eastern edge of the prairie has been under restoration by a farmer and conservationist, who has been honoured as a master in each of those categories.

As a naturalist, he is a keen observer who has followed nature's laws in building up the fertility of much of the soil of 1,800 acres by using the choices of wildlife and of his livestock as guides for proper additions of calcium, magnesium, phosphorus, copper, cobalt and even iodine, some of the latter three coming to the soil via their presence in the salt.

"Science does not yet know all the biological values Mother Nature produces in the soil," says Mr. E. M. Poirot, senior partner. "Animals just below man in the pyramid of life strata, are a part of the natural balances. Their choices and response are, therefore, valuable guides.

"Observations of them are our best helps until the chemical laboratory can point out the 'why' of the effects of the soil restoration on animal health.

"Before I applied any phosphate, now nearly forty years ago," he says, "my cattle were so hungry they chewed bones whenever they found one, and in the absence of them they would chew oakwood brought in from elsewhere ... At any place where phosphate had been applied, cows would crop the plants, literally, down into the soil.

"Where lime and phosphate had been applied on part of the field, the cattle would mark the place to the line by avoiding the grass growing four inches from the drill-line of the applied treatment.

"The animals seemed to want more of the elements applied. When those were offered, either in the soil or in feed boxes in their pasture, diseases all but disappeared, their weights and general conditions improved, and they began to bear normal calf crops.

"My cattle are now living in good health, without need of any veterinary services for infectious diseases during the last eighteen years.

"They are reproducing normally and giving a calf-crop to nearly 100 percent, without winter shelter and without grains, silage, legume hay or other feeds, save a special protein mixture during the winter at one pound per head daily, along with the Bluestem hay left in the field at the spot where each bale was dropped while baling.

"Through restoring the soil, over 200 head are now enjoying margins of food, self-protection and reproduction on the same land area, which less than four decades ago could not supply an adequate ration for eight head of their ancestors."

From the preceding examples of natural self-preservation and careful observations of the autoimmunities of the lower forms of life below man, we cannot escape the deduction that each living unit, from the simple cell to the most complex organism, survives, to a large degree, according as it develops its own self-protection.

Better health of plants and animals are readily demonstrated as results from the more fertile soils.

Each body establishes many immunities which are not yet catalogued. Nor have we comprehended and explained many well enough to make them successfully manageable as uniformity throughout the crowd.

No epidemic is 100 percent disastrous. There are always those who survive on their own. Nor is health in any group 100 percent perfect.

But there is much to be gained in the latter by the individual's own effort of learning about his own nutrition, with buoyant health as a studied objective by concern with the natural qualities and nutritional values grown into, and preserved within, the foods we eat.

CHAPTER 16

Soil Fertility and Food Quality

FOOD IS THE DOMINANT factor in the control of all forms of life. Food stands out as the major objective of our struggles, whether in peace or in war. Reduced to its agricultural chemical fundamentals, food production is a matter of mobilizing some dozen nutrient elements into our bodies from the soil by way of plants and sunshine power. For nutritional service, these essential chemical elements must come, not singly, but variously and properly compounded. When synthesized into myriads of chemical complexes they serve to build the body and to keep it going. Their fitness as to supply in total amount and in proper chemical combinations determines the quality of our foods.

Every kind of creation starts with this handful of dust, or with the five percent of vegetation, or finally of our bodies, that is the ash. It is this soil-borne mite that controls the fabrication of the other ninety-five percent — that is four elements coming from air and water — into either mainly carbohydrates, cellulose, lignin, and wood of energy value only, or into proteins, vitamins, and more complex compounds of higher service in body-building. The soil fertility, or these mundane chemical potentialities of life, are then the real material basis of our bodies. We are, in actual fact created from the soil.

Plants Feed by Exchange, or by Barter with the Clay

Plants get their nourishment by means of chemical exchanges between the hydrogen or acidity on their root surfaces and the nutrients held on the surfaces of the innumerable particles constituting the clay fraction of the soil. Of the three soil separates, sand, silt, and clay, named in order of decreasing particle size, it is the clay that offers the greater possibilities of rapid chemical reaction. As for its own breakdown, the clay is a relatively inert mineral. But it is of infinitely small crystal size and holds on its immense surface in exchangeable condition the many elements of nutrient service to plants. It is there that these elements of service in feeding plants and peoples are held in this condition against loss by water as a leaching agent, but ready for a quick transfer to plant roots offering acid or hydrogen in trade. It is the clay with its supply of essentials that has adsorbed or taken these out of solution. It is the clay that is the jobber to provide the plant with its needs quickly when the growing root comes along. It is the clay, which within its own crystal structure offers a little, but which on its surface can hold much that has been given it, and which plays the soil's essential and active part in provisioning our crops at the high speed required during their short growing season.

The silt and the sand as minerals in the absence of the clay offer so little active surface, and are so insoluble that the root in direct contact with them can get very little from their slow chemical breakdown. The sand, in particular, that has survived weathering forces to remain in particles of larger size, is naturally harder and more insoluble as this resistance to disintegration and decomposition testifies. Then, too, its main mineral constituent is quartz. This mineral carries no element of nutritive value. The silt, however, that is softer and is therefore more readily ground to smaller size by weathering agencies, is richer in nutient minerals and is more readily broken down chemically. It is, therefore, the soil's main reserve supply of nourishing elements in the rocks and minerals that by their slow decomposition keep these passing to the clay in adsorbed form for plant nutrient service.

Clay as the Jobber Handles Acidity as Well as Nutrients

It is this mineral assembly line that is giving supplies to the plant. The rock is passing the essentials to the clay and the clay is passing them on to the root. The root in turn is passing hydrogen, the acid element — and possibly other compounds — in the opposite direction. The root, as a growing body, goes through the soil only as it can do so, by growth. It does not advance into a sterile soil. As a respiring organism it gives off carbon dioxide, which unites with the water to form nature's widely disseminated and most common solvent, carbonic acid. This acid is the provider of the hydrogen, a very active element that is exchanged to the clay for the nutrient stock it carries. As the clay gives up its store of nutrients and takes hydrogen in exchange, this soil separate becomes more acid. The resulting acid clay, then, or acid soil in nature, is merely a soil of lower supply in fertility elements or in possibilities of plant production.

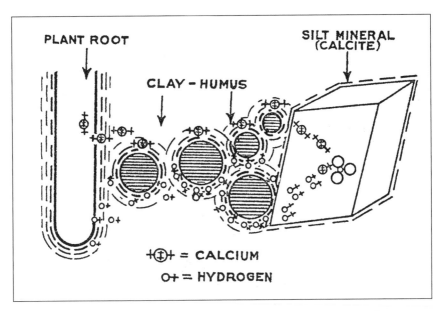

Fig. 1. Plant nutrients, like calcium, held on the colloidal clay or humus, are exchanged to the plant root for the hydrogen or acidity it gives off. As the nutrient supplies on the colloid become exhausted the excessive hydrogen substituted for them serves to break down the mineral reserves to pass their stock of nutrients to the colloid and to the root.

Soil Rest to Restock the Clay with Plant Nutrients

This acid clay, or this jobber that has traded its stock of fertility for acidity, must then take a rest from crop production while it trades its acidity for fertility in the silt reserve minerals to restock itself for more business with the plant roots. Natural acidity, then, is merely a case of significant depletion of the soil. It indicates that the clay is not quickly restocked from the reserve minerals and rock fragments. The soil's mineral assembly line that is ordinarily passing essential nutrient elements from the silt to the clay and then to the roots, is beginning to run too slowly and to deliver less. Soil acidity is merely nutrient deficiency of the clay and of the mineral reserves.

Humus, Too, May Be a Nutrient Jobber

In our virgin soils that have had myriads of generations of plants to come and go and to pass on their dead tops and incorporated roots as decayed organic matter to form colloidal humus, there was this stock of prefabricated soil fertility for our crops. As we plowed these virgin soils to fan the microbial fires of humus destruction, and to use this additional organic colloidal exchanger of nutrients taking hydrogen from the plant roots and breaking down the mineral silt fraction, we were running, at high speed, this humus assembly line that made for high crop yield. We had little thought of soil depletion. We worried little about impending deficiencies in the crops as animal feeds or as human foods. It was this destruction of natural humus in the soil that made such good crops on land freshly cleared of forest. It was this destruction that spelled early American prosperity and pushed high the unearned increments of our lands. It is this destruction that calls for soil conservation and soil fertility restoration today.

This high production of crops occurred on land that, without the drop of forest leaves as natural "forest manure" and as returning fertility to go into trees again, could scarcely produce even the wood crop by which few animals or higher life forms can be nourished. It is this waning humus supply in the soil that has been pushing nutritious vegetation westward except as the soil is bolstered up through lime and other fertilizers with the nutrients that make crops more than merely woody bulk of value only as fuel.

Restored humus by means of fertilizers and sod crops grown for that purpose is essential to keep this second assembly line running in our soils. As it runs almost empty there come in the less nutritious crops, or those which as volunteers in pastures are called weeds because their fabrication with so little soil fertility makes the animal disregard them even under the threat of starvation. The animal is discriminating against photosynthesis only and is looking for crops that also give compounds of biosynthesis. In our cultivated lands the grain crops, too, fail to yield regularly. Some of the soils have become alternate year yielders, as demonstrated by the plot in continuous wheat on Sanborn Field at the Missouri Experiment Station. This is bearing a wheat crop only every other year regardless of annual seedbed preparations and seedings. *Both the humus and mineral assembly lines need to be running at full delivery capacity for the higher yields of nutritious foods and feed from our soils.*

Differences in the Stage of the Soil's Development Give Differences in the Plant's Chemical Composition

Soil may be said to be a temporary rest stop of the rocks enroute to solution and to the sea. When the trip has just been started, the soil is not yet significantly developed. As the rock nears solution, or represents those remaining minerals of high resistance to weathering, the soil is overdeveloped. Thus, we may have soils *in construction* and *in destruction* in a geological sense. Soils at their best, however, are those with the rock broken down sufficiently to provide a fair amount of clay, and to have the adsorptive, or exchange, capacity of this soil separate fairly well saturated with the nutrient elements like calcium, magnesium, potassium, and others of positive electrical charges, and commonly called the bases. The better soils have not been weathered far enough to remove completely the softer rocks and minerals carrying the essential nutrients as reserves to be weathered out later. The silt separate still carries a supply of nourishing mineral reserves to be mobilized to the clay as it gives up its adsorbed nutrient supply to plants. Nor has the weathering gone far enough to load much of the clay's exchange capacity with acid, the non-nutrient hydrogen. *Better soils are midway between construction and destruction, both of which, as processes, contribute to the productive capacity of our soils.*

While soils are in construction, vegetation gains its foothold and starts to conserve fertility by combining it with carbon of atmospheric origin and to hold it as humus against the forces of destruction and removal. Soils barely started in construction, or when they are little more than crushed rock, mobilize so little of the materials in the absence of clay that forest trees and other woody vegetation are all they can produce. There the organic matter produced is left on top of the soil. Soils farther along in the construction process under higher rainfall, but with insignificant soil leaching, build humus within the soil by means of leguminous, herbaceous growths. These latter soil improvements are possibly only on calcium-laden soils. Here also nitrogen is captured from the atmosphere to contribute its special humus compounds of blacker color that make choice soils.

This special humus of narrower carbon-nitrogen ratio moves its nitrogen downward readily; gives a fine, stable, granular structure to the soil; and develops those prairie soils of deep, dark profiles on which the production of food and feed of high quality is so universally recognized.

Under still higher rainfalls to leach soils more toward their destruction, the acid dominance and fertility deficiency encourage a carbonaceous vegetation rather than a proteinaceous one. Humus made from this material has a wide carbon-nitrogen ratio. Consequently, nitrogen is hoarded near the soil surface by microbial competition for it. This magnifies the differences in color and makes more prominent the surface and subsoil horizons in the profile. While the leaching forces are pulling nutrient elements downward, plant roots and struggles by surviving vegetation are pulling them upward to magnify the contrasting darker color and higher fertility in the surface layer against the fertility deficiency in the lighter colored subsoil. This second soil horizon becomes a kind of a "No man's land" over which both forces have fought for the nutrient elements, leaving little of fertility value for crop production after the surface soil is eroded. *Humus, by its prominence and scarcity in different degrees; its distribution in the profile in different extents; its different carbon-nitrogen ratio; and its differing speeds of nitrogen mobilization during the growing season, is associated with the mobilized soil fertility and the crop-producing power of high value as nutrition to higher forms of life.*

Climatic Geography Locates Mainly Carbonaceous or Proteinaceous Crops According to the Requisite Soil Fertility

Differences in climate are basic to differences in the degree of soil development and therefore to differences in the degree to which the soil provides the elements of plant nutrition. Too readily have we accepted the belief that the chemical composition of plants is controlled by the differences in rainfall rather than by the differences in soil fertility brought about by those differences in precipitation. Too readily have we accepted the belief that a single variety of plant is always of the same composition and that it delivers seeds or fruits of constant nutritive value. So-called "hard" wheat is grown in regions of lower annual rainfall. Its higher protein content, which is responsible for the "hardness" and better properties for so-called "light" bread, originates, however, only on soils still well supplied with calcium,

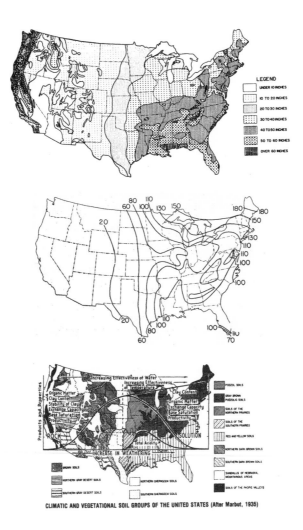

CLIMATIC AND VEGETATIONAL SOIL GROUPS OF THE UNITED STATES (After Marbut, 1935)

Fig. 2. Rainfall is the natural force weathering rock to soil. Exclusive of the western coast of the United States there is an increasing amount of rainfall from west to east and southeast to serve in soil construction in the western half and in soil destruction in the eastern half (upper figure).

When rainfall is divided by evaporation from free water surface (both as inches/ acre/year times 100, or as percentage) the high evaporation in the Cornbelt to lessen the leaching effect of the rain, it is readily understandable why the Cornbelt was "prairie" soils (middle figure).

The weathering agencies as climatic forces of the United States serve clearly to give us the soil areas as they were mapped, with soils "in construction" in the western half, and soils "in destruction" in the eastern half, and the properties of the soils as they minister for or against particular crop production (lower figure).

and hence with other fertilizer elements, whereby a good supply of nitrogen is properly mobilized to make the protein production possible. Similarly "soft" wheat is ascribed to higher rainfall areas. Yet by providing the proper soil fertility, the wheat in the so-called "soft" wheat areas can be made as "hard" as any ever grown in the drier, hard wheat regions.

Starchiness of the wheat results from the process of photosynthesis within the leaves of the plants. Starch represents the carbon taken from the atmosphere and the water drawn up from the soil and both fabricated into this carbohydrate form by sunshine power in the chlorophyllous part of the leaf. It is an animal or human food having only energy value. Other carbohydrates, including cellulose, fiber, lignin, and less digestible forms represent plant bulk that increases rapidly with increasing dependence on constituents obtained from water, air, and sunshine. Plant bulk, or the size of the plant factory for fabricating products of weather origin, is rapidly increased with the advancing season of growth. This carbohydrate production or the increase in plant bulk is therefore closely related to the weather.

The production of protein within the plant, or of the many other essentials for body construction and bone-building in humans and animals, is, however, more than a matter of weather. This process represents the mobilization of the soil fertility through the plant factory. The output in the form of these compounds as bulk is not so large. The amounts of these essentials within the crop are not so readily represented by the bulk of vegetative mass. Rather, their elaboration within the plant during the entire growing season may result in only the small amount finally delivered as the seed crop. It is these complex elaborations, however, that have high value as foods in terms of body building rather than in terms of provisioning it with fuels. They come only from the soil fertility. In consequence, they are apt to be deficient in the plant's crop delivery because of our failing soils.

Proteinaceousness of the crop is connected with soils that are less leached of their calcium and other elements of soil fertility. Only the more fertile soils can therefore give us, in abundance, the feeds and foods so essential for growing young animals with good bone and good brawn. Soils in regions of lower rainfall, then, provide the soil fertility to serve this function. On the other hand, the carbonaceous crops are readily produced on soils more highly leached and of lower content in soil fertility. Such soils still supply the potassium requisite for carbohydrates synthesis but they are deficient in the calcium, the phosphorus, the nitrogen, and other requisites by which these carbonaceous compounds of energy values can be converted through biosynthesis into proteins, vitamins, and other

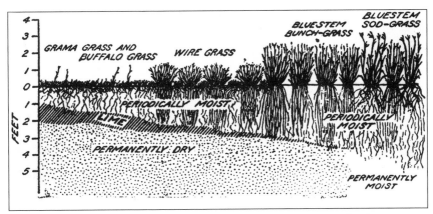

Fig. 3. The native vegetation of Kansas increases in tonnage production per acre from west to east as the rainfall increases from 17 to 37 inches. Its chemical composition is related to the fertility of the soil, as indicated by the bison's choice of buffalo grass because of its nutritive value more than its tonnage yield per acre.

complexes serving in body construction rather than as energy for keeping it going or maintaining its temperature.

The climatic geography of the United States and its crop distribution serve very effectively to illustrate this general principle of soil fertility depletion as basic to the natural incidence, or to the success on their introduction, of carbonaceous or woody crops in contrast to the more fertile and less leached soils as natural areas for proteinaceous products. In the rainfall of the United States (exclusive of the western coast) the lowest annual precipitation is in the West with less than ten inches. As one goes eastward, there are longitudinal zones of increasing amounts until one reaches the belt of 30 to 40 inches of rainfall. This amount runs north and south in the southern half as a longitudinal belt but more like a blanket over the northern portion of the eastern half of our country. In the southeastern states the annual rainfall figures are not so zonally arranged as they climb to the serious soil-leaching amounts of 50 to 60 inches per annum.

In terms of this picture of the precipitation one can see that the rainfall increase up to about 30 inches is an ascending force in soil construction. Beyond this figure, and particularly as one goes southeastward to higher temperature, one can see the increased rainfall as a force in soil destruction. Fortunately for the area known as "the cornbelt", its location so far from seashore and within the center of a large land mass conferring the properties collectively known as "continentality", gives it a higher summer evap-

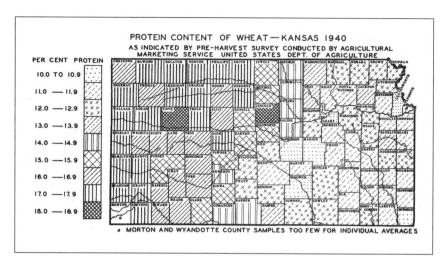

Fig. 4. Protein production demands more than air and water. The elaboration of this food complex depends on soil fertility. As the soils are less leached by lower rainfall the wheat grain is higher in protein. Using the lower tier of counties in Kansas going from the East (37 inches rainfall) to the West (17 inches rainfall), the protein content of the wheat in 1940 went from 10 to 17 percent.

oration which reduces the leaching of the nutrients by its higher rainfall. Its soils have therefore retained significant amounts of those mineral reserves representing the plant nutrients in the original rocks. The low ratios of the annual rainfall to annual evaporation from a free water surface as they can be delineated on the map serve to show that the fertility of the cornbelt is similar to that of the grassy prairie areas farther west. It was the fertility of the soil that presented the cornbelt pioneers with the highly productive plains of the prairies. It was not the prairie grasses that made the fertile soils, as one might erroneously be led to believe. Conversely, the fertile soils made the nutritious grass.

Unfortunately for Florida and the southeastern part of the United States, this is an area of high rainfall. This weathering agent has not only depleted the soil of its nutritive mineral reserves common in the silt and sand, but has also given a clay that in its chemical makeup is different from clay under lower rainfall and temperature. In addition, the clay is lower in its exchange capacity and therefore in its ability to serve as a jobber. It can take less out of solution of fertilizers and can therefore give less to crops growing on it. Then, too, with soils formed from marine deposits or marine-worked materials it is not surprising that soils should be segregations and made up mainly of peat deposits in one area, sand or silt deposits in another, and not of the well blended combinations of sand, silt, and clay serving more uniformly for crop production. In the region of southeastern United States, then, the climatic forces in soil construction and soil destruction stand out prominently as the agriculture, modified accordingly, so forcefully testifies.

The Soil Fertility Pattern of the United States Is Replicated in Other Centers of Civilization in the World

Here is a pattern of soil conditions, as determined by climatic forces, by which we can locate areas of similar soil productivity on the globe. Within the temperate zone these areas with annual rainfalls approaching the 30-inch figure, represent the combination of conditions that gave us soils which provision life with its food essentials. It was in this narrow belt of soils running north and south across the United States that the pioneer found the buffalo roaming in thundering herds. It is on these same soils that the cattle production is centered today with possible shipment eastward to higher rainfall areas for fattening purposes. It is on this belt that wheat as the staff of life can be produced. But even this food grain demonstrates its high protein content of eighteen percent in the 17-inch rainfall area of western Kansas in contrast to the ten percent of protein in wheat grown in eastern Kansas with its 37 inches of annual rainfall. It is this fortunate combination of climatic forces operating on a fortunate combination of mineral resources originally left to the climate for construction of soil that makes the midlands of the United States the well-laden breadbasket and meat basket that it is.

It is on similar soil patterns that other parts of the world are supporting corresponding populations and have established civilizations of similar accomplishments. That hard wheat has been the staff of life so universally the world over is not wholly due to inborn powers in the crop. Rather it is the soil fertility by which this crop can be both a protein-producer of growth values and a starch-former of energy values that locates civilizations on the higher rainfall sides of the hard wheat belts of the world. It is this soil fertility condition that is closely linked with all civilizations, not only in the United States but in other parts of the globe. A close scrutiny of the world for similar climatic soil combinations demonstrates that

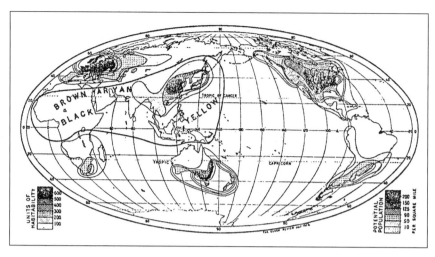

Fig. 5. The settlements of peoples in different parts of the world suggest the higher concentrations of them according as the climatic forces have made soils of such fertility levels that guarantee survival and permit development of their civilizations. (Map according to Griffith Taylor.)

wherever civilizations of higher accomplishments have been established they are built on such soils of similar fertility levels serving as their basic resource. Europe with its hard wheat belt in Russia and higher rainfalls to the west is the picture of the United States with its East and West reversed. Similar soil and climatic combinations prevail in the Argentine, South Africa, Australia, New Zealand and to a similar degree in northeastern China. Studied in terms of the world wars, the basic food resources at the disposal of the warring nations loom as factors in the combat as well as any military or political maneuverings.

Plant Ecology Indicates the Vegetations Changing in Chemical Composition with the Declining Soil Fertility

The distribution of plants across the United States reveals a pattern of their chemical composition in terms of service as animal and human foods as well as of an organized array of plant varieties. The higher concentration of fertility in the less leached soils gives a prairie grass vegetation. Among these plants are the many proteinaceous, mineral-rich legumes growing naturally to stock the soils with nitrogen and humus by which the more proteinaceous and more mineral-rich non-legumes as well as legumes can flourish. These blacker soils, with a relative dominance of calcium over potassium within them and therefore a corresponding dominance of protein synthesis in plant functions, produce a physiological basis for the fine bone and big brawn of the buffalo, native there.

Forests abound where quite the opposite fertility condition prevails, or where potassium is in relative dominance to calcium. This is the situation in rocky regions not yet developed into soils, also on highly weathered soils from the clay of which sufficient potassium is still delivered to the deeply penetrating tree roots to support this plant's activities that are predominantly photosynthetic as it builds its body mainly of wood. Even this carbonaceous construction mainly by means of air, water, and sunshine — all supra-soil in origin and action — can proceed only as the annual drop of fertility elements in the leaves keeps going back to maintain this annual cycle of self-fertilization. *The plant pattern is as the soil permits and not as the plant wills.*

The processes of soil development and soil depletion then give us the ecological pattern of plant composition and therefore the pattern also of the possibilities of feeding wild animal life, domestic animal life, and human life as well. They point the warning finger to the waning of human health, too, when cropping depletes the soil and when the same crop, that once was a life-sustaining food with body-building powers, has shifted its chemical output to products that are neither proteinaceous nor mineral-rich as they once were, but have become carbonaceous or woody materials of fuel value only. Our depletion of the soil or our failure to restore the removed nutrients is therefore an insidious under-miner of health in its many ramifications. As our soils are becoming deficient through our exhaustion of them, or as they had serious natural deficiencies originally, our foods have been or are becoming deficient and our health and growth along with them. And, unfortunately, the popular demand is for cures for these troubles, not for prevention by way of more fertility put back to give us restored soils.

Animal Instincts Offer Helpful Suggestions

Careful observations of the behavior of wild animals in their selection of herbages on different soils and of domestic animals according to soils differently treated will give optimism to our efforts in soil improvement for better foods and hence for health's sake. It is a common observation that in the spring of the year cattle break out on to the highway and railroad right-of-ways. Little have we reminded ourselves that they will face possible body injury while going through the fence in order to get the more nutritious grass growing where the soil has not been so highly depleted of its fertility by excessive crop removal. Much has been said about keeping cows at home by means of better fences to avoid loss of valuable meat animals in highway or railway casualties. More might well be said about making the pasture soils as fertile and as productive of nutritious forages as the highway soils. We would thereby avoid the need for excessive fencing when the quality of the feed on the farm tempts the cow more than does that of the grazing on the highway. Soil treatments can be tested against the animal choices to indicate the better feeding values in the crop. Animal assays of the crop can be guides for the proper soil treatment by which our soils, seemingly threatening danger to our health as well as to that of our animals, can give us better qualities of feed and food.

The deer has demonstrated by its choice of browse in the forest that even trees give different chemical compositions in their growing buds and different feeds to wild animals. Sheep have selected the early growing rye where manure from alfalfa was applied, and in the same field where the soil was enriched by lime. Cattle have chosen pastures fertilized with 200 pounds of fertilizer in preference to that with only 100 pounds of this soil treatment. Hogs have taken the grain from the part of the field first where the soil was once fertilized to grow alfalfa. They have taken the corn at different rates from different compartments of the self-feeder according to the treatments of the soil where the grain was grown. The choices of the rats in cutting the bags of the same stored grains corresponded with the choice by the hogs. The rats failed to cut the bags of the corn that was disregarded by the hogs.

These animal choices are in accord with the demonstrations by Dr. Curt Richter using experimental rats to demonstrate their appetite as an attempt to maintain their physiological condition at the proper level for their best nourishment and survival. We are just beginning to appreciate the fine discrimination exercised by animals with reference to the chemical composition of their feeds as these feed qualities are dependent on the fertility of the soils producing them.

Diseases of domestic animals suggest that in their confinement by fences and barns to feeds provided for them, the animals are merely making manifest our failure to nourish them properly. Rickets, "loin disease",

Fig. 6. Hogs put into this field to "hog down" the corn selected this area of the forty acres where this Missouri farmer had treated the soil and grown alfalfa some years previously. It was Prof. Evvard, the inventor of the self-feeder, who said, "If you will give the pig a chance it will make a hog of itself in less time than you will."

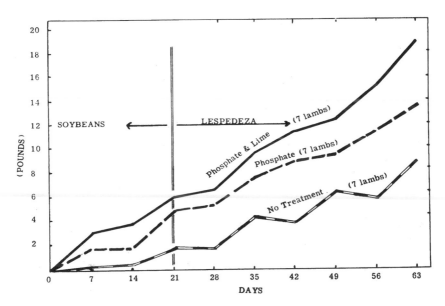

Fig. 7. Three lots of lambs were fed for nine weeks on equal amounts of grains and of hays from adjoining plots given the different soil treatments. Those fed with hay from the plots given lime and phosphate gained twice as much as those fed from the hays grown without soil treatment.

"creeps", acetonemia, pregnancy disease, and other ailments forcefully suggest that we need to look to the quality "grown into" the feed rather than antidotes or remedies "thrown into" it and into the animals.

Experiments Demonstrate Improved Feed Quality Through Fertilization of the Soil

Experiments using the animals to assay the value of the soil treatment in producing better feed quality have demonstrated the validity of the belief that we can feed our animals by treating the soil. The use of equal amounts of supplements and of hay per head per day with the hay coming from three plots with different soil treatments demonstrated clearly that the animals' meat-making machine can run no more efficiently than is made possible by the raw materials supplied as feed.

Three soil treatments were used in growing the hay, namely (a) no treatment, (b) superphosphate, and (c) lime and superphosphate. The gains — as pounds per head — during sixty-three days corresponding to these treatments were 8, 14, and 18, respectively. By giving attention to the soil, the meat output by the animal from the same bulk of feed and during the same

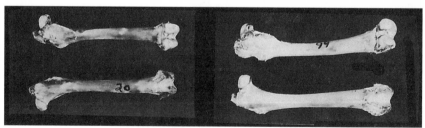

Fig. 8. Fertilizer treatments of the soil register their beneficial effects in the plant, but more noticeably in the physiology of the animal, as indicated by better weight, wool, fur, bones, or other body products and functions. On the left, the rabbit and bones record the lack of soil treatment, in contrast to the effect of treatment measured by similar gauges on the right.

time was more than doubled where lime and phosphate were the fertilizers for the soybean and the lespedeza hays. The soil treatments doubled the feed efficiency or the animal's efficiency in making meat.

Rabbits selected for uniformity in sexes and weights as litter mates, were fed the lespedeza hay grown on the five different soil types of the experiment fields in five different parts of Missouri both with and without soil treatment, only to find that the animals on hays from untreated soils in final appearances suggested five distinctly different kinds of rabbits. Those fed the hay from treated soils were similar. Studies of their various body parts, as glands, bones, and others, revealed the extensive variations as the result of the differences, not in initial animal, not in kind of plant, but in the quality of the same feed originating in the differences in the fertility of the soil growing it. Differences in the soils made differences when the animals were originally alike in age, size, pedigree and other properties of controlled uniformity at the outset. They were eventually different because the soils supporting them were different and therefore the qualities of their forage feeds were different.

Human skeletal parts are well hidden away and are not subject to measurements of size, breaking strength or chemical composition. Teeth are, however, an exposed skeletal part. By their failures to develop properly or to maintain themselves permanently, they reflect the deficient

Fig. 9. Human, as well as plant and animal health, declines as the fertility of our soils is leached or washed away.

body physiology. Other body weaknesses are also well hidden so that most body organs can be defective or failing almost fifty percent before the body's buffer capacity can no longer keep the deficiency hidden. Defective body parts represent deficiencies in the means of constructing them. They speak for failure in body-building foods more than for shortages in energy foods. They suggest the possibility of foods lower in quality as growth promotors than expected. These changed qualities may be the difference within the same plant species due to changes in the level of the soil fertility growing it.

Declining soil fertility, then, as it provokes the plant's failing synthesis of growth essentials may be the fundamental cause in the declining food quality. These qualities cannot be adequately bolstered by mineral additions to the ration. If these are the facts, then, we may well look to the treatment of our soils with those fertilizer essentials that contribute to plant composition in terms of the elaborated compounds that give food its life sustaining values of the highest service in terms of good health. In this respect all of us, and our children need to appreciate the great fact, that food quality for all life is no higher than the fertility of the soil producing it. If our declining soil fertility is not to sweep us down with it, our efforts in soil conservation must be to push the fertility of the soil back up by a proper treatment of the land. Our future health as well as our wealth depends on the restoration of our soils.

CHAPTER 17

Soil Fertility, Food Source

Efficiency in Mobilizing Reserves of a Dozen Elements in Earth's Crust is to Be Regarded as a Determinant in World Affairs

FOOD IS FABRICATED soil fertility. It is food that must win the war and write the peace. Consequently, the questions of who will win the war and how indelibly the peace will be written will be answered by the reserves of soil fertility and the efficiency with which they can be mobilized for both the present and the postconflict eras. National consciousness has recently take notice of the great losses by erosion from the body of the surface soil. We have also begun to give more than passive attention to malnutrition on a national scale. Not yet, however, have we come to recognize soil fertility as the food-producing forces within the soil which reveal national and international patterns of weakness or strength.

What is soil fertility? In simplest words, it is some dozen chemical elements which are being slowly broken out of mineral and rock combinations in the earth's crust and hustled off to the sea. Enjoying a temporary rest stop en route, they are a part of the soil and serve their essential roles in nourishing all the different life forms. They are the soil's contribution — from among a large mass of nonessentials — which empowers the germinating seeds and the growing plants to use sunshine energy in the synthesis of atmospheric elements and of rainfall into the many crops for our support. The atmospheric and rainfall elements are carbon, hydrogen, oxygen, and nitrogen, so common everywhere.

Soil fertility constitutes the 5 percent that is the plant ash. It is the handful of dust that makes up the corresponding percentage in the human body. Yet it is the controlling force that determines whether Nature in her fabricating activities shall construct merely the woody framework, with leaf surfaces catching sunshine and with root surfaces absorbing little more than water or whether inside that woody shell there shall be synthesized the innumerable life-sustaining compounds.

Soil fertility determines whether plant foods of only fuel and fattening values, or plant foods capable of body service as complicated as growth and reproduction, shall be grown in a given area. Because the soil accounts for only a small percentage of our bodies, we are not generally aware of the fact that this 5 percent can predetermine the fabrication of the other 95 percent into something more than mere fuel.

Realization is now dawning that a global war is premised on a global struggle for soil fertility as food. Historic events in connection with the war have been too readily interpreted in terms of armies and politics and not as actions calculated to mobilize soil fertility. Gafsa, merely a city in North Africa, was rejuvenation for phosphorus-starved German soils. Nauru, a little island speck in the Pacific, is a similar nutritional savior to the Japanese. Hitler's move eastward was a hope looking to the Russian soil-fertility reserves. The hoverings of his *Graf Spee* around Montevideo and his underground workings in Argentina, much more than being maneuverings for political or naval advantage, were designs on that last of the world's rich store of less exploited soil fertility, to be had in the form of corn, wheat, and beef. Some of these historic martial events serve to remind us that "an empty stomach knows no laws" and that man is in no unreal sense an animal that becomes a social and political being only after he has consumed some of the products of the soil.

In view of our youthfulness as an extensive country, our different geographic areas have registered themselves mainly as differences in body comfort, whether hot or cold, wet or dry. Because of the free flow of foods and food constituents by means of cheap transportation, we have not been cognizant of the differences in quality as well as in kinds of foods produced in adjoining districts that differ in soil. We have not yet marked out our country into smaller patchwork districts with distinctive local colorings, as the Old World has in the opinion of visitors from the New World. Limitations in travel, difficulties in food delivery, and all the other

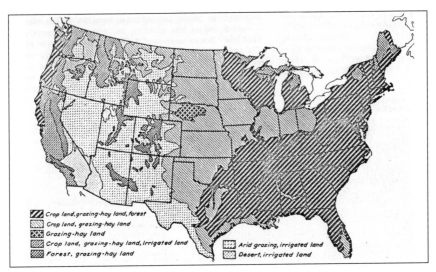

The regions of major rural land uses as mapped by F.J. Marschner. Though the main natural vegetation types — forest, grassland, and desert shrub — are indicative of major rural land uses, other factors are influential. In the eastern corn belt, originally timber covered, forestry now scarcely exists, because the fertility of the soil and the gentleness of the surface relief favor crop production.

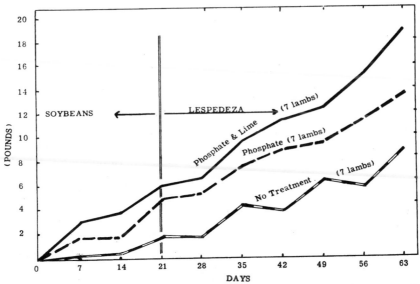

The effect of fertilizer treatment of soils is indicated by this chart. It measures in pounds against days the gain in weight of sheep which were fed equal amounts of hay (and supplements) grown on soils essentially similar but given different fertilizer treatments.

restrictions now making us more local will soon emphasize differences and deficiencies according to the soils by which we live.

Geographic divisions give us an East and a West in the country as a whole, while a North and a South for the eastern half are commonly interpreted as separations according to differences in modes of livelihood, social customs, or political affiliations. Variations in rainfall and temperature are readily acknowledged. But that these make soils so different in nutritional quality as to control differences in vegetation, animals, and human beings is not so readily granted. That "we are as we eat," and that we eat according to the soil fertility, are truths that will not so generally and readily be accepted. Acceptances are seemingly to come not by deduction but rather through disaster.

Vegetation has been distinguished by names of crop species and by tonnage yields per acre. Plants have not been considered for their chemical composition and nutritive value according to the fertility in the soil producing them. This failure has left us in confusion about crops and has put plant varieties into competition with one another rather than in support of one another. Now that the subject of nutrition is on almost every tongue, we are about ready for the report that vegetation as a deliverer of essential food products of its own synthesis is limited by the soil fertility.

Proteinaceousness and high mineral contents of distinct nutritive values are more common among crops from soils receiving comparatively low rainfall and in less leached areas, as, for example, in the midwestern part of the United States. Hard wheat — so called because of its high protein content, which makes it useful in the milling of the patent flour for light bread — is commonly ascribed to regions having lower annual rainfalls. Soft wheat is similarly ascribed to areas of more abundant rain. The high calcium content, the other liberal mineral reserves, and the pronounced activities of nitrogen within the less leached soil must be accepted as the reasons for this distinction, in view of the fact that experimental trials supplying these fertility items to the soil in regions of high rainfall can result in hard wheat where soft wheat is common.

The proteinaceous vegetation and the synthesis by it of many unknowns which, like proteins, help to remove hidden hungers and encourage fecundity of both man and animal are common in the prairie regions marked by the moderate rainfalls. It is fertility of the soil, rather than low precipitation, which gives the Midwest, or those areas bordering along approximately the 97th meridian, these distinctions: (1) selection of it as a feeding ground by the thundering herds of bison, which multiplied to

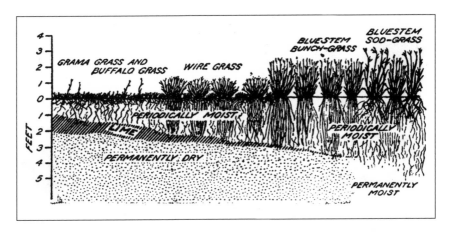

An array of native vegetation from western Kansas (17-inch rainfall) to eastern Kansas (37-inch rainfall). This calls attention to the buffalo's location on lime-laden soils with proteinaceous, mineral-rich but sparse vegetation named for him, rather than on the leached soils with more bulky, carbonaceous growths farther east. (Drawing by Schantz.)

untold numbers on the buffalo grass; (2) the wheat which, taken as a whole rather than as refined flour, is truly the staff of life; (3) areas where cattle, on unhampered range, nourish themselves so well that they reproduce regularly without being pampered; and (4) the more able-bodied selectees for military service of whom seven are chosen out of ten, in contrast to seven rejected out of ten in one of the southern states where the soils are more exhausted of their fertility.

Protein production, whether by plant, animal, or man, makes demands on the soil-given elements. Body growth among forms of higher life is a matter of soil fertility and not one of photosynthesis only. It calls for more than rainfall, fresh air, and sunshine.

Heavier rainfall and forest vegetation characterize the eastern United States, where the soils have been leached of much fertility. Higher temperatures in the southern areas have made more severe the fertility-reducing effects of the rainfall. Consequently, vegetation there is not such an effective synthesizer of proteins. Neither is it a significant provider of calcium, phosphorus, magnesium, or the other eight or more soil-given fetus-building nutrients. Annual production of vegetation per acre is large, particularly in contrast to the sparsity of that on the western prairies. The East's production is highly carbonaceous, however, as the forests, the cotton, and the sugar cane testify. The carbonaceous nature

Fertilizer treatments of the soil register their beneficial effects in the plant, but more noticeably in the physiology of the animal as indicated by better weight, wool, fur, bones, or other body products and functions. On the left, the rabbit and the bones record the results of lack of soil treatment, in contrast to the effect of treatment measured by similar gauges on the right.

is contributed by air, water, and sunlight more than by the soil. Fuel and fattening values are more prominent than are aids to growth and reproduction.

Here is a basic principle that cannot be disregarded. It has signal value as we face nutritional problems on a national scale. It is, of course, true that soils under higher rainfalls and temperatures still supply some fertility for plant production. Potassium, however, dominates that limited supply, to give prominence to photosynthesis of carbonaceous products. The insufficient provision of calcium and of all the other requisite elements usually associated with calcium does not permit the synthesis, by internal performances in plants, of the proteins and many other compounds of equal nutritive value. The national problem is largely one of mobilizing the calcium and other fertility elements for the growing of protein and not wholly one of redistributing proteins under Federal controls. As the distribution pattern of soil fertility is etched on the map, it delineates the various areas of particular success or particular trouble in nutrition. It coincides also with the regions where the starving plants can be given relief by particular soil treatments.

The more concentrated populations in the United States are in the East and on the soils of lower fertility. To those people, Horace Greeley gave good advice when he said, "Go west, young man." It was well that they trekked to the semihumid Midwest, where the hard wheat grows on the chernozem soils and where both the breadbasket and the meat basket are well laden and carried by the same provider — the soil. It was that move which spelled our recent era of prosperity. In Europe the situation is similar but the direction of travel was reversed and the time period has been longer. Western Europe represents the concentrated populations on soils of lower fertility under heavier rainfall. Peoples there reached over into the pioneer United States for soil fertility, trading for it the goods "made in Germany." More recently the hard-wheat belt on the Russian chernozem soils has been the fertility goal for Hitler's *Drangnach Osten*. Soil fertility is thus a cause of no small import in the world wars.

Life behaviors are more closely linked with soils as the basis of nutrition than is commonly recognized. The depletion of soil calcium through leaching and the almost universal deficiency of soil phosphorus affect animals directly, since their bones are the chief body depositories for these two elements. In the forest, the annual falling of leaves and their subsequent decay, to pass their nutrient elements through the cycle of growth and decay again, are almost a requisite for tree maintenance. Forest soils offer very little fertility and offer it very slowly. Is it any wonder then that dropped antlers and other skeletal forms are eaten by animals to keep calcium and phosphorus in their cycle? Pregnant squirrels gnaw bones in their nests. Deer will select in their browse those trees that have been given fertilizers in preference to those that have not been treated. Pine-tree seedlings along the highway, transplanted from fertilized nursery soils, are eaten by deer while the same species in the adjoining forests go untouched. Wild animals truly "know their medicines," which they take as plants from particular levels of soil fertility.

The distribution of wild animals during pioneer days, the present pattern of domestic animal distribution, and that of concentrations of animal diseases can be visualized as superimpositions on the soil-fertility pattern as it furnishes nutrition. We have been prone to believe that these patterns of animal behaviors conform wholly to climate. We have forgotten that the eastern forest areas gave the Pilgrims only limited game, among which a few turkeys were sufficient to establish for us a nation-wide tradition of Thanksgiving. It was on the fertile prairies existing in the Middle West, however, that bison were so numerous that only their pelts were commonly taken. The distribution of domestic animals today reveals a similar pattern, but it is characterized more by freedom from disease (more properly, freedom from malnutrition) and by greater regularity and fecundity in reproduction. It is on the lime-rich, unleached, semihumid soils that animals reproduce well. There the concentrations of diseases are lower and some diseases are rare. There the beef cattle are multiplied and grown to be shipped to the humid soils where they are fattened. Similar shipments of cattle from one fertility level to another are common in Argentina.

In going from midwestern United States eastward to the less fertile soil, we find that animal troubles increase and become a serious handicap to meat and milk production. The condition is no less serious as one goes south or southeast. The distribution patterns of milk fever, of acetonemia, and of other reproductive troubles that so greatly damage the domestic animal industry parallel the soil-fertility pattern. Troubles in the milk sheds of eastern and southern cities are more a challenge for the agronomists than for the veterinarians.

Experimental soil treatments have demonstrated the important roles that calcium and phosphorus can play in animal physiology and reproduction. Applied on adjoining plots of the same area, their effects on sheep were registered as differences in growth per unit of feed consumed and as differences in the quality of the wool. Rabbits also grew more rapidly and more efficiently on hay grown where limestone and superphosphate had both been used than where phosphate alone had been used.

The influence of soil fertilizers registers itself pronouncedly in the entire physiology of the animal, seemingly so far removed from the slight change in chemical condition in the soil. This fact was indicated, in the study mentioned, not only by differences in the weight and quality of the wool but in the bones and more pronouncedly in semen production and reproduction in general. Rabbit bones varied widely in breaking strength, density, thickness, hardness, and other qualities beside mass and volume. Male rabbits used for artificial insemination became sterile after a few weeks on lespedeza hay grown without soil treatment, while those eating hay from limed soil remained fertile. When the hays were interchanged during the second feeding period, a corresponding interchange of sterility and fertility took place between the groups of animals. This factor of fertility alone is an economic liability on less fertile soil but is a great economic asset on the soils which either are more fertile naturally or are made so by soil treatments.

Instincts for wise choice of food are still retained by animals in spite of our attempts, for example, to convert the dairy cow into a chemical engineering establishment wherein her ration is as simple as urea and phosphoric acid mixed with carbohydrates and proteins, however crude. That milk cannot as yet be reduced to the simplicity of chemical engineering is demonstrated by calves which have rickets despite ample sunshine and plenty of milk if they grow on certain types of soil having distinctly low fertility. Rickets as a malnutrition "disease" according to soil type need not be a new concept, at least as far as this trouble affects calves.

Notwithstanding our attempt to relegate the cow into the lower levels in the biotic pyramid, even down to that of plants and microbes that alone can live on chemical ions not requisite as compounds, she still clings to her instincts of selecting particular grasses in mixed herbages. Fortunately she strikes up a partnership with the microbes in her paunch, with the result that some seven essential vitamins are synthesized there for her. We tend to forget, however, that these paunch dwellers cannot be refused in their demands for soil fertility to enable them to meet this expectation. England's allegiance in wartime to the cow as a ruminant that can carry on these symbiotic vitamin syntheses, and England's reduction of pigs and poultry that as nonruminants cannot do so, are more effective in bringing the soils more directly into efficient service for national nutrition than we have been prone to believe.

The instincts shown by animals are compelling us to recognize soil differences: Not only do the dumb beasts select herbages according as they are relatively more carbonaceous or proteinaceous but they select offerings from the same kind of grain according to the different fertilizers with which the soil has been treated. The fact that animal troubles are engendered by the use of feeds in mixtures only should be weighed against the fact that hogs select different corn grains from separate feeder compartments with disregard of hybrids but with particular and consistent choice among grains produced by different soil treatments. Rats indicate the same discrimination by cutting into the bags of corn that were chosen by the hogs but leaving uncut the bags holding the corn the hogs refused. Surely the animal appetite that calls the soil fertility so correctly can be of service in guiding animal production by means of soil treatments.

Curt P. Richter of the Johns Hopkins Hospital has pointed to a physiological basis for such fine distinctions by rats. Deprived of insulin, for example, they ceased to take sugar. But dosed with insulin, they increased consumption of sugar in proportion to the insulin given. Fat was refused in the diet similarly in accordance with the incapacity of the body to digest it.

The soil takes on national significance when it prompts the Mayor of the eastern metropolis to visit the Gateway to the West to meet with farmers discussing their production problems. More experience in rationing should make the simple and homely subject of soils and their productive capacity household words among urban as well as rural peoples. Patterns of the distribution of human beings and their diseases, which can be evaluated nationally on a statistical basis as readily as can crops of wheat or livestock, are not yet seen in terms of the soil fertility that determines one about as much as the other. Man's nomadic nature has made him too cosmopolitan to permit his physique, health, facial features, or mental attitudes to label him as of the particular soil that nourished him. His collection of foods from far-flung sources also handicaps ready correlation of his level of nutrition with the fertility of his soil. We have come to believe that food processing and refinement are denying us some essentials. We have not yet, however, come to appreciate the role that soil fertility plays in determining the nutritive quality of foods, and thereby our bodies and our minds. Quantity rather than hidden quality is still the measure.

Now that we are thinking about putting blanket plans over states, countries, and possibly the world as a whole, there is need to consider whether such regulations can blot out the economics, customs, and institutions which have established themselves as a counterbalance to the soil's fertility, if not, indeed, as a mirror image of the distribution pattern of soil fertility. Since any civilization is actually premised on its resources rather than on its institutions, changes in the institutions cannot usefully be made in disregard of so basic a resource as the soil.

Researchers in soil science, plant physiology, ecology, human nutrition, and other sciences have given but a few years of their efforts to human welfare. These contributions have looked to hastened consumption of material surpluses from unhindered production for limited territorial use. They are now to be applied to production, and a production that calls for use of nature's synthesizing forces for food production more than to simple nonfood conversions. When our expanded chemical industry is permitted to turn from wartime to peacetime pursuits, it is to be hoped that a national consciousness of declining soil fertility can enlist our sciences and industry into rebuilding and conserving our soils as the surest guarantee of the future health and strength of the nation.

CHAPTER 18

Soil Fertility and Nutritive Value of Foods

WE ARE GRADUALLY coming to believe that the soil, in terms of the food it grows, is a controlling factor in agricultural creation. The pattern of the soil fertility, according to the climatic forces determining it, has only recently been worked out. That this fertility pattern maps out the nutritional quality of feeds and foods is not yet widely recognized or appreciated. That it should be is not so expectable when we have been measuring our agricultural output in terms of only bulk and weight increase rather than in terms of nutrition, reproduction, and better survival of the species.

By subscribing to the production criteria of more tons and more bushels, we have watched the crops but have forgotten the soils that grow them. Accordingly, we have introduced new crops which pile up carbohydrates and caloric bulk readily instead of those which consume much of their own fuel foods in converting a part of them into proteins through help from the soil fertility. When the dwindling fertility makes-protein-producing, mineral-providing crops "hard to grow," we fail to undergird them with soil treatment for their higher nutritional values in growing young animals. The soil fertility as help towards more protein within the body, as protection against microbial and other invasions, has not impressed itself. Instead we have taken to the therapeutic services of protective products generated by animals, and even microbes, in our blood-stream as disease fighters. The life of the soil is not attractive. The death of it is no recognized disaster. Hence, it may seem farfetched to any one but a student of both the soil and nutrition to relate the nutritive quality of feeds and foods to the soil.

The provision of proteins is our major food problem. Carbohydrates are easily grown. Any growing plant is synthesizing carbohydrates mainly from the elements of the weather by sunshine energy. For the output of these energy foods very little soil fertility is required in terms of either the number of chemical elements or the amounts of each. But, in order for the plant to convert its carbohydrates into proteins by its life processes and not by the sunshine power, calcium, nitrogen, phosphorus, and a long list, including the trace elements, are required. Plants and microbes — even those in the cow's gut — synthesize the amino acids that make up the proteins. Animals cannot fabricate these amino acids. They only collect them from the plants and assemble them into their proteins of milk, meat, eggs, and other body-building foods. Both plants and animals assemble their proteins to provide their reproductive functions since these are the only compounds through which the stream of life can flow.

It is in the protein synthesis and in the reproduction of life, that the control by the soil of the nutritive quality of food is pronounced. Our ignorance of this control is suggested when we classify as proteins anything that gives off nitrogen upon burning in sulfuric acid. By this we include nitrogenous compounds that are not proteins. Yet we recognize about two dozen different amino acids as components of the proteins. We know that life is impossible without providing the complete collection of at least eight of them. When even the trace elements, manganese and boron, applied to the soil at rates of but a few pounds per acre for alfalfa increase the concentration of these essential amino acids in this crop — especially those amino acids deficient in corn — there is evidence that the nutritive quality of this forage is connected with the fertility of the soil.

The assessment of the contributions by the soil through only the ash analyses of the crops, has left us ignorant of the numerous roles played in the plant's synthetic processes by the elements of soil origin. In believing that we need "minerals" according to such analyses of our bodies and our foods for their inorganic contents, we consider the soil as the supply of these and the plants as conveyors of them. We conclude therefrom that limestone fed to the cow in the mineral box is the equivalent in nutritional service to lime used as soil treatment coming through the plant.

Likewise have we been content to accept and use average figures for ash analyses. In the same year and in the same state, for example, the protein of wheat has varied from a low of 10 to a high of 18 percent of the grain. Ash elements may double or treble their concentration in the crop on one soil over that on another. Such variations go unappreciated if we are content to believe that "plants are good feed and good food if they make a big crop." Crops that are doing little more than to pile up carbo-hydrates, as was demonstrated with soybeans, make big yields of bulk. But when fertilized to produce proteins, the hay yields are smaller. To be content with the above simple faith is to be as agronomically gullible as the youngster content with the knowledge of reproduction that credits this process to the delivery services by the stork.

Our reluctance to credit the soil with some relation to the nutritive qual-ity of our feeds and foods is well illustrated by the belief persistent during the last quarter of a century, namely, that the acidity of the soil is injurious and that the benefit from liming lies in its helps in fighting this acidity when, in truth, it lies in its nourishment of the plants with calcium and its activities in their synthesis of proteins and other food essentials. To say that we don't believe there is a relation between the nutritive values of feeds or foods and the fertility of the soil is a confession of ignorance of all that is to be known of this fact and is not a negation of it.

As yet we do not appreciate the pattern of soil fertility in the United States, that in pre-colonial days was allowing only wood crops, or forests, on the soils in the eastern half. It grew protein as meat in the bison on the buffalo grass in mid-continent, and in some scattered areas farther east like particular valleys of Pennsylvania or the present race horse area of Kentucky. It permitted corn in the forested New England when each hill was fertilized with a fish. Corn on the eastern prairies grew well without such stimulation.

We may well ask whether the soil in its fertility pattern is of no import relative to nutritive quality of what it produces (1) when we grow cattle and make beef protein more effectively today in the former bison area; (2) when that area is now growing the high protein wheat; (3) when we fatten cattle farther east on the more weathered soils and combine this specu-lative venture with pork production that puts emphasis on fat output by carbohydrates and the lessened hazard by marketing these smaller animals nearer their birthday; (4) when soil fertility exhaustion has pushed soft wheat westward; (5) when the protein in corn has dropped, because of soil exploitation, from an average figure of 9.5 to 8.5 percent; and (6) when the pattern of the caries of the teeth of the Navy inductees in 1942 reflects the climatic pattern of soil fertility. Such items related to the national pattern of soil fertility suggest that many of our agricultural successes (or escapes from disaster) have been good fortunes through chance location with respect to the fertility of the soil when we have too readily, perhaps, credited them to our embryo agricultural science.

When a crop begins to fail we search far and accept others if they make bulk where the predecessor didn't. We credit the newcomer with being "a hay crop but not a seed crop." If it cannot guarantee its own reproduction via seed, we call it feed for the cow. With the cow's failure to reproduce under such poor nutritional support we, apparently, economize on the bull's energy by resorting to repeated artificial inseminations. The grazing animals have been selecting areas according to better soils. They have been going through fences to the virgin right-of-way. They have been grazing the very edges of the highway shoulders next to the concrete to their own destruction on the Coastal Plains soils. All these are animal demonstrations that the nutritive quality of feeds is related to the soil that grows it. But to date, the animals rather than their masters, have appreciated this fact most.

Shall we keep our eyes closed to the soil's creative power via proteins, organo-inorganic compounds, and all the complexes of constructive and catalytic services in nutrition? When the health and functions of our plants, our animals and ourselves indicate the need, isn't it a call for agricultural research to gear production into delivery of nutritional values related to the fertility of the soil rather than only those premised on bulk and the ability to fill? By directing attention to the soil for its help in making better food, we may possibly realize the wisdom in the adage of long standing that tells us that "to be well fed is to be healthy" and that good nutrition must be built from the ground up.

CHAPTER 19

Our Soils, Our Food
and Ourselves

THE WEATHER HAS ALWAYS been considered a very important factor in our agricultural production. Located as we are in the cornbelt, for example, of the central United States, we talk much about the seasonal rainfall and temperature as they determine, our crop yields. While the daily variations of the meteorological conditions, which we call the weather, have long been recognized as important, the climate, which is the average of the weather over a long time, is even more important in controlling both the kind and the quantity of what we can grow.

It is the long-time effect of rainfall and temperature combined as climate that determines what kind of soil has been produced by weathering the rocks going to make it. The kind of soil determines the kind and quality of the foods that can be grown. Then, if we are what we eat, as some German put it when he said *"Mann ist was er esst,"* there is a close connection between our soils, our food, and ourselves.

Some Climates
Bring About Soil Construction

The soil is a temporary rest stop by the rocks on their way to solution and the sea. How far the rocks have travelled on this journey depends on how much rainfall and high temperature have been crowding them along on their route. In regions of low rainfall the soils are still rocky and sandy. There has not been enough rainfall to carry rock decomposition so far as to make much insoluble clay. Nor has there been enough water to wash the soluble materials away. Consequently the soils are alkaline. They are loaded with too many salts to permit good plant growth even if we make up the shortage in seasonal rainfall by irrigating the crop.

This condition of insufficient rainfall in the past to have made the better soils is illustrated in western United States. If one starts in the west from near the Coast Range and goes eastward across the country to experience gradually increasing amounts of annual rainfall, one meets with a succession of different soils. By the time we reach the middle of the United States the soils are darker in color. They are deeper, higher in clay content, and more productive under the annual rainfall there amounting to near 35 inches. Going upward toward this figure for rainfall in the temperate zone means going toward better soils.

Coming eastward in the western part of our country means more soil construction. It means coming from the desert and its soil that supports very little life to where the bison once roamed and where wheat and livestock grow today. It means enough lime and other active fertility left in the soil that legumes have grown bountifully enough in the past so that the soils are well stocked with nitrogen. It means soils that have not been leached. They have not had most of their fertility washed out, nor have they had hydrogen take its place on the clay to make them "acid." It means mineral-rich and productive soils because the lesser rainfalls have made enough clay and have loaded it with fertility. But those lower rainfalls have not carried that fertility down through to leave an acid clay subsoil below a shallow surface soil layer, which is the common condition in eastern United States under high rainfall.

Some Climates Give Us Soil Destruction

Increasing rainfall as one goes eastward from the midcontinent, particularly in the northern part of eastern United States, means soil destruction. This results because there is more rainfall than evaporation. This puts considerable water down through the soil. The percolating water loaded with its carbonic acid takes the lime, magnesia, potash, and many other nutrient elements off the clay by putting hydrogen or acid — a non-nutrient — in their place.

With much rainfall to have weathered the rocks extensively, there is enough clay residue in the soils to make us say, "They are heavy." They require much plowing and working to make a good seedbed. Fortunately, their clay is still somewhat like the original rocks. It is still a silicate and has a high filtering capacity. By this property it can catch and hold nutrients by taking them out of any solutions, should they come along. This same high exchange capacity of the clay for nutrients can mean a high degree of acidity in case the fertility has been washed out. But it is the same big capacity to hold fertility if we put it back into the acid soil. Such are the clays and soil conditions in the cooler, northern half of eastern United States, where higher rainfalls mean soil destruction in terms of better foods.

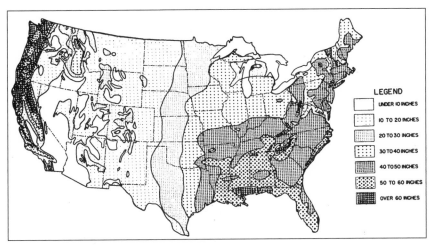

Distribution of mean annual rainfall in the U. S. The pattern of rainfall with the higher amounts in eastern U. S. suggests that the mineral elements have been leached out of the soils there, hence forest in pioneer days and carbohydrate-producing crops today rather than protein-rich and mineral-rich products grow there.

High Temperatures Coupled with High Rainfall Means More Soil Destruction

If the climate is a combination of higher temperature as well as higher rainfall, as is the case when in eastern United States one goes from the North to the South, then the rocks and even the clay are broken down much more completely. They do not leave a gray silicate clay. Instead a red, iron-aluminum clay results. This clay does not have much filtering or exchange capacity. If solutions of nutrients pass through, it does not take

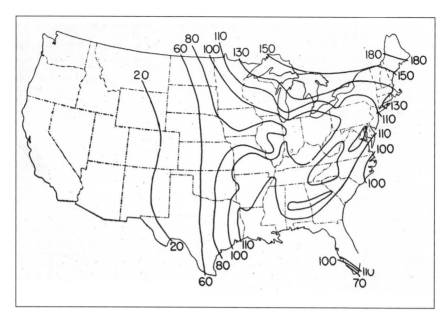

Lines of constant ratios of rainfall to evaporation from free water surface (times 100) give pattern to the fertility in the soils. Corn Belt soils are similar in this respect to those farther west under less leaching. Southeastern, eastern, and northeastern soils are highly leached and low in mineral fertility supplies. Map according to Professor Transeau, Columbus, Ohio.

the nutrients out so effectively nor hold them for rapid exchange to the growing plant roots. It will not hold much acid either. Consequently in the southeastern states it has often been said "Because there is so little acidity in the soil no lime is needed to remove it."

Such reasoning fails to appreciate the difficulty of growing crops on soils of which the clay has so little exchange capacity. It disregards the high needs for the calcium in lime as a fertilizer even if those soils do not need the carbonate of lime to neutralize any acidity. Such soils are low in capacity to grow mineral-rich, protein-rich crops. They grow wood instead.

They require considerable fertilizing to grow even the simple carbohydrates like sugar and like cellulose in cotton fiber. So much of the fertilizer is washed out to require fertilizer for every crop following.

The soils, then, in the western states are still rich in un-weathered minerals. Their clay is well stocked with nutrients. They have a high producing power for proteins. In the eastern states the soils are highly weathered with the clays in the soils of the cooler regions quite different from those in the tropical soils. This climatic pattern that makes the soils from the rocks determines, then, what nutrient elements the soils contain. Thereby it determines also how well those soils will feed our crops, our animals, and ourselves.

Plant Species and Chemical Composition of any Plants are Determined by the Fertility of the Soil

In accordance with the long-held belief that only the weather controls the kind of virgin plants in any locality, we have been scouring the world and making transplants from everywhere to everywhere with little regard for the soil fertility required to nourish the shifted crops. When alfalfa grows dominantly in Colorado soils; when sugar cane grows abundantly in Louisiana; and when the rubber tree quickly takes over in Brazil; are these merely matters of differences in temperature or rainfall with no dependence on the soil? Can plants be successfully shifted merely by keeping them properly heated and moistened?

Alfalfa is a protein-bearing, mineral-containing forage of especially high lime content. It demands large supplies of mobile nutrients from the soil. It grows well where lower amounts of rainfall have not depleted the lime and other fertility elements from the surface soil. When planted on soils in regions of higher rainfall, it demands lime and other soil treatments for its successful growth.

Cotton delivers mainly carbon products in its fibers, only seeds, and shrub-like form. It demands less fertile soils than alfalfa. Lime helps cotton but is not an absolute requisite to grow it. Cotton responds more to fertilizing it with potassium, the nutrient which encourages carbohydrate production in plants more than protein production which is encouraged by calcium. Cotton is not a forage feed for livestock, then, because the products it manufactures under its soil limitations are not necessarily feed.

The rubber tree is another carbon — or wood — delivering crop. Its product, rubber, is neither edible nor digestible. Like other forest trees, it uses much less fertility than alfalfa for growth and each annual supply of that is dropped back to the soil almost wholly in its leaf crop. Through decomposition, this fertility supply in the leaves completes the cycle as it rotates from the soil up into the tree to the leaves and from the fallen and decomposed leaves back to the soil again. While making this cycle it does

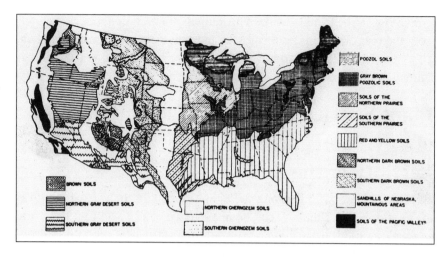

Climatic and vegetational soil groups in the U. S. according to Marbut 1935. The soil map shows itself a composite of the maps of rainfall and the ratios of rainfall to evaporation. The soils divide us into an East and a West. They divide the East into a North and a South.

little more than make wood. Even that product consists mainly of air and water elaborated by sunshine into compounds of fuel value only for flames and not for the physiology of animals and folks.

Fertility Pattern of Soils Gives Pattern of Food Composition

Perhaps you have never thought much about the variation in chemical composition of the food crops in the various parts of the country according to the climatic soil pattern. It is true that we have different plant species, alfalfa, cotton, and rubber on different levels of soil fertility. More significant, however, is the great fact that the same kind of crop has different chemical compositions on these different soils. The plant's pedigree is no control of this. So when Nature has washed out a soil by pouring excessive rainfall on it, or when we have taken out its fertility by crop removal and no fertility return, there is a change in the chemical composition in such common crops like corn or wheat, for example. Unfortunately, that change is not in the carbohydrate part so much where it would register as recognizable change in bulk. Rather such change consists of the reduction in the protein and mineral contents, the smaller and unrecognized, but very significant fraction of the crop. Plants keep right on making carbohydrates as fuel and fattening foods for us in less fertile soils. But they do less in converting those carbohydrates into proteins and mineral compounds that help grow bodies and help in their reproduction.

The protein concentration in wheat, often spoken of as its "hardness," illustrates this fact very well. On Missouri soils under her 40 or more inches of annual rainfall to make them badly leached and acid, wheat does well to have as much as ten percent protein. Going westward across Kansas, according to data of 1940, the protein in the wheat there went up from the above figure in eastern Kansas to one as high as eighteen percent in the western part. Putting extra fertility into the Missouri soils at the proper times made equally as high a protein wheat there, according to experimental trials.

While some one may believe that the dry weather of western Kansas makes wheat "hard," the dry year of 1936 in Missouri did not push the protein in the latter state's wheat crop up to where it was a competitor with the former state's "hard" wheat. Rainfall as seasonal water is not in control directly of the concentration of protein in the wheat. Rather it controls indirectly through the fertility it has left in, or removed from, the soils in the course of developing them from the rocks during centuries past.

This variation in the chemical composition of wheat is a part of the soil fertility pattern. High protein accompanies the starch or carbohydrate farther west. On coming eastward there is still plenty of starch as indicated by the high yields as bushels per acre, but there is a decrease in the protein. On the lime-laden, nitrogen-providing soils this grain crop makes carbohydrates and converts a good share of them into protein by the help of this extra soil fertility. On the less fertile, commonly called "acid" soils under the higher rainfall of the temperate zone, the crops make carbohydrates as the bushels per acre measure it. But they do not produce much protein.

Consequently then in feeding our animals we are faced with the problem of purchasing the protein supplements. These must be grown, and brought from soils somewhere. These once consisted of the by-products of the wheat milling business that also has gone west. Along with the problem of feeding the animals on such soils comes the fact that human foods are not so mineral-rich when the nutrients from the soil required by the plants to synthesize their proteins are not there.

Any Plant Can Deliver Carbohydrates, But Only Fertile Soils Give Complete Proteins

Any plant that grows is making carbohydrates by that process. These are built from air and water by sunshine energy. The plants that make proteins need the fertility from the soil to help make these complexes which the animals can only collect from the plants, but can not synthesize themselves. Carbohydrates pile up readily as bulk to give big yields as tons and bushels. But when plants are converting this sunshine product into proteins, they do not pile up such yields so rapidly. Our selection of a crop merely for big bulk as yields has brought into prominence those crops that are mainly producers of carbohydrates. It encourages the "soft" wheats and the low protein corn. It has encouraged production of the fattening foods and less of those for body-building and fecund reproduction.

The pattern of the chemical composition of feeds and foods reflects the pattern of soil fertility beneath and in control of it. Less weathered soils in the Midwest grow alfalfa, high protein wheat, beef cattle and sheep. Those same soils were growing big crops of protein when they had thundering herds of bison on their short grass. The more weathered soils in the east central and eastern states grow carbohydrate crops and fattening power as we recognize readily in corn and hogs. Such soils pile up the crop bulk, but they give us the problems of protein supplements and the troubles in animal reproduction.

In the quality of our foods we must recognize the soil and its fertility in control. By the traverse from the more fertile soils in the West to the less fertile in the East there is the change from both carbohydrates and proteins to mainly carbohydrates. When less fertility means more carbohydrates and less proteins we can understand that the depletion of the soil is responsible for the decline in the protein of corn from 9.5 to 8.5 percent during the last ten years of higher yields and much-mentioned hybrid vigor. The chemical composition of our food suggests that it takes its pattern for the country from the pattern of the fertility of the soil by which it is created.

In Giving the Food Pattern the Soil Fertility Also Gives the National Health Pattern

Because we have given so little thought to health and so much more to disease, the national health pattern has not very generally called itself

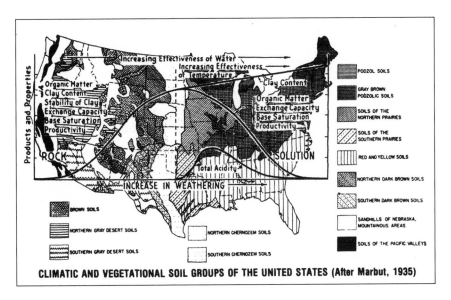

CLIMATIC AND VEGETATIONAL SOIL GROUPS OF THE UNITED STATES (After Marbut, 1935)

The pattern of soil development of the U. S. shows the maximum of soil construction in the Mid-Continental area. It is there that the maximum of protein and inorganic nutrient delivery by crops is possible as good feed and food. Carbohydrate crops are more prominent on less construction of soil to the West and on more destruction of the soil to the East.

to our attention. We have been slow to believe that the pattern of variable health is a reflection of the variable nutritional values of our foods that go in good measure with the variations in the fertility of the soil. That we should grow cattle in the West and fatten them in the East has not been considered a pattern of animal health even by some of the folks of the experiment stations. They have been prone to consider this a matter controlled by economics. Likewise some folks have been content to believe that the same economics, rather than the exhaustion of the soil fertility, is responsible for the westward march of high-protein wheat from the Geneseo River Valley in New York — where big milling works were originally set up — across the continent as far west as Kansas to date. While economics are connected — more as a result than a cause — with such changes, one needs only to look deeper and consider the question, "What controls the economics?"

Certainly if one can grow only fattening feeds it will be more economical for the farmer, but healthier for the animals, to use them to hang fat on the animals grown near to adulthood somewhere else than to face the odds of trying to breed and raise them with no better nutritional help than such feeds bolstered by imported protein supplements, mineral mixtures and drug concoctions. When our dairy calf crops in eastern United States are less than sixty percent of the cows bred; and when in Missouri, for example, we get to market less than sixty percent of the pigs the brood sows deliver as their litters; there is the suggestion that some significant economics are coming into play. Unfortunately, such is bad economics. There is the further suggestion that a nine month period of gestation by the cow and the life span of but six months of the porker are even too extended a period for us to carry successfully our responsibilities as animal feeders. These bad economics seemingly are crowding the marketing dates for our livestock closer and closer to their birthdays. Instead of attributing these troubles to disease and calling for more veterinarians it looks as if we need to see the health pattern of our animals and of ourselves in relation to the map of soil fertility as it makes the map of crop composition, especially the proteins and minerals.

Better Teeth Go Along with Better Soils

Maps of the variable health of our folks need to be made as a means of relating health to the soil and helping agricultural production serve in giving better food for better health. Health records of the draftees for the Army are numerous for areas as small as a county. There is no shortage of data that might well be studied on a national scale to give helpful information. Data for the condition of the teeth of nearly 70,000 inductees into the Navy in 1942 are a good illustration of what such records tell us about our soils and ourselves in terms of dental health.

The Navy reported its records of the number of cavities and fillings per mouth gathered as a means of estimating the number of dentists needed to keep the masticating section of the Navy in a good state of repair. These data were assembled for the different sections of our country. When arranged by longitudinal belts two states wide and considering these in going both westward and eastward from the Mississippi River, this map of dental health of our young men reflects the soil fertility pattern clearly.

For the area two states wide adjoining the Mississippi River on the west each Navy inductee had, as an average, 8.38 cavities, 3.70 fillings, or a total of 12.08 caries in his mouth. Farther west by two states, each mouth reported 8.80 cavities, 4.30 fillings, and 13.10 caries. For the west coastal states the corresponding figures were 9.10, 6.40 and 15.50, respectively.

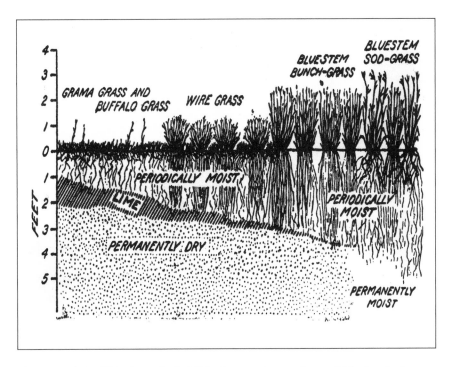

Kansas with its 17 inches of rainfall in the west increasing to 37 inches in the east had different virgin grasses because of the different soils. Diagram by H. L. Shantz.

Thus, in going from the midcontinent westward the numbers of cavities and fillings of the teeth per inductee mounted by more than 25 percent as poorer health.

Much more serious are the implications concerning the health of the teeth, according to these data, in going from the midcontinent eastward. For the belt of two states wide just east of the Mississippi River there were 10.06 cavities, 4.89 fillings, or 14.95 total caries. Much worse are the conditions for the Altantic belt of states where the records give 11.45 cavities, 6.10 fillings, and 17.55 total caries.

While we have none too good a health condition of our teeth even in the midcontinent with its soils of maximum protein-producing power in the better fertility supply, the teeth are poorer as one goes westward to the less developed soils, and much poorer in going eastward to those excessively developed and less fertile. Only the soils more fertile in terms of making more protein in plants give better health of the teeth.

PROTEIN CONTENT OF WHEAT—KANSAS 1940
AS INDICATED BY PRE-HARVEST SURVEY CONDUCTED BY AGRICULTURAL MARKETING SERVICE, UNITED STATES DEPT. OF AGRICULTURE

PER CENT PROTEIN

10.0 TO 10.9
11.0 — 11.9
12.0 — 12.9
13.0 — 13.9
14.0 — 14.9
15.0 — 15.9
16.0 — 16.9
17.0 — 17.9
18.0 — 18.9

* MORTON AND WYANDOTTE COUNTY SAMPLES TOO FEW FOR INDIVIDUAL AVERAGES

The protein, or "hardness," of wheat increase from 10% in eastern Kansas to 18% in western Kansas more because of the soil than because of the seasonally less rainfall.

192   *The Albrecht Papers*

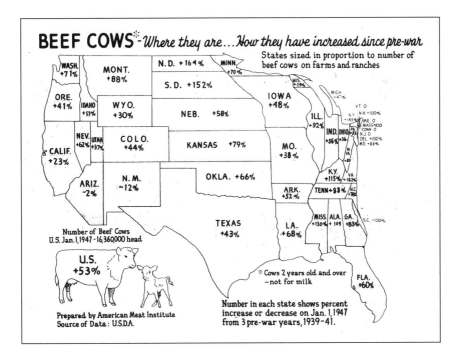

BEEF COWS*—Where they are... How they have increased since pre-war

States sized in proportion to number of beef cows on farms and ranches

WASH. +71%
MONT. +88%
N.D. +164%
MINN. +70%
WIS. +29%
MICH +4%
ORE. +41%
IDAHO +57%
WYO. +30%
S.D. +152%
IOWA +48%
VT. 0
N.Y. N.H. +100%
ILL. +92%
IND. +56%
OHIO +36%
ME. 0
MASS +100
CONN 0
N.J 0
DEL. +100%
MD. +33%
NEV. +62%
UTAH +37%
COLO. +44%
NEB. +58%
KANSAS +79%
MO. +38%
W.VA. +80
CALIF. +23%
ARIZ. -2%
N.M. -12%
OKLA. +66%
KY. +115%
VA +162%
TENN +33%
N.C. +78
ARK. +52%
MISS. +130%
ALA. +109
GA. +83%
S.C. +100%
TEXAS +43%
LA. +68%

Number of Beef Cows
U.S. Jan. 1, 1947 – 16,360,000 head

U.S. +53%

* Cows 2 years old and over —not for milk

FLA. +60%

Prepared by American Meat Institute
Source of Data: U.S.D.A.

Number in each state shows percent increase or decrease on Jan. 1, 1947 from 3 pre-war years, 1939-41.

The western states produce proteinaceous mineral-rich forages to make animals with protein rather than fat as their choice food quality for us. Courtesy American Meat Institute.

The Healthy Man of the Future Must be Created from a Fertile 'Handful of Dust'

When we make more health maps of our country in terms of other body parts and functions, very probably we shall find the same suggested relations between their health and the soil as is indicated for our teeth. Since the teeth are an exposed part of the skeleton, shall we not expect a map of our "creaking bones" to point back to the map of the soils' contents of lime and phosphate of which bones consist almost completely? Since we can build no better bodies than is permitted by the quality of the foods we eat; and since the agricultural business of food creation can scarcely put the quality of its products higher than is allowed by the fertility of the handful of dust into which the warm moist breath of air, rainfall and sunshine is blown; is it a fantastic stretch of the imagination of any one

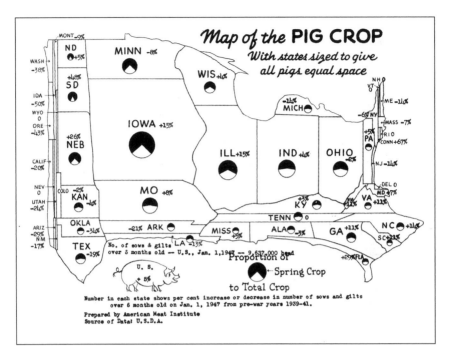

The eastern states produce carbohydrates to make animals with fat more than lean as protein. Courtesy American Meat Institute.

who tills the soil to believe in the close relation between our soils, our foods, and ourselves? The growing science of the soil is reminding us more and more that already two thousand years ago they were emphasizing the importance of a handful of dust in the creation of man.

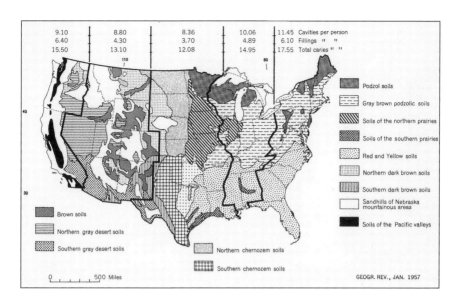

9.10	8.80	8.36	10.06	11.45	Cavities per person
6.40	4.30	3.70	4.89	6.10	Fillings " "
15.50	13.10	12.08	14.95	17.55	Total caries " "

Podzol soils
Gray brown podzolic soils
Soils of the northern prairies
Soils of the southern prairies
Red and Yellow soils
Northern dark brown soils
Southern dark brown soils
Sandhills of Nebraska mountainous areas
Soils of the Pacific valleys

Brown soils
Northern gray desert soils
Southern gray desert soils
Northern chernozem soils
Southern chernozem soils

0   500 Miles

GEOGR. REV., JAN. 1957

The distribution of dental caries according to data from the Navy inductees is a reciprocal curve of that for soil development (Fig. IV). Maximum soil construction in the Mid-Continental area gives minimum of dental caries. Either less soil construction to the West, or more soil destruction to the East give more caries.

This picture is typical of large parts of entire counties. Proteins and minerals are lacking in proper amounts in plants produced from such soil. Human erosion and soil erosion go hand in hand.

Our Soils, Our Food and Ourselves   195

CHAPTER 20

Soils in Relation
to Human Nutrition

FOOD IS FABRICATED soil fertility. It was food that was called upon to win the war. The call now to maintain the peace of the world is a still greater one for food. A call in that direction is one to the soil.

National consciousness has recently taken consideration of the great losses by erosion from the body of the surface soil. We have also come to give more than passive attention to malnutrition on a national scale. Not yet, however, have we recognized soil fertility as the food-producing forces within the soil that reveal national and international patterns of weakness or strength. Soil fertility, in the last analysis, must not only be mobilized to win the war, but must also be preserved as the standing army opposing starvation for the maintenance of peace.

What is soil fertility? In simplest words it is some dozen chemical elements in mineral and rock combinations in the earth's crust that are being slowly broken out of these and hustled off to the sea. Enjoying a temporary rest stop enroute, they are a part of the soil and serve their essential roles in nourishing all the different life forms. They are the soil's contribution — from a large mass of non-essentials — to the germinating seeds that empowers the growing plants to use sunshine energy in the synthesis of atmospheric elements and rainfall into the many crops for our support. The atmospheric and rainfall elements are carbon, hydrogen, and nitrogen, so common everywhere.

It is soil fertility that constitutes the five percent that is plant ash. It is the handful of dust that makes up the corresponding percentage in the human body. Yet it is the controlling force that determines whether Nature in her fabricating activities shall construct merely the woody framework with leaf surfaces catching sunshine and with root surfaces absorbing little more than water, or whether inside of that woody shell there shall be synthesized the innumerable life-sustaining compounds.

Soil fertility determines whether plants are foods of only fuel and fattening values, or of body service in growth and reproduction. Because the soil comes in for only a small percentage of our bodies, we are not generally aware of the fact that this five percent can predetermine the fabrication of the other ninety-five percent into something more than mere fuel.

History Records Changing Politics Rather Than Declining Soil Fertility

Geographic divisions to give us an East and a West, and a North and a South for the eastern half of the country, are commonly interpreted as separations according to differences in modes of livelihood, social customs, or political affiliations. Differences in rainfall and temperature are readily acknowledged. But that these weather the basic rock to make soils so different that they control differences tion with the war have been too readily interpreted in terms of

In view of our youthfulness as an extensive country, our different geographic areas have registered themselves mainly as differences in body comfort, whether hot or cold, wet or dry. The free flow of foods and food constituents by means of cheap transportation has not allowed recognition of differences in quality as well as in kind of our foods in adjoining districts according to soil differences. We have not yet marked out our country into the smaller patchwork districts with distinctive local colorings as the Old World has in the opinion of visitors from the New World. Limitations in travel, difficulties in food delivery, and all the other restrictions now making us more local, will soon emphasize differences and deficiencies according to the soils by which we live.

Patterns of Nourishment Are Premised on the Pattern of Soil Fertility

We have been speaking about vegetation by names of crop species and by tonnage yields per acre. We have not considered plants for their chemical composition and nutritive value according to the fertility in the soil producing them. This failure has left us in confusion about crops and has put plant varieties into competition with — rather than in support of — one another. Now that the subject of nutrition is on most every tongue, we are about ready for the report that vegetation as a deliverer of essential food products of its own synthesis is limited by the soil fertility.

Proteinaceousness and high mineral contents, as distinct nutritive values, are more common in crops from soil formed in regions of lower rainfall and of less leaching as for example the "midlands," or the midwestern part of the United States. "Hard" wheat, so-called because of its high protein content needed for milling the "patent" flour for "light" bread is commonly ascribed to regions of lower annual rainfalls. "Soft" wheat is similarly ascribed to regions of higher rainfalls. The high calcium content, the other liberal minerals reserves, and the pronounced activities of nitrogen within the less-leached soil, however, are the causes when experimental trials supplying the soil with these fertility items in high rainfall regions can make hard wheat where soft wheat is common.

The proteinaceous vegetation and the synthesis by it of many unknowns, which like proteins, help to remove hidden hungers and encourage fecundity of both man and animal are common in the prairie regions marked by the moderate rainfalls. It is the soil fertility, rather than the low precipitation, that gives the midwest, or those areas bordering along approximately the 97th meridian these distinctions: (a) its selection by the bison in thundering herds on the "buffalo grass"; (b) the wheat which taken as a whole rather than as refined flour is truly the "staff of life"; (c) animals on range nourishing themselves so well that they reproduce regularly; and (d) the more able-bodied selectees for military service of whom 7 out of 10 were chosen in Colorado in contrast to 7 rejected out of 10, in one of the southern states where the soils are more exhausted of their fertility.

Protein production, whether by plant, animal, or man, makes demands on the soil-given elements. Body growth among forms of higher life is a matter of soil fertility and not only one of photosynthesis. It calls for more than rainfall, fresh air, and sunshine.

The heavier rainfall and forest vegetation of the eastern United States mark off the soils that have been leached of much fertility. Higher temperatures in the southern areas have made more severe the fertility-reducing effects of the rainfall. Consequently, vegetation there is not such an effective synthesizer of proteins. Neither is it a significant provider of calcium, phosphorus, magnesium, or the other soil-given, foetus-building nutrients. Annual production as tonnage per acre is large, particularly in contrast to the sparsity of that on the western prairies. The East's production is highly carbonaceous, however, as the forests, the cotton, and the sugar cane testify. The carbonaceous nature is contributed by air, water, and sunlight more than by the soil. Fuel and fattening values are more prominent than are aids to growth and reproduction.

Here is a basic principle that cannot be disregarded. It has signal value as we face nutritional problems on a national scale. It is, of course, true that soils under higher rainfalls and temperatures still supply some fertility for plant production. Potassium, however, dominates that limited supply to give prominence to photosynthesis of carbonaceous products. The insufficient provision of calcium and of all the other requisite elements usually associated with calcium does not permit the synthesis, by internal performances of plants, of the proteins and many other compounds of equal nutritive value. The national problem is largely one of mobilizing the calcium and other fertility elements for growing protein and not wholly one of redistributing proteins under federal controls. The soil fertility pattern on the map delineates the various areas of particular success or particular trouble in nutrition. It marks out the areas where, by particular soil treatments, the starving plants can be given relief.

The Fertility Pattern of Europe
Is a Mirror Pattern of Our Own

The more concentrated populations in the United States are in the East and on the soils of lower fertility. For those people, Horace Greeley spoke with good advice when he said, "Go west young man." It was well that they trekked to the semi-humid midwest where the hard wheat grows on the chernozem soils, and where both the breadbasket and the meat basket are well-laden and carried by the same provider, viz., the soil. It was that move that spelled our recent era of prosperity.

In Europe the situation is similar but the direction of travel was reversed and the time period has been longer. It is western Europe that represents the concentrated populations on soils of lower fertility under heavier rainfall. Peoples there reached over into the pioneer United States for soil fertility by trading for it the goods "made in Germany." More recently the hard wheat belt on the Russian chernozem soils was the fertility goal under the Hitlerian move eastward. Soil fertility is thus a cause of no small import in the world wars.

Calcium and Phosphorus are Prominent in the Soil Fertility Pattern as it Determines the Pattern of Nutrition of Plants and Animals

Life behaviors are more closely linked with soils as the basis of nutrition than is commonly recognized. The depletion of soil calcium thru leaching and cropping, and the almost universal deficiency of soil phosphorus, connect readily with animals when bones are about the complete

Even the animals struggle desperately to find the necessary calcium and phosphorus coming out of the soils to make their bones, when antlers are quickly consumed by the porcupine, the pregnant squirrels, and other animals living on the highly weathered, or rocky, forest soils. (Courtesy Florence Page Jaques, Snowshoe Country, The University of Minnesota Press).

body depositories for these two elements. In the forests, the annual drop of leaves and their decay to pass their nutrient elements thru the cycle of growth, and decay again, are almost a requisite for tree maintenance. Is it any wonder then that dropped antlers and other skeletal forms are eaten by animals to prohibit their accumulation while their calcium and phosphorus stay in the animal cycle. Deer in their browse will select trees given fertilizers in preference to those untreated. Pine tree seedlings along the highway as transplantings from fertilized nursery soils are taken by deer when the same tree species in the adjoining forests go untouched. Wild animals truly "know their medicines" when they take plants on particular levels of soil fertility.

The distribution of wild animals, the present pattern or distribution of domestic animals, and the concentrations of animal diseases, can be visualized as superimpositions on the soil fertility pattern as it furnishes nutrition. We have been prone to believe these patterns of animal behaviors wholly according to climate. We have forgotten that the eastern forest areas gave the Pilgrims limited game among which a few turkeys were sufficient to establish a national tradition of Thanksgiving. It was on the fertile prairies of the midwest, however, that bison were so numerous that only their pelts were commonly taken.

Distribution of domestic animals today reveals a similar pattern, but more by freedom from "disease" — more properly freedom from malnutrition — and by greater regularity and facundity in reproduction. It is on the lime-rich, unleached, semi-humid soils that animals reproduce well. It is there that the concentrations of diseases are lower and some diseases are rare. There beef cattle are multiplied and grown to be shipped to the humid soils where they are fattened. Similar cattle shipments from one fertility level to another are common in the Argentine.

In going from midwestern United States eastward to the less fertile soil, we find that animal troubles increase and become a serious handicap to meat and milk production. The condition is no less serious as one goes south or southeastward. The distribution patterns of milk fever, of acetonemia and of other reproductive troubles, that so greatly damage the domestic animal industry, suggest themselves as closely connected with the soil fertility pattern that locates the proteinaceous, mineral-rich forages of higher feeding values in the prairie areas but leaves the more carbonaceous and more often deficient feeds for the East and Southeast with their forest areas. Troubles in the milk sheds of eastern and southern cities are more of a challenge for the agronomists and soil scientists than for the veterinarians.

Experiments using soil treatments have demonstrated the important roles that calcium and phosphorus can play in the animal physiology and reproduction by way of the forages and grains from treated soils. Applied on adjoining plots of the same area, their effects were registered in sheep as differences in animal growth per unit of feed consumed, and as differences in the quality of the wool. Rabbits also grew more rapidly and more efficiently on hay grown where limestone and superphosphate had been used together than where phosphate alone had been supplied.

The influence of added fertilizers registers itself pronouncedly in the entire physiology of the animal. This fact was indicated not only by differences in the weight and quality of the wool, but in the bones and more pronouncedly in semen production and reproduction in general. Rabbit bones varied widely in breaking strength, density, thickness, hardness and other qualities beside mass and volume. Male rabbits used for artificial insemination became sterile after a few weeks on lespedeza hay grown without soil treatment, while those eating hay from limed soil remained fertile. That the physiology of the animal, seemingly so far removed from the slight change in chemical condition in the soil, registered the soil treatment, is shown by the resulting interchange of the sterility and fertility of the lots with the interchange of the hays during the second feeding period. This factor of animal fertility alone is an economic liability on less fertile soil, but is a great economic asset on the soils that are more fertile either naturally or made so by soil treatments.

Animal Instincts are Helpful in Meeting their Nutritional Needs

Instincts for wise choice of food are still retained by the animals in spite of our attempts to convert the dairy cow into a chemical engineering establishment wherein her ration is as simple as urea and phosphoric acid mixed with carbohydrates and proteins, however, crude. Milk which is the universal food with high efficiency because of its role in reproduction, cannot as yet be reduced to the simplicity of chemical engineering when calves become affected with rickets in spite of ample sunshine and plenty of milk, on certain soil types of distinctly low fertility. Rickets, as a malnutrition "disease" according to soil type, need not be a new concept, so far as this trouble affects calves.

Even if we try to push the cow into the lower levels in the biotic pyramid, or even down to that of plants and microbes that alone can live on chemical

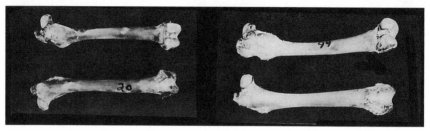

Lime and other fertilizer treatments of the soil register their beneficial effects in the plant, but more noticeably in the physiology of the animal as indicated by better weight, wool, fur, bones and other body products and functions. On the left, the rabbit and the bones record the soil deficiencies in contrast to the effects of correcting these as measured by similiar gauges on the right.

ions not requisite as compounds, she still clings to her instincts of selecting particular grasses in mixed pasture herbages. Fortunately, in her physiology she strikes up a partnership with the microbes in her paunch where they synthesize some seven essential vitamins for her. We are about to forget, however, that these paunch-dwellers cannot be refused in their demand for soil fertility by which they can meet this expectation. England's allegiance in war time to cows as ruminants that can carry on these symbiotic vitamin syntheses, and her reduction of the population of pigs and poultry that cannot do so, bring the matter of soils more directly into efficient services for national nutrition than we have been prone to believe.

The instincts of animals are compelling us to recognize soil differences. Not only do the dumb beasts select herbages according as they are more carbonaceous or proteinaceous, but they select from the same kind of grain the offerings according to the different fertilizers with which the soil was treated. Animal troubles engendered by the use of feeds in mixtures only stand out in decided contrast. Hogs select different corn grains from separate feeder compartments with disregard of different hybrids, but with particular and consistent choice of soil treatments. Rats have indi-

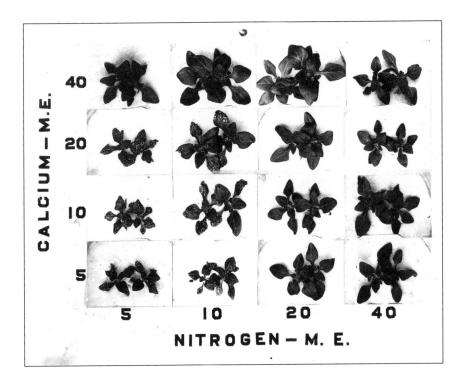

Good Nutrition Protects Plants From Insect Attacks

Spinach grown with limited supplies of nitrogen in the soil (two vertical rows on left) was attacked by the thrips while that grown alongside with more nitrogen (two vertical rows on right) was free of this trouble. Also, more lime or calcium (upper horizontal rows) was helpful in reducing the attacks.

cated their discrimination by cutting into the bags of corn that were chosen by the hogs and left uncut those bags not taken by the hogs. Surely the animal appetite, that calls the soil fertility so correctly, can be of service in guilding animal production more wisely by means of soil treatments.

Dr. Curt Richeter of the Johns Hopkins Hospital, has pointed to the physiological basis for such fine distinctions by rats, as an example. Deprived of insulin delivery within their system, they ceased to take sugar. But dosed with insulin they increased consumption of sugar in proportion to the insulin given. Fat was refused in the diet similarly in accordance with the incapacity of body to digest it. Animal instincts are inviting our attention back to the soil just as differences in animal physiology are giving a national pattern of differences in crop production,

Cattle Select Hay From Fertilized Soil
The discriminating tastes of cattle led them to cut the haystack in two (upper photo) consuming first the part of hay into which some was mixed that had grown on fertilized soil and to leave the remnant stack of unfertilized hay. This remnant stack (foreground lower photo) was no more tempting than the other stacks of hay grown on soil without treatment. (Photos by E. M. Poirot, Golden City, Missouri).

animal production, and nutritional troubles too easily labeled as "diseases" and thus accepted as inevitable when they ought to have remedy by attention to the soil. The soils determine how well we fill the bread basket and the meat basket.

Patterns of Population Distribution are Related to the Soil

The soil takes on national significance when it prompted the mayor of the eastern metropolis to visit the "Gateway to the West" to meet the farmers dealing with their production problems. More experience in rationing should make the simplest and homely subject of soils and their productive capacity household words amongst urban as well as rural peoples. Patterns of the distribution of human beings and their diseases, that can be evaluated nationally on a statistical basis as readily as crops of wheat or livestock, are not yet seen in terms of the soil fertility that determines one about as much as the other. Man's nomadic nature has made him too cosmopolitan for his physique, health, facial features, and mental attitudes to label him as of the particular soil that nourished him. His collection of foods from far-flung sources also handicaps our ready correlation of his level of nutrition with the fertility of the soil. We have finally come to believe that food processing and refinement are denying us some essentials. We have not yet, however, come to appreciate the role that soil fertility plays in determing the nutritive quality of foods, and thereby our bodies, and our minds. Quantity rather than hidden quality is still the measure.

Now that we are thinking about putting blanket plans as an order over states, countries, and possibly the world as a whole, there is need to consider whether such can blot out the economics, customs and institutions that have established themselves in relation to the particular soil fertility. Since any civilization rests or is premised on its resources rather than on its institutions, changes in the institution cannot be made in disregard of so basic a resource as the soil.

National Optimism Arises Through Attention to Soil Fertility

Researchers in soil science, plant physiology, ecology, human nutrition, and other sciences have given but a few years of their efforts to human welfare. These contributions have looked to hastened consumption of material surpluses from unhindered production for limited territorial use. Researchers are now to be applied to the production that calls for use of Nature's synthesizing forces for food production more than to simple nonfood conversions. When our chemical industry so expanded by wartime needs is fully turned to peacetime pursuits, it is to be hoped that a national consciousness of declining soil fertility can enlist our sciences and industries into rebuilding and conserving our soils as the surest guarantee of the future health and strength of the nation.

CHAPTER 21

Soil Fertility and Its Health Implications

IT IS SCARCELY NECESSARY to say that dentists have more than a passing interest in soil fertility, since they know that strong, healthy teeth contain a high concentration of calcium and phosphorus — nutrient elements that head the list of minerals drawn from the soil for sustenance of plant and animal life. Of the total gross weight of the teeth as part of the human skeleton, one-fourth is calcium and one-eight is phosphorus. Of the tooth enamel, one-third is calcium and one-sixth is phosphorus.

As cardinal requisites of a fertile soil, calcium and phosphorus in the form of limestone and superphosphate are the two foremost fertilizers or soil treatments used by well-informed farmers. Too frequently, however, these treatments are regarded merely as a means of obtaining greater tonnage or more bushels of crops per acre.

But when shortages in bulk of foods confront us, it is all the more essential that we improve the quality of that bulk. It is the soil on which, after all, the health qualities of foods depend. When teeth are calling for much calcium and phosphorus, defective teeth are not far removed from crops that are calling in vain on the soil that is deficient in these two mineral constituents of man's skeleton and teeth.

The Dental Profession has a Real Stake in Soil Fertility

In addition to calcium and phosphorus, there are about ten more growth-promoting, body-building nutrients on the list of fertility elements that soils must provide for vigorous, healthy bodies and sound teeth. Shortages in any one of these elements needed in body construction, or in catalytic service in body or plant growth, will reappear in the human family as health deficiencies. We cannot therefore afford to tolerate shortages in the soil's store of these truly "grow" foods.

Besides these dozen so-called "grow" foods, or elements coming from the soil, every growing body and every growing plant must have what can conveniently be called energy providers or "go" foods. The elements constructing such compounds are, in the main, carbon, hydrogen, and oxygen. They come from the air and water. Nitrogen also comes from that source, so that as much as 95 percent of plant mass or animal body weight is combustible. It serves in provision of energy and in giving bulk and weight.

Photosynthesis and Biosynthesis

Because the recognition of mass is a simple mental impression, the concept of bulk is always easily and quickly caught. So commonly are crops measured by weight that we are just now coming to realize that the "growth" quality, or the nutritional value of herbages is not the same as the tonnage value. A bushel of corn is always 56 pounds, but one bushel may be nourishment while the other is not, as judged by livestock growth. Plants attain mass of growth through the service of sunshine as it makes carbohydrates through use of the sun's energy in the chlorophylous leaves. This process of chemical synthesis of carbon, hydrogen, and oxygen into carbonaceous products gives tonnage, but surely this photosynthetic behavior does not guarantee animal or human nourishment when it results in trunks of trees consisting only of just so much woodiness. Sunshine, fresh air, and water — processed through the suprasoil activities by plants — may be responsible for 95 percent of plant bulk, yet contribute nothing to nourishment of higher life forms.

Nutritive values of herbages result from the synthesis of compounds within the growing plants, as for example, those that give rise to the seed and will feed our animals. These values are dependent on the calcium, phosphorus, magnesium, etc., that come from the soil. Animal life finds plenty of bulk for consumption. Recall hastily, if you will, the many plants which animals refuse to eat, or the many we call weeds. Nutritional deficiencies result from the failure of that vegetative bulk to have within itself the products of synthetic activities by the plant quite aside from products directly from photosynthesis. We need to appreciate what may well be called the "biosynthesis" or the synthesis by the life of the plant that depends not on air and water, but on the delivery by the soil of its complete list of soil fertility elements to be constructed by the plant into what is truly food substance.

In considering plants as phenomena of growth, we may well think of them first as a photosynthetic performance. This builds the woody frame of the plant, uses only limited amounts of soil fertility, mainly potassium, as catalytic agents, to set up the factory and provide its fuel supply. In the second place, plants are a biosynthetic performance, into which the soil fertility enters more directly to have its phosphorus, sulfur, nitrogen, etc., synthesized into proteins, vitamins, and other compounds truly valuable for body construction rather than for fuel only. It is the soil fertility much more than the sunshine and fresh air that determines how well the plant really gives us nourishment. It is this biosynthesis and not the photosynthesis whereby soil fertility takes on its significant implication in your health, in my health, in your teeth and in my teeth.

Virgin Plant Growth Concentrated the Soil Fertility in the Surface Soils for Help to Man

That the entire land surface of the earth cannot be generous in its provisioning of human and animal life becomes almost axiomatic when it is known that the soil must deliver about a dozen chemical elements. Soils constructed under good physical conditions, and stocked with such a large number of nutrient elements, must of necessity be the exception rather than the rule. Plant life in virgin, condition has been sending its roots down and searching through large volumes of soil to collect and assemble in the surface layer as organic matter or humus, these many elements needed. Hundreds of years of virgin condition have kept within the plant life, as a cycle of growth, death, decay, and re-use, these nutrient mineral elements from the soil. It is this feature that makes surface soil so valuable while subsoil is so unproductive.

Soil Construction and Soil Destruction

Naturally, soils vary widely as to their fertility since soils are temporary rest stops of rock en route to the sea and to solution. In lower rainfall areas the soil is finely ground rock. It is mainly mineral, with little clay and little water for plant growth. The plants grown there are mineral-rich, however. More rainfall gives more clay, more plant growth, more organic matter to decay. It also leaves a rock reserve to supply the clay as it gives up its nutrients to the plants. In central United States with its prairie areas, we have soils now in the stage of maximum of construction of clay that is in balance, or equilibrium, with a generous reserve of rich minerals to maintain productivity. With no more than 30 inches of rainfall along approximately the 97th meridian of the United States, we have the Midlands, where the animals raise themselves and human health is good as indicated by the fact that seven out of ten draftees pass inspection in Colorado while only three out of ten do so in a southern state.

With higher annual rainfalls and higher temperatures, the rocks are so highly weathered and the clay is so changed that it represents soil destruction. This is the prevailing condition in eastern and southeastern states. In terms of this degree of soil development we can see the basic principles

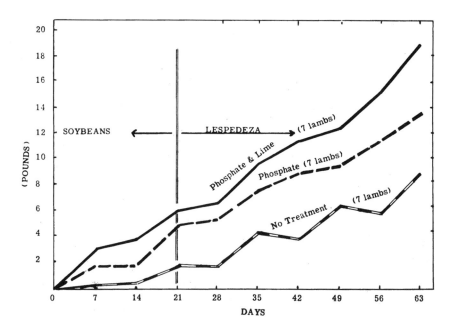

Fig. 1. The curves represent the gains in weight per head by lambs consuming constant weight of grains and hays per day, but with the different hays grown on adjoining plots given different soil treatments. The efficiency of the meat-making animal depends on the efficiency of the food synthesis by the plant in terms of the soil that controls it.

of nutritional troubles in the southern states, of limited populations in the tropics, of population concentrations into limited areas of the temperate zones, of customs whereby aborigines survive while the white man fails utterly, and numerous seemingly uncanny situations where the influence of soil fertility upon the human species is not yet appreciated.

Crop Juggling Disregards Soil Fertility

An ecological survey with tabulations of plant species is not needed to locate the forests in the northern regions, in the tropics, and in eastern and southeastern United States, nor to locate the prairies in central United States, and the barrens in the West, excluding the western coast. Underlying this seeming agreement of greater vegetative production in forests with higher rainfall, and vice versa, there is the soil fertility. We have not been connecting the different crops, their tonnage production per acre, and their chemical composition in terms of nutritive value for animals with the soil fertility. That the scantily growing buffalo grass of western Kansas was more nutritious because of more fertile soils than the lush bluestem of eastern Kansas on the less fertile, more leached soils was recognized by the buffalo. This brawny beast stayed on his scant grazing because it meant growth, muscular and bony body, and good reproduction. There was no natural obstruction to prevent his coming eastward, had he desired to move to get more bulk per acre.

More protein in the wheat as we move westward across Kansas follows the same course, with the less leached soils in central and western Kansas giving high protein in wheat. But in place of recognizing soil fertility as the controlling factor, we have been ascribing the difference to rainfall or to plant pedigrees. Plant breeding has been credited with wonders when we think of hybrid corn. But to date no geneticist's creation has yet come forward that can tolerate starvation or the lack of soil fertility.

Crops have been introduced, moved from place to place and pushed to the very fringes of starvation, while we have kept our attention fixed on the pedigree in place of the plant's nutrition. During this crop juggling, the chemical composition of the plant has shifted. Photosynthesis has come into prominence while biosynthesis has almost disappeared. The crop has retained its service in giving energy values but lost much of its service as a growth food and carrier of soil minerals elaborated into organic complexes of nutritive value. We have gone from proteinaceousness and high mineral contents in plants grown on soils under construction through lower rainfall to carbonaceousness and mineral deficiencies in plants grown on soils under destruction through higher rainfalls. Nutrition at the same time has rescended from a level of bone-building, brawn-making, and fecund reproduction to hydration, obesity, fattening performances and other excesses of weights with weakened bones and flabby muscles, to say nothing of carious teeth, alveolar bone disintegration, and other oral troubles.

Declining Soil Fertility
Brings the 'Sweet Tooth'

Declining soil fertility has been pushing out of the agricultural program those crops drawing heavily on the soil fertility, and naturally of high nutritive values. As such crops failed to produce tonnage, we have sought other crops maintaining the tonnage production per acre but failing to provide the nutritive equivalents per acre and the nutritive concentration or food value per pound. Carbonaceousness, consequently, has come

Fig. 2. Animals discriminate very judiciously by grazing different plants to different degrees. That the animal is balancing its diet according to the plant composition determined by the soil is not commonly appreciated. This instinct may be serving the animal better than it is in the human.

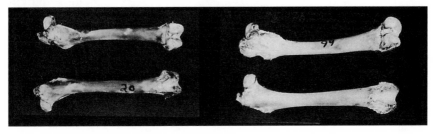

Fig. 3. Fertilizer treatments of the soil register their beneficial effects in the plant, but more noticeably in the physiology of the animal as indicated by better weight, wool, fur, bones, and other body products and functions. On the left, the rabbit and bones record the results of lack of soil treatment in contrast to the effect if treatment measured by similar gauges on the right.

into prominence, while proteinaceousness and high mineral contents have dwindled.

Declining soil fertility has been provoking the shift to feeding our animals on fattening feeds, and our own shift to soft wheats, and to starchy and saccharine elements in our diet. Our "sweet tooth" in a dietary sense has become a carious tooth in a dental sense as a result of the unobserved and unappreciated exploitation of the soil fertility, and shift in dominant plant composition.

Failing Skeletons Go with Failing Teeth

When the simplest expression of the chemical composition of bones and teeth puts these two together in the same category with their ash containing 894.6 parts of calcium phosphate per thousand parts, these two soil-borne elements, calcium and phosphorus, are lifted into prominence. This dare not, however, crowd out the 15.7 parts of magnesium phosphate, the calcium fluoride, the chloride and the carbonate of calcium as 3.5, 2.3, and 101.8 parts, respectively, and the 1.0 lone part of iron oxide. That this complexity in chemical composition of the teeth is no mere accident is well worth considering, and that it is a specific combination which makes for sound teeth only by good metabolism to maintain its specificity is also worthy of serious consideration. Shifts in the fluorine content, that makes up less than .013 percent of the enamel of the teeth, are known for the troubles they cause. Can we not then appreciate the inevitable incidence of tooth and skeletal troubles when the supplies of calcium and phosphorus in the foods fluctuate widely in amounts and in chemical combinations ingested, while we keep our eyes fixed on food bulk only?

Animal studies are pointing out the widely variable thickness, size, strength, and other properties of bones of animals according as they are fed different hays, the same hays from different soils, or the same hays from the same soil given different soil treatments, such as limestone and phosphate. Hidden away as it is within the animal's body, the skeletal structure may be undergoing drastic shortages in calcium and phosphorus that are readily passed over without concern. Surely the jaws carrying the teeth cannot escape registering these same irregularities taking place in the other skeletal parts.

To the Drugstore for Cure Rather than to the Soil for Prevention

Even though the practice of salting domestic animals has been with us for scarcely a century and a half, we have taken readily to the belief that the deficiency in any essential element in the diet can be met by its ingestion as a simple chemical salt in its ionic and molecular forms. With sodium and chlorine, both of which are monovalent and extremely soluble, accepted in the common salt form by domestic animals and searched out in the "salt lick" by wild animals, there may be serious error in concluding that deficiencies of calcium phosphates in the diet may be met by ingesting the salts of tricalcium phosphate or calcium and phosphorus in one or the other acid phosphate forms. Calcium is a divalent and phosphorus is a pentavalent ion. The two are closely associated or combined chemically wherever phosphorus is found in Nature. They serve such important roles in plant life where sodium and chlorine are not considered essential that it should seem fallacious even to postulate that calcium and phosphorus as salts can serve as effectively in both processes as when they are part of the compounds elaborated by plant synthesis.

The eating habits of the animals themselves offer suggestions. The eating of bones by cattle is not common. It occurs only after the animal arrives at certain stages of emaciation resulting from feeds deficient in phosphorus. This is quite different from their behavior relative to sodium chloride of which the consumption does not suggest itself as an act of desperation.

The behavior of rachitic bones suggests that the advent of calcium and phosphorus into the digestion via the plant as it has taken them from the soil is more effective when these come through this route whereby it is synthesized as organo-complexes rather than simple mineral salts. When a rachitic bone is cut longitudinally and immersed in ionic calcium phosphate solutions, the calcium and phosphorus are not readily deposited in the unmineralized bone parts. However, when such a bone is placed in a solution of calcium hexose monophosphate or calcium glycerophosphate, it absorbs the calcium and phosphates, to deposit them as minerals in the zone of the rachitic bone prepared for calcification. Such behaviors suggest that the organo-calcium phosphate may be a much more efficient means of introducing these bone-building ions into the skeleton and teeth than are calcium and phosphorus ingested simply as ionic salts.

Yeasts, as fermenters of sugars, require phosphates in order that this reaction giving off carbon dioxide may proceed. The phosphate acts seemingly as a catalyst. It enters into combination in one step in the process, but is not a part of the product. Thus, the phosphate is not serving in construction of the body of the yeast cell, or as a part of it. Rather it is serving in the chemical reaction that provides the energy for the life of the yeast. Calcium phosphate, as it serves in the energy reactions or metabolism of higher life, is still not a known phase of its behaviors in nutrition.

Here is the suggestion that the calcium and phosphate ions do not use the plant merely to hitchhike from the soil to the stomach of the animals. Rather it suggests that while these nutrient elements are helping in the biosynthetic performances within the plant, they are functioning in its metabolic performances and putting themselves into some unique organic combination through which they can move into the construction of the bones and teeth so much more effectively.

Then, too, when calcium gluconate, another calcium or gano-complex injected into the blood stream, is an effective cure for milk fever, it emphasizes the plausibility of the belief that calcium and phosphorus in the blood stream in non-dialyzable or colloidal form may be playing far more essential roles than we have been inclined to appreciate while focusing attention on them mainly in their ionic behaviors. Much about the physiologic activities of these two nutrient elements remains to be learned, but surely there are strong suggestions that as they play these roles we can aid their functions more from the soil forward by using them as fertilizers in the plants and thus for preventions, than from the drugstore backward and thereby as cures for nutritional troubles by which havoc has already been wrecked in the body.

Other Aspects of Soil Fertility

Your attention has been focused specifically on but two nutrient elements of the dozen (possibly more) essential ones coming from the soil for human sustenance. If recognition of the deficiencies of these two in the soil has led us to understand the irregularities in plant physiology of the food crops we eat, and deficiencies in our teeth, our skeleton, and our own body physiology as all these provoke bad health, we need to prepare ourselves for more troubles arising as the remaining nutrient elements are being drawn from the soil. Potassium has long been registering its shortages for crops, but fortunately is so bountifully supplied by food plants that our bodies excrete rather than hoard it. Magnesium, however, which is the next on the list, cannot be viewed with so little concern. Shortages of this element in the soil are already impending. Heavy limings with calcium limestone only and soil conservation activities without attention to magnesium may throw a panic into body physiology and sound teeth. Elements no more plentiful than fluorine required in drinking water by quantities as low as one part per million and coming in milk in from 5 to 25 parts per ten million are only beginnings in our thinking about several elements to which quantitative attention for health's sake has not been directed. We are soon to face the health problem linked with all the dozen (possibly more) nutrient elements contributed by the soil as we have just begun to connect rickets, teeth decay, and other troubles with calcium and phosphorus. With such a large list to be compounded into medicine by the drugstore, surely in desperation we ought to turn away from medicinal concoctions for cure and learn to put fertility into the soil so as to give help to Nature to nourish us for disease prevention instead.

Public Health Calls for Conservation of Soil Fertility

The importance of the soil as the basis of our nutrition has not yet been appreciated. For too many of us, food comes only from the grocery and the meat market in paper bags, fancy cartons, glass bottles, and tin cans. We are measuring it only by weight or cost per plate. Milk is still sold by the gallon and by its fuel value in terms of fat content, when milk may be so deficient as to give rickets even to the calf taking it, uninjured by aeration and pasteurization, directly from the mother cow. Milk, which is closely connected with reproduction, is lowered in its quality even as the function of reproduction, itself, is impaired by nutritional deficiencies resulting from neglect of the soil. Reproductive cells, both as egg cells in the female or sperm cells in the male, are a physiologic output by the body for reproduction — just as milk is food for service to the young in the same reproductive process. Egg cells and sperm cells defective because of deficient soil fertility and malnutrition are just as possible physiologically as is defective milk.

To the observant dentist, teeth and the mouth as a whole reflect the nutritional plane of his patient and thereby reveal not only the irregularities in the quality of his food, but should point much farther back to the plane of soil fertility in the region where the patient's food was grown. With that extension of the view of your mind's eye as you look into the mouths of children, we trust you will catch some suggestion that you in an office on the paved street have some share in conservation of the soil that is owned and managed by the man of the country who may seemingly be miring in the mud. That mud is becoming more precious for health's sake.

Man is going to be controlled in his behavior by the extent to which there is mobilized in the soil about a dozen simple chemical elements commonly found in mineral and rock combinations. Consequently, we want to see man in his behavior in that ecological picture with all other life forms wherein the fertility of the soil is at the controls. Those who are in the limestone industry are dealing with one of the ten elements — probably two if you are dealing with dolomitic limestone — that is at the control of agriculture, at the control of food, and at the control of all life, including man.

We think of food in terms of bulk, weight, volume. We seldom think of it in terms of its quality as nourishment. In the making of food, we have two objectives as to its quality; first, it should five us power and energy; but before we can use that power and energy we must construct the body, and food must meet the second objective, namely provide growth substances.

Reduced to its chemical simplicity, the body is about 96 percent of these four elements that find their origin in air and water. It is about 5 percent of a list of 10 or more elements that find their origin in the soil. We have been keeping our eyes keyed on bulk. We have been keeping our eyes fixed on those four substances, namely carbon, hydrogen, oxygen, nitrogen, that are liquid or gaseous in form and that flow and move freely. Therefore, they do not represent much of a struggle for us to get them. We have not given enough attention to the other elements that are fixed in their position in the soil and to which the plant or the animal must go for their service.

We have literally been in a blind alley for a number of years on this matter of liming, we have been thinking that the lime is serving a great function in fighting soil acidity. That is a fight that ought now be over. It should have been over a long time ago. Peace along these lines ought to be declared. We are no longer liming for the purpose of fighting soil acidity. We are now liming in order to introduce calcium and magnesium as fertility elements to be mobilized for better plant and animal production.

Soil Areas, Medical Rejectees Give Similar Maps

THERE IS AN INTERESTING similarity in the map of medical rejectees for World War II and the map of the major Missouri soil areas, says Dr. W. A. Albrecht, chairman of the University of Missouri soils department.

Now that there is increasing concern about growing population pressure on the land, workers are finding that soil has four dimensions instead of two as has been commonly supposed. In addition to the two customary dimensions of length and breadth, Albrecht adds the two dimensions of depth and fertility.

Also, workers are becoming concerned about how bountifully people in this country shall be fed. Quantity has been the common measure of the supply of food but Albrecht points out that food quality is important for food may be filling but not nourishing.

The maps of different crops in this country have long been connected with maps of soil fertility. Alfalfa has been "natural" on less weathered, mineral-rich soils. A liberal supply of essential plant nutrients in these soils has made alfalfa the high-protein, bone-building forage commonly used to supplement protein-poor corn in feeding livestock.

Red clover, another prized protein-rich forage, seems to be failing. Albrecht explains this is caused by declining soil fertility not being able to provide complete proteins for its growth, its protection against diseases, and its generous seed delivery.

Carbohydrate-producing crops are "easier to grow" than protein-rich crops. Dwindling soil fertility does not, nourish crops well enough to con-

Soil Areas, Medical Rejectees Give Similar Maps   221

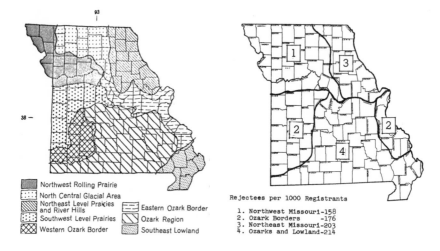

Northwest Rolling Prairie

North Central Glacial Area

Northeast Level Prairies and River Hills

Southwest Level Prairies

Western Ozark Border

Eastern Ozark Border

Ozark Region

Southeast Lowland

Rejectees per 1000 Registrants

1. Northwest Missouri-158
2. Ozark Borders   -176
3. Northeast Missouri-203
4. Ozarks and Lowland-214

A comparison between maps showing major Missouri soil areas, left, and medical rejectees per 1,000 registrants for the World War II Selective Service, center, shows definite similarities. Draft rejections were lowest in northwest Missouri counties where, on the average, the best soil in the state is located. And, rejections were highest in the Ozarks and southeast lowlands where soil is poor or where living conditions are not average.

vert carbohydrates into high-quality protein feed as readily as it helps to pile up carbohydrate bulk of less nutritional value.

The similarity between maps of different crops and soils maps is evident, Albrecht says, since soil fertility represents protein possibilities in crops and thereby in animals. Also, the similarity between soils and both wildlife and domestic animals is evident.

Soil is connected with these lower life forms in that soils are the cause of them through better nutrition — of quality rather than quantity.

And the maps of the quality of the human body, as determined by the selective service system, suggest that humans, like the animals in the lower part of the biotic pyramid, rest on the soil foundation for nutrition.

CHAPTER 23

Human Health Closely Related to Soil Fertility

MAN, IN THE BEGINNING, was created from a handful of dust. Darwin stated the carefully observed natural phenomenon of physical existence as the Law of the Survival of the Fittest. Too many of our modern technologies have kept our thoughts and study away from soil fertility, that handful of dust, as the basis for our being fit. Should we not, then, consider the soil and its fertility from this point of view?

The development of any soil from the natural minerals and the resulting fertility are consequences of the climatic forces, water and heat, working on the particular parent rocks. Missouri is geographically located so that the differing climatic effects may be readily observed. Northwest Missouri receives 30 inches of precipitation annually, whereas the Southeast Lowlands receive 50. This increasing amount of water is made more efficient in its chemical reactions for rock decay into soil, but also more damaging through leaching and fertility destruction when the increasing temperatures follow the same pattern to magnify those effects. This is shown by the evaporation-transpiration curves in figure 1. Rainfall less than evaporation (less than 100) prevails in Northwest Missouri, but rainfall in excess of evaporation (more than 100) is characteristic in the Lowlands of Southeast Missouri.

Other factors are also responsible for the differing fertility areas of Missouri. Unweathered material from the arid west, washed in by the Missouri River and left in its flood plains, is annually blown over and deposited as fertilizer on the Northwestern section of the state. This material then breaks down to replenish the supplies of plant food elements which produce protein- and mineral-rich crops for good nutrition.

The Ozarks, without such windborne additions, are the oldest and most weathered soils in the state with little to offer as plant nutrition. The Southeast Lowlands were formed mainly of materials already highly weathered before they were brought in from the East Central States. Their low fertility is evidenced by their production of cotton, vegetable oil, and watermelons, mainly combinations of air, water and sunshine (carbon, hydrogen and oxygen) with little protein and minerals to offer for nutrition.

Man can be healthy only as the food he consumes supplies him with protein and minerals which are made available to the plants growing on the soil. Soil fertility suggests itself as the determiner of man's physical health by the correlation between the rejectees (per 1,000 registrants) and the major soil regions (Compare figure 3 with figure 2).

Mental ability and better mental health, dependent as they are on good physical health, are therefore, also related to the soil fertility. This relation is shown by the distribution of honor students in the College of Agriculture, as tabulated for a period of eight academic years, 1949-50 through 1956-57.

The mental quality, as a product of the soil, was measured in terms of square miles required to produce one honor student per year. General soil areas, urban counties excluded, produced one honor student for the number of square miles indicated for each soil area shown in figure 4, namely, Northwest 307, Ozark Borders 376, Northeast 431, and the Ozarks and Lowlands 617.

In terms of population, 7,455 were required to produce one honor student in Northwest Missouri, whereas 15,740 were required in the Ozarks and Lowlands. The percentage of enrollees who had a 3.50 (B+) or higher grade average varied from 5.1% in the Northwest to 3.26% in the Ozarks and Lowlands, with no students of this quality from the bootheel, another indication of student quality according to the soil fertility pattern.

Do these measurements, square miles and population per honor student and percentage of enrollees with high grades, not suggest fertility of the soil as the basis of mental as well as physical health? Should we not remove the haze of Sputnik from before our eyes so that we might study the soil and work with it to nourish ourselves for health and education rather than exploit the soil? Let us therefore consider the fact that man's mobility has not removed his "roots" from the soil as his best nutrition, and teach physiology and nutrition of and for healthy plants and animals, bodies and minds.

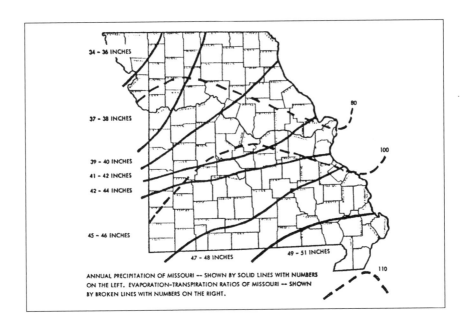

ANNUAL PRECIPITATION OF MISSOURI -- SHOWN BY SOLID LINES WITH NUMBERS ON THE LEFT. EVAPORATION-TRANSPIRATION RATIOS OF MISSOURI -- SHOWN BY BROKEN LINES WITH NUMBERS ON THE RIGHT.

The increasing rainfall and temperature in going from northwest Missouri to southeast Missouri (figure 1, above) give higher degrees of soil development, or declining fertility, and different soils (figure 2, below).

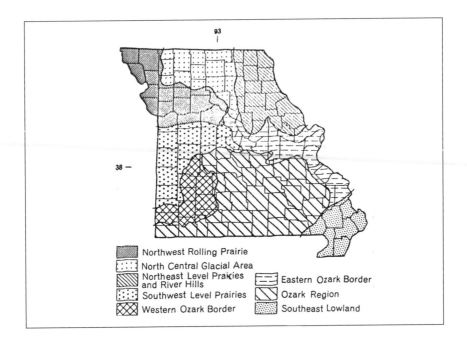

Northwest Rolling Prairie
North Central Glacial Area
Northeast Level Prairies and River Hills
Southwest Level Prairies
Western Ozark Border
Eastern Ozark Border
Ozark Region
Southeast Lowland

Human Healthy Closely Related to Soil Fertility   225

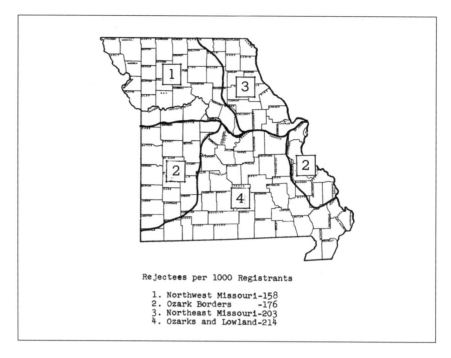

Rejectees per 1000 Registrants

1. Northwest Missouri-158
2. Ozark Borders   -176
3. Northeast Missouri-203
4. Ozarks and Lowland-214

Draftee rejections per 1,000 registrants (figure 3, above) and sections of soil area producing one honor student per year in the College of Agriculture, (figure 4, below).

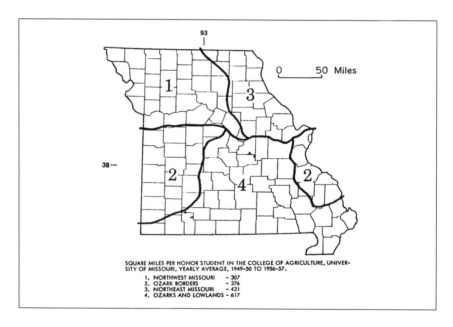

SQUARE MILES PER HONOR STUDENT IN THE COLLEGE OF AGRICULTURE, UNIVERSITY OF MISSOURI, YEARLY AVERAGE, 1949-50 TO 1956-57.

1. NORTHWEST MISSOURI   - 307
2. OZARK BORDERS   - 376
3. NORTHEAST MISSOURI   - 431
4. OZARKS AND LOWLANDS - 617

Section 4

Soil Fertility
& Human and
Animal Health

CHAPTER 24

The Fertility Pattern

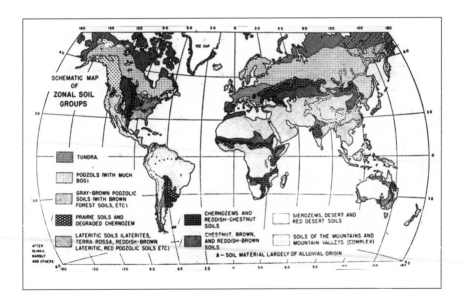

THE LARGER PATTERN of man's distribution over the earth is premised on the pattern of the soil and by the soil's creative potential.

Man is human and sociable in his behaviors only when he is well fed. When he is hungry his behavior confirms the truth in the Russian proverb: "An empty stomach knows no laws."

Man's height above other animals, is a dangerous loftiness. He stands at the top of the biotic pyramid. The other life forms below him are (a) animals, (b) plants, and (c) microbes. Then, below the microbes and supporting the entire pyramid there is the soil. The soil is not merely the site or the foundation, but it is the contributor of the creative means of all life forms in the pyramid of successive biotic dependencies on each other.

Man is only beginning to realize the hazard to himself, located in that high place. He has now overrun the earth in his exploitation. His technologies have lengthened his life lines, reaching from the hazardous areas back to the less hazardous ones. He has pushed out on the fringes of fertility and on to deficiencies in nutrition that are disastrous if he is limited to those fringe areas. Now that some of those life lines are shortening, he is worshipping economics and politics rather than conceding to the natural laws that are in final control. But man's loftiness becomes more hazardous as the basic forces extending various hungers are becoming more powerful in their dictates.

The seashores and the droughty, windswept land provided the first nutritional security. Primitive man stayed near the seashore. He migrated inland to significant extents, but survived there only in semi-arid regions. Semi-arid soils are high in fertility. They are such because they have not been seriously leached or washed out.

On droughty, windswept land, moreover, the wind brings in unweathered minerals from everywhere to increase the chances that our soil contains all the essential elements for compounding foods and feeds of the highest nutritional order. Particles of silt size, or windblown, unweathered dust, represent speedy mineral decomposition to make available their elemental contents. Soils that are windblown are nutritional security of high order in quality, if not in quantity, because of the fertility.

Food of quality is first and economics is second in determining man's location (with survival) *on the earth.*

The seashore with its complete array of the essential inorganic elements in solution, or in protein compounds of sea animals as human food, and the semi-arid land areas with limited tonnage yields of many crops, permitted man to wander freely. They allowed him to multiply in the new areas without their starving him out through nutritional shortages. Egypt and other parts of the semi-arid and arid Orient, the Missions of our pre-Colonial Spanish Southwest, and other dry areas, record ancient civilizations as possible illustrations of this principle.

From the Orient the expansions and migrations of peoples moved westward around the shores of the Mediterranean. There it could have been both the sea and the soils under lower rainfall that provided the foods which were then — and still are — more than just carbonaceous bulk and calories of energy.

It was from there that lucerne, or alfalfa, expanded to make good forage and to be the basic nitrogen-fixing legume in southern Europe. Today this nitrogen-rich feed is the major means of providing the manure pile on which food production of the southern European farm is so highly dependent. Those areas of winter rainfalls, threatening summer shortage of water for crops, but of mineral-rich soils to grow alfalfa naturally, have grown nutritious foods. An agriculture that retained there much of its seeming primitivity to the point of derision when we speak of "the slow, old-fashioned European peasant out on the land" has not been a hazard. Instead, it has been security of the human species according to the soil fertility under the course which those migrations followed. Other illustrations of similar character may be familiar enough to you for additional citations.

Fortunately for the nomad, the cow went ahead of the plow. Grazing flocks and herds may have determined the direction rather than man himself. The animals led the way to new areas of grazing. Man followed them to pitch his tent where his herds had been the advance soil chemists. The herds went ahead assaying the nutritional qualities of the herbage and thereby approving the fertility of the soil for his nutrition as well as their own. For assaying the feeds, the cow's criterion, or that used by the sheep, is not tons of hay or bushels of grain. Nor is it the feed's qualities for the speedy laying of body fat on a castrated male. Instead, the criterion by which animals judge their feeds is its provision of proteins and all that comes along with them.

Animals seem to recognize nutritional shortages, not only in proteins as the crude forms designated only by nitrogen presence, but they seem to suggest also the shortages in any of the nearly two dozen amino acids of which the proteins are composed. By their choices and behaviors the animals reflect the deficiencies in the many other compounds depending for their syntheses by plants and by animals on the long list of inorganic elements originally in the minerals of the soil.

Therefore, man's expansion over land areas chosen under guidance of the biochemical services of his flocks and herds was not hazardous, but secure. It was a movement to lands found equal to the needs for his good nutrition, and thereby his reproduction, because it was so judged by animals almost duplicating his food requirements in those for themselves.

For modern man, the plow went ahead of the cow. His technological aids to help him go farther into the more humid soils pushed him into the interior of larger land masses and continents. It was a case in reverse of that of the primitive farmer.

At the same time some technological aids, such as medical science, food preservation, conversion processes and extensive transportation, moved agriculture away from its concern about production of good nutrition, toward more and more concern about speculation and sharp trading. Sections of the population began to make their living at the expense of other sections of it. A larger and larger share of it was less secure with less of the food and shelter requirements provided so directly by the work of their own hands. Cities began to develop. Man pushed himself more and more out on the areas so limited in soil fertility that they permit little more than a single salable crop.

With that expansion of population came more purchase and importation of necessities and less of one's own production of them in place. Under these economic compulsions, the single crop agriculture became an extensive and mechanical one on the less fertile soils compelling such with its associated troublesome social consequences.

Today, high population per unit of land area and the declining fertility of the soils are emphasizing the difficulties in maintaining life lines for our active support. Now we have taken to talking about *soil conservation.* We are soon to be taken with a more inclusive concern about *human ecology,* under the simpler, but more forceful term of *conservation,* with all that it can entail.

Man's expanded knowledge in the sciences and the resulting technologies may have goaded him on in his expansion, in his over-running of territory, and in his exploitation of natural resources to the point of matching sections of population against others in warfare of atomic caliber. Now those same sciences are being challenged to bring order out of the chaos they have wrought.

Soil conservation dare not be a cry suggesting urban condemnation of the rural neglect of this resource, suddenly appreciated as the supplier of food and nutrition. It must be a universal effort by all. All shared in the exploitation. Now all must share in the restoration.

Chemical tests of the soil and analyses of the crops are pointing to the increasing failure of the crops to deliver the more significant nutritional values. This is the fact in spite of increasing tonnages of vegetative mass and bushels per acre about which boast and bombast are so common. Unwittingly in our crop juggling to maintain high yields per acre, we have brought in those exotic crops maintaining delivery of carbohydrate foods but failing more and more to create the protein foods and all the inorganic essentials of mineral origin coming to us by way of the plants.

The suitcase wheat farmer of the Dust Bowl; those rushing to take over land in every newly irrigated region; the adventurer following Horace Greeley's admonition to "Go West Young Man"; the novice sugar cane farmers that responded to the revised version of that journalist's slogan suggesting "Go South Young Man"; the cotton farmers of the South now shifting to diversified farming where the "Piney Woods" and palmetto brush starve native cattle while filling their bellies; the tenant farmers under sudden economic shifts; and many other pathetic human cases making appeal to public sentiment, all tell us that we have seen ourselves losing individual grip on *that one true security, namely, real food from fertile soil.*

Such a loss is the major of all hazards to a stable society. Technologies of exploitation, of rapid movements of peoples, and of long hauls of products coupled with the economics of speculation rather than those of production, have given us the fringes of human ecology that are already seriously frayed out.

The climatic pattern of our country has had much discussion as a matter of external comfort, namely, how warm, or how cold, and how wet or how dry. Escapes from the costs of better shelter, and of more fuels for longer winter seasons have moved peoples to warmer climates. Various aspects of climate have entered into the ecological pattern of humans without their recognition of the great fact that climate controls Man's inner comfort, namely, the freedom from, or the torment by, hidden hungers according to the fertility of the soil which the climate develops in the particular setting in question.

It is in terms of the rainfall coupled with temperature that these two factors, combined, give us the climate and determine the human ecology by way of the soils. Peoples are well nourished; they present few problems which they do not solve readily themselves, when the climatic combination gives soil construction or the fertility for production of proteins as well as carbohydrates in our foods. Peoples are poorly nourished and present themselves as problems to the rest of society in climates that tend toward soil destruction or soils permitting production of carbohydrates generously but proteins too niggardly to keep folks healthy and free of hidden hungers. We have emphasized the temperate zone; we have complained much about limited rainfalls; but we fail to appreciate the food security in terms of those soils that once grew the bison, grow the high protein wheat now, and make the good beef proteins we enjoy.

Those are the fertile soils illustrated by the Midwest. In that area of the Mid-continent we have soils that feed us rather than soils that fail us. It represents a distinct part in our national soil fertility pattern. It is there that we find the *maximum of soil construction* and the *minimum of soil destruction* in terms of the production of food of the high order that truly *feeds rather than only fills and fools us.*

Proteins are not created from the elements by animals. Livestock only assembles them from the components of proteins created from the essential elements by plants and microbes. Life flows by means of proteins. Proteins reproduce themselves. Carbohydrates and fats do not. Proteins represent true growth, not merely increase in weight, as may be true for the watermelon, for example, or a fattening animal.

Only very slowly are we coming to see that the ecological pattern of the human species in the United States would mark itself out according to the fertility pattern of soils as the climate makes it. That pattern would exhibit itself more readily were we not shipping proteins from the Mid-continent meat centers to the rest of the country, or milk from there to distances scarcely believable. All this protein transport and meat price squabble is still viewed as economics and business. It is not yet visualized as a struggle

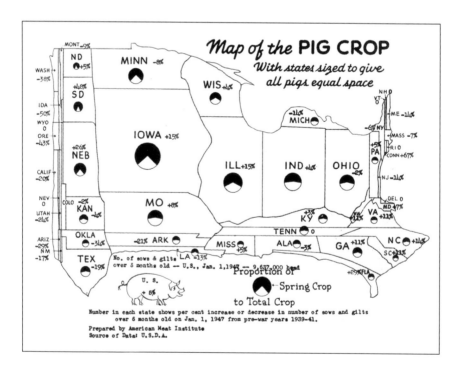

by the human species on less fertile soils to get proteins that can be grown only on soils more fertile.

As we go to the west of the Mid-continent, the agriculture dwindles and the population becomes sparse. It is not always well with the folks on arid sands which Nature has not yet developed into soils.

To the east of the Mid-continent under increasing annual rainfalls, there are the corn and the hogs where once the forests primeval were dense. Fuel foods in the carbohydrates and in the fats — spelling deficiencies in health in extra body fats — grow abundantly. They grow where high rainfalls for soil destruction made much clay, and washed it severely with carbonic acid to remove the fertility and leave acidity of the soil in its place.

Here the human species struggles for its proteins, while consuming carbohydrate products from plants that grow profusely. That is where bulk production for sale is the criterion of agriculture. But hidden hungers and insufficient health are reasons for more and more hospitals until soon we shall have one-half of the crowd in bed and the other half caring for them.

In the southeastern United States we condemn the single-crop agriculture of cotton farming, and propagandize diversification. There the racial problems have been a constant menace and sharp color lines have persisted. Politics have been blamed as causative by some, but have been considered the remedial hopes by others. Underneath these social troubles there has been the poor soil that could grow only poor foods in terms of proteins and all the essential nutritional compounds coming with these essentials on fertile soils.

A glimpse of the soil map of the United States will show that the soils and not the people give us our East and our West. Soil also divides the East into the North and the South.

The soil map puts the beef cattle market in Kansas City as the beef protein center, with production of it to the West. The soil map puts the pork market in Chicago with the animal fat production nearby and east thereof. Only soils of a particular fertility level according to a specific degree of development under less drastic climatic forces of the moderate rainfalls in the temperate zone give the nutrition and the higher security for larger numbers of the human species. On those soils, peoples are assets to themselves and to others, instead of liabilities.

Let us now use our own United States, with its Midwest as a standard, or as a help, in looking at the soil map of the world, and our international problems.

Where in the rest of the world do you find soils similar to our protein belt in our Midwest? In the Union of the Socialistic Soviet Republics. Not in Great Britain, which along with Russia was recently one of the triumvirate in world power.

However, on further study of the soil map with Britain's present plight in mind, you see our Midwest soils duplicated in Canada, South Africa, India, and Australia. There you can see the wheat-producing and meat-producing soils of her outlying colonies as the basis for the past strength of the British Empire.

Now we begin to recognize other aspects in the ecological pattern, interpreting some of the behaviors of the human species in recent world turmoils. Soils in North China suggest reasons for Japan's stealthy infiltration there. Soils in South America, making it extensive cattle country, suggest reasons for a naval battle between the Graf Spee and British Men-of-War in that vicinity in World War II.

The soils of the world that produce proteins mark out the so-called Powers of the World and have been more basic in control of human behaviors in war as well as in peace than most of us have been ready to believe. When the so-called "those who have not" are in strife with the so-called "those who have" we may well characterize those two groups more specifically *as those who have not soils fertile enough to produce proteins* and *those who have fertile soils supplying them with proteins.*

Serious symptoms call for drastic treatments to bring about recovery. As yet, no depletion allowances in income taxes, for example, are made for soils, when similar allowances are as high as 25 percent annually for some other mineral properties. For taxation purposes it is claimed that soils do not depreciate.

And yet, for nutritional purposes, one generation of farming may be mining the soil enough to almost liquidate the health of the family if the economics of trying to pay for the farm doesn't liquidate both the soil and the family completely before then. During all these past years while the soil fertility has been thrown into the bargain by the farmer in making a sale of his products, his economics have been the equivalent of liquidating his capital while everybody was calling it profit or pay.

In consequence of such economics without a soil foundation, a distorted ecology of the human species has come about with fewer rural people owning poorer land and poorer food security. We have a bad economics aggravating itself into a worse one with increasing urban people owning no soil and no food security at all. Increasing populations and dwindling

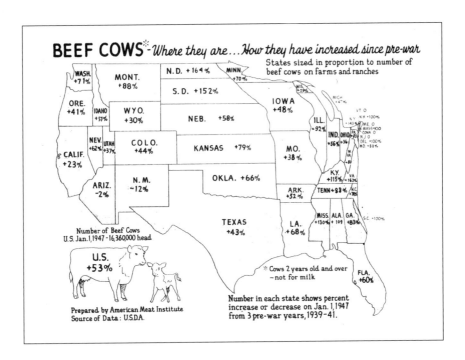

BEEF COWS* — *Where they are...* *How they have increased since pre-war*

States sized in proportion to number of beef cows on farms and ranches

WASH. +71%
MONT. +88%
N.D. +164%
MINN. +70%
WIS. +5%
ORE. +41%
IDAHO +57%
WYO. +30%
S.D. +152%
IOWA +48%
MICH. +4%
VT. 0
N.Y. +43%
N.H. +100%
ME. 0
MASS. +100%
CONN. 0
NEV. +62%
UTAH +37%
COLO. +44%
NEB. +58%
ILL. +92%
IND. +56%
OHIO +36%
PA. +31%
N.J. 0
DEL. +100%
MD. +81%
CALIF. +23%
ARIZ. -2%
N.M. -12%
KANSAS +79%
MO. +38%
KY. +115%
VA. +162%
OKLA. +66%
ARK. +52%
TENN. +88%
N.C.
MISS. +130%
ALA. +109%
GA. +83%
S.C. +100%
TEXAS +43%
LA. +68%
FLA. +60%

Number of Beef Cows
U.S. Jan. 1, 1947 - 16,360,000 head.

U.S. +53%

* Cows 2 years old and over — not for milk

Number in each state shows percent increase or decrease on Jan. 1, 1947 from 3 pre-war years, 1939-41.

Prepared by American Meat Institute
Source of Data: U.S.D.A.

soil resources combined are bringing a greater consciousness of the basic truth that rural welfare is too closely connected with food production for any of us in the urban group to neglect the rural segment in the ecological pattern.

The issue must be faced squarely. An increasing number of people on shrinking soil acreage of which the fertility is declining even more speedily, will mean a quarrel for food. It will be a quarrel bringing on wars unless the larger ecological pattern premised on soil fertility serves to guide the thinking and the planning to prevent such. Shrewd bargaining by our individual selves, or by sections of the country under leadership of politicians in state capitols and in our National Capitol, or by our representatives under the United Nations, does not make more productive soil per person, nor does it feed us better. We are coming face to face with the necessity of accepting one of two alternatives, or possibly both, (a) either give more restorative attention to our soils so they can feed more of us properly, or (b) limit our population accordingly.

CHAPTER 25

Proteins and Reproduction

THE QUESTION THAT I am asked to discuss is the probable relationship between the protein supply of a land or area and the birth rate of the people there. We are, of course, only at the beginning of knowledge in such matters; but from all that I have been able to gather in studying the intricate relationship between soils and the protein pattern I am not inclined to believe that high-protein diets, in themselves, diminish either fecundity or survival, and thereby lighten the population load on the land.

Other factors, economic and social, that customarily accompany the higher standards of living achieved by richer lands and peoples may lead, as Sir John Boyd-Orr, Dr. Josué de Castro and others indicate, to a lower birth rate; but a high intake of proteins seems to me, in the light of a whole chain of living evidence, to increase both fecundity and longevity.

Let us first get away from the myopic view that sees shortages of food only in the quantitative terms of calories, or shortages of "crude" proteins in terms of human need alone. Let us start in the soil and examine the evidence logically — and ecologically — from the ground up.

Protein shortages are intricately connected with the behavior of animals, plants, and microbes, all of which are successive parts in the biotic pyramid that has man as its apex, and the soil as the foundation of the whole structure.

The soil's pattern of fertility elements for various countries was possibly the determiner of man's migrations on the face of the earth. The soil's pattern may be more subtle, but it is more uncompromising than any politics, policies of colonizations, recommendations by Councils of United Nations, or other politico-sociological forces. For it is the soil that determines the proteins by which we have *reproduction.*

The provision of proteins in any area does more to delineate the different life patterns than almost any other ecological factor. It is these protein compounds that alone can keep life flowing. They build the body tissue. In fact, only they represent growth as cell multiplication. This stricter interpretation of the term "growth" is quite different, of course, from considering it simply as the increase in body weight. Weight has been the common concept of growth applied to animals in the pasture and the feedlot, and naturally so, when the hanging on of fat and the loading of the tissues with water serve so well to make the practice of buying low and selling high a lucrative one.

But even then, the success of this speculative venture demands the exclusion of the animal's reproductive potential. The feedlot phase of agriculture restricts itself largely to fattening the castrated males. Significantly, this practice finds itself located mainly on soils where the native crops serving as fattening feed are so deficient in proteins — not only in totals but also in nutritional quality thereof — as to demand protein supplements imported from other more fertile soils, or from places where the plants can provide more complete proteins.

The fattening of our beef cattle in the eastern half of the United States (grown largely farther west), and the growing of pigs in that eastern part as animals mainly fat — may seem an arrangement in accord with natural economic controls, but it goes deeper. Underneath the control by economic forces there is in reality the specific control by a deficiency, of proteins, going back to the soil. This deficiency is not necessarily one of totals of proteins, as we measure their amounts when we determine the element nitrogen considered as making up 16 percent of the "crude" proteins. This controlling deficiency is more often the shortage within the feed and food supply of some of the protein's constituent parts, namely, the amino acids. Eight or possibly ten of the amino acids are considered absolutely essential (and required regularly) for the survival of the experimental white rat — and inferentially for the human species.

Man and the animals must be given these amino acids. These creatures cannot create their proteins from the simpler chemical elements (except to limited extent by microbial helps in the intestinal tract). Only plants and microbes are equal to this accomplishment. These lower life forms struggle for their required proteins too. But they can grow and reproduce by means of a more limited list of the amino acids. Consequently, the mere growth of plants is no assurance of their serving as a feed which will guarantee growth of the animals consuming them.

We are coming slowly to realize that the array of the amino acids within the same plant species in uniform ratios is not the rule, except as the soil fertility contributes the required creative elements accordingly. In consequence, the animal may be able to cover enough territory, or to find enough of particular plants so as to provide itself with complete proteins. It is through the proteins in the main that the soil controls the many forms of terrestrial animal life. Even for the marine forms, the sea supports them mainly where the soil inwash and the shallow, well-lighted waters grow microscopic plants to feed proteins to the little fish so they in turn can be feed for the bigger ones.

The soil fertility pattern as it expresses itself in the pattern of protein potential is, then, a significant determiner in any ecology. This holds true even for the ecology of man, save as his technologies give him life lines to drag the required fertility to his more nearly local soil from distant ones, or periodically let him make excursions out far enough and often enough to satisfy his hidden hungers before they extinguish him.

The areas favorable to man and the food animals supporting him are those where the soil processes under the particular climatic forces are breaking down the rocks and minerals to provide the flow of all the essential chemical elements to the plant roots. These must come in such amounts and ratios as will support those plants synthesizing the complete proteins. Such conditions prevail mainly in the temperature zones under moderate rainfalls, or the equivalents in the chemo-dynamics for providing the fertility within the soil.

High rainfalls, then, to wash nutrients out of the soil into the sea do not represent protein potential in the vegetation, though they represent voluminous production of carbohydrates in cellulose, starch, and sugars. Low rainfalls, too, fail to provide proteins, for they fail to build the rocks into a soil that will sufficiently provide plants with protein, even when water is provided for the crops.

The favorable place, then, for our protein-rich plants in the climate-soil-ecological pattern is on the moderately weathered soils. Those plants include not only the legumes, but also the protein-rich herbage that puts our protein-producing beef cattle (lean meat) and sheep (lean meat and wool) on these same soils under range conditions. These animals will seek the same soils which in their virgin state made the brawn and bone of the buffalo, but supported no extensive animal-fattening industry. It is those same soils where today wheat makes more protein of itself to give us the "staff of life" when protected from the ultra-refining processes to make the "white" bread. Those are the soils considered under too little rainfall for big yields per acre, even if it was there where the cow went ahead of the plow while assaying them with favorable report for reproduction of herself and for like performances by man. As man pushes himself off these protein-producing soils on to the "fringe" soils, he must extend his life lines from the latter back to the former, except as he can tolerate increasing degrees of malnutrition and partial starvation.

Now that we have overrun the earth by means of technologies, have exploited our soils by them, and have extended our life lines to the point of fishing the Antartic for proteins in whale meat, we are seeing those life lines shortened gradually if not already breaking and often severed. That shortages of proteins originate in our soils is as yet unrecognized. We are failing to see man in the larger picture.

We hold post-mortems and offer explanations but fail to comprehend causes. We run the motion picture film backwards, as it were, in our delusion that we control the ecology. Man, like other animals, is an expression of the natural forces ruling him far more than he can rule Nature. Thus is generated a blind faith that man can extend himself over the vast acreages of land unused, with no thought as to the reasons why they are so. History makes little of its record that man has already tried such areas with a resulting failure to maintain himself there.

Much land remains as acres but the serious shortages in the soil as source of complete proteins offers provocation for a revival of remarks once made by Malthus. There are qualitative deficiencies, and while many phases of man's behavior are subjects of debate, no one to date has come up to take the negative side of the proposition that "Man must eat, and particularly of the proteins."

Our use of antibiotics is acceptance by us of the synthetic services for our protection by the lowly microbes. From next to the soil, at the bottom of the biotic pyramid, these chemical services approaching those represented in the synthesis of proteins are passed up to us at the top for our protection against other but dangerous microbes. Plants, too, offer protection in their many compounds simulating proteins, when they give us vitamins, hormones, via catalytic and stimulating effects still unknown. Proteins are still the major protection against disease and degeneration of the body.

It is in terms of specific proteins that our animals give us protection when we use the serums, vaccines, and various inoculants made from animal blood proteins. It is the cow that can take our disease of smallpox, can live through the scourge of it, can build proteins in her bloodstream to protect herself against recurrence of it, and then can share those proteins with us for the vaccination and protection of hundreds of humans. Yet she does that by support of no specific drugs, but by support of nutritional compounds no more startling than those in green grass growing on fertile soil.

The horse takes our form of typhoid fever. With apparently no serious disruption of his health, he creates proteins to combat the effects of the typhoid bacteria, and shares those disease-fighting compounds as inoculative protection for human beings. Our bodies may often suffer from insufficient ability to corral and to create antibiotic, protein-like substances for protection against invasions by foreign, death-dealing microbial proteins. Yet with a little help from proteins brought to us by the microbes, the plants, and the animals, we carry or create sufficient of our proteins for protection.

Plants also protect themselves by means of proteins. Experimental trials have demonstrated that by increasing those fertility elements in the soil which were serving for increasing proteins in the young plants, there was provided increasing protection against the attack by a fungus suggesting one connected with the "damping off" disease. In another experiment, more nitrogen and more calcium offered to vegetable plants for higher concentrations of proteins in these food crops, gave more protection against attack on the plants by leaf-eating-insects. Here was suggested the possible converse of this demonstration, namely, that the increasing fungus diseases of our crops and the increasing insect attacks on them seem to be premised on deficiencies of protective proteins in the plants, and these in turn on the deficiencies of the fertility in the soil.

Shall we not, then, open our minds to the possibility that the shortages of proteins and shortages of all that is associated with them in their synthesis by microbes, by plants, and by animals, are prohibiting us through a kind of malnutrition from collecting and creating the necessary list of proteins by which our bodies can protect themselves, or build their own immunity?

Seemingly, our wild animals gather their own "medicines" by instinctive selections, not only among different plant species, but also amongst the plants of the same species according to differences in the fertility of the soils growing it. Our domestic animals manifest similar selections within the limits permitted by our enclosure of them within fences, barns, stanchions, and other hindrances to their exercise of choices for their own better nutrition and better protection against diseases. While proteins are the major nutritional "cure" for tuberculosis, we are still unmindful of the many other diseases against which complete proteins may possibly be a protection.

It was some experiments using sheep as farm animals and rabbits under more carefully controlled procedures which demonstrated the fact that the soils and proteins can control reproduction possibilities. Ewe lambs were fed on legume hays grown on a less productive soil given (a) no treatment, (b) phosphate, and (c) both lime and phosphate. Their growths as increases in body weights were in the proportion of 8, 14, and 18 pounds per animal for the above treatments, respectively, when equal amounts of hay per head per day were consumed. The wool from those lambs fed hay grown on the soils with the more complete treatment was the only one among the three lots which could be scoured and carded without the destruction of the fibers. More significant, however, than the failure to secrete this protein fiber of normal quality in the case of the two lots of lambs fed the hay given only phosphate, or no soil treatment, was their failure also in their possibilities for *reproduction.*

When at the age of eighteen months the three lots of lambs were put with the ram, these two failed to mate and failed to give a lamb crop while those fed previously on hays grown on soils given both lime and phosphate for soil fertility improvement gave a lamb crop as the result of mating with the same male.

As additional test of the possible causal connection between soils, proteins, and reproduction, the two hays grown on the soil treatments of phosphate only and both lime and phosphate were fed to two lots of male rabbits in use for artificial insemination. Their regular delivery of semen was measured carefully and studied critically, only to find (a) the delivered volume decreasing, (b) the concentration of spermatozoa falling, and (c) the percentage of live spermatozoa declining rapidly, for those rabbits fed the hay grown on the soil of which the fertility was improved by no more than only a phosphate treatment.

Such was not the case, however, for those rabbits feeding on the hays grown on the soil given both lime and phosphate. No significant irregularities in the production and delivery of the semen was manifested by this second lot.

When these differences between those two lots were especially wide, the males of the former lot were approaching sexual impotency so closely that they were indifferent to the presence of a female in oestrus. At the same time, those in the latter lot manifested their interest in her the moment she was brought near their hutches.

Still more significant, as evidence of the relation of soils and crop proteins to reproduction, were the marked changes in reproductive potentials resulting when the feeding program was modified by merely interchanging the hays for the lots of rabbits. Only three weeks had elapsed after this shift in feeding, when the lot of originally impotent and indifferent animals was restored to sexual vigor with all the characteristics of potent males. The formerly potent ones exhibited falling curves for all the measurements. In the same short period of three weeks those on the hay grown with the limited soil treatment, had fallen to the same low level of the other lot before the hays were interchanged.

When, in these tests, the soil treatments for improved production of protein by legumes, as measured in terms of increased nitrogen in their hays, were the only variables responsible for shifting the sexual vigor from impotence to potence and vice versa, one can scarcely refute the causal connection between soils, proteins, protection, and reproduction. It appears as if the proteins as food compounds are connecting the animal, (a) in its survival as an individual via nutrition and protection against disease, and (b) in its survival as a species via fecund reproduction, very definitely with the combinations of the essential nutrient elements in the soil.

When plants get their proteins in varying degrees of completeness for their reproduction via seed according as the more complete suites of fertility elements in the soil permit; when herbivorous animals must depend on the plants for their proteins as a collection of all the required amino acids; when protection against invasion of our own bodies by death-dealing agencies is given us by proteins; and when the stream of reproduction of any life can be kept flowing only by means of proteins, shall we envision man as capable of sidestepping this pattern of controls? Would it not be more logical to build our conceptual scheme of his behaviors as merely that of another animal more complex in its physiological requirements, of less privilege for variance from these controls, and subject to greater potential disaster if he disregards these controls?

Man's extension of his kind over the earth as a nomad following his herds was according to the protein-producing capacities delineated by the reliable animal instincts. But man's extension of his kind under his own technologies pushed him away from the fertile soils that were guaranteeing proteins, protection, and reproduction of himself and his species. It pushed him on to the "fringe" soils in these respects, but at the hazard and necessity of using his technologies to reach back to, and keep connected with, those same fertile soils (or the sea) his life lines bringing him the protein foods and all that comes with them for supplementing his hazardous location. Those life lines may soon become tangled with lines of economics and politics. They may be shortened or cut off and such fringe soils supporting only mono-cultures of crops then demonstrate man's nutritional insecurity. They generate hungers apt to be interpreted in most any other way except that they are the result of a protein shortage going back to fertility shortages in the soil. Man is a social animal when well fed, but if put under starvation he even becomes cannibalistic, or gets his proteins at the price of murder.

When the pre-death struggle of the protein-starved man to save himself as an individual rises to the desperate height of cannibalism, is this not akin to the immediate pre-death struggle of the processes of our bodies manifested by increased rate of heart beat, increased blood pressure, and temperature rise as fever? If then a segment of the human species under protein-starvation makes a desperate survival effort in the form of increased reproduction when other efforts for that have appeared in vain, would this not seem to aggravate the hazards for survival all the more? Would not such a manifestation seem of more logical interpretation when considered mainly as the pre-death struggle by the species?

Naturally, there are possibilities for wide variances between our individual conceptual schemes for man's behavior under severe hunger. But when in his fundamental physiologies man is viewed as another animal, he can scarcely set himself outside of the natural forces which seem so completely in control. If the complete proteins determine body protection and reproduction of our animals; if the life forms just below man depend on plants for these essential foods still non-synthesizable by either science or industry, and if plant proteins are determined by the soil, then the soil fertility as it controls the animals in their reproductive potential would seem to be also the logical power in control of man's reproduction too.

CHAPTER 26

Our Teeth and Our Soils

THE KNOWLEDGE ABOUT the human body and its many functions has been accumulating seemingly very slowly. The additions to our information have awaited the coming of each new science and the contributions by them in their respective fields. Dentistry as well as the medical profession has been ready and quick to accept and use any new knowledge that might alleviate human suffering. In medicine, for example, one can list the major successive additions almost as separate sciences coming at the slow rate of about one per century. Anatomy was the beginning one making its debut in the sixteenth century. The seventeenth century brought us physiology; the eighteenth added pathology; and the nineteenth emphasized bacteriology, all these for our better health.

Very probably the twentieth century will be credited with the addition of the science of nutrition as a major contribution to the better life of our people. Better nutrition is leading us to think less about medicine as cures and less about fighting microbes with drugs. In a more positive way it is helping us to think more about helping the body defend itself by being well-fed and therefore healthy.

If we are to bring about good nutrition by means of good food, to build up a good defense for the body, that defense must be strong, not only against enemy invasions, as it can be against tuberculosis, but also against the degenerative diseases like the heart troubles, cancer, diabetes, etc. For such defense then of necessity, the science of the soil and its fertility, by which alone high quality foods can be provided, may well be an addition during the present century to our knowledge of the better functions and better health of our bodies. It is proposed therefore in this discussion to lead you to think about the health condition of only one part of our body, namely, our teeth as they are related to the fertility of our soils.

Some Basic Facts Involved

In dealing with the subject of soil fertility and its implications for our teeth, or for any other part of our anatomy and our physiology, it is essential that one establish certain facts and principles at the outset and then follow through as these seem to have causal connections with the phenomena under consideration.

The first fact that may well be considered is the observation that under moderate temperatures the increase in annual rainfall from zero to 60 inches, for example — as is the range in going across the United States from near the Coast Range eastward — gives first an increased weathering of the rocks. That change represents increased soil *construction.* Going east from zero rainfall means increasingly more productive soils until one reaches about the mid-continental area. Then with still more rainfall, there comes excessive soil development under the higher rainfall which means increased soil *destruction* in terms of soil fertility considered both in quantity and in quality.

The second important fact in connection with this climatic pattern of soil development is the observation that at the maximum of soil construction (and in the approach to it), which is near the 100th meridian of longitude, there is a wide ratio of the exchangeable calcium to the exchangeable potassium on the colloidal clay of the soil. There is a similar ratio of these two in the chemical composition of the crops and other vegetation grown thereon.

Then there is the third significant fact, namely that calcium is associated with the synthesis of proteins by plants, while potassium is associated with their synthesis of carbohydrates. The latter process, which is commonly spoken of as "photosynthesis", may well be considered a supra-soil performance. This classification is proper since photosynthesis is a compounding of carbon, hydrogen and oxygen — all weather-given elements taken from the air and water — into carbohydrates by sunshine energy. The process of synthesizing proteins is a biosynthetic process, that is, one by the life processes of the plant. It seems to be a case in which some of the carbohydrates serve as the raw materials out of which the proteins are made. This is brought about by combining with these carbohydrates some nitrogen, some phosphorus, and some sulfur, all coming from the soil. At the same time, some calcium, and possibly several other soil-borne nutrient elements are required, while more of the carbohydrates are consumed as energy materials for this conversion process.

The fourth significant truth that brings the soil fertility into control of the composition of our food, and therefore of our health, comes out of the facts (a) that in soils under construction by the limited climatic forces, or those with a wide calcium-potassium ratio, proteinaceous and mineral-rich crops and foods as well as carbonaceous ones are possible, and (b) that in soils under destruction by excessive climatic forces, or those with a narrow calcium-potassium ratio, protein production is not so common while production mainly of carbohydrates by the crops is almost universal.

Out of these climatic, pedologic, and physiological facts there comes the major principle of concern to the dentists, namely, we have in the regions of higher rainfall the excessive carbohydrates in Nature and therefore may expect them in the human diet. Where rainfall is high enough to encourage vegetation in abundance there we have a hindrance to sound teeth from Nature herself, because of too much carbohydrate, or conversely, insufficient proteins and minerals, a fact — all too familiar to those in the dental profession — that militates against sound teeth. We need then to realize these facts and consider them by remembering our geographic location and in our management of the soil with human nutrition in mind.

Excess of Carbohydrates is Natural

In considering soil fertility as it provokes excessive carbohydrates but deficiencies of proteins and minerals, we need only to look at the chemical composition of the human body in comparison with that of plants (Table 1). From these analytical data we can see that potassium is taken into the plants in largest amounts of all the mineral elements from the soil, while calcium and phosphorus are next in that order. In the human body, these same elements are the major three, but calcium is first, phosphorus second, and potassium third. Of amounts still higher than any of these in the human body is nitrogen. This is the key element distinguishing protein synthesized as amino acids from the elements only by plants. Plants offer us mainly carbohydrates with only small amounts of proteins. Plant composition, considered as our food, represents possible shortages of proteins, of calcium, of phosphorus, and of probably other essential elements. We, like other animals, are constantly

Table 1

Chemical Composition of the Human Body in Comparison with that of Plants and of Soils

Source	Elements*	Human Body % Weight	Vegetation % Dry Weight	Soil† % Dry Weight
Air and water	Oxygen	65.00	42.9 (2)*	47.3
	Carbon	18.00	44.3 (1)	.19
	Hydrogen	10.00	6.1 (3)	.22
Air and soil	Nitrogen	3.00	2.63 (4)	—
Soil	Calcium	1.50	.88 (6)	3.47
	Phosphorus	1.00	.34 (8)	0.30‡
	Potassium	.35	2.14 (5)	0.0075
	Sulfur	.25	.30 (10)	0.03
	Sodium	.15	.70 (7)	2.46
	Chlorine	.15	.70 (7)	.12
	Magnesium	.05	.31 (9)	2.46
	Iron	.004	.0251 (11)	.12
	Manganese	.0003	.01 (12)	2.46
	Iodine	.00004	.00004	.06
	Copper	Very small amount	.0011	2.24
	Zinc	Very small amount	.0041 (13)	4.50
	Fluorine	Very small amount	.0005	.08
	Aluminum	Very small amount		.10
	Boron	Very small amount		7.85
	Silicon		.004 (14)	27.74

* Order of magnitude.
† Collected from various sources.
‡ % readily exchangeable in soils.

in danger of deficiencies of proteins and minerals, especially as we are more vegetarian. By the very nature of the creative processes that start with the soil, carbohydrates are plentiful while there are deficiencies of minerals and proteins. Man is therefore always faced with the shortages of minerals and proteins relative to the carbohydrates and fats. It is this nutritional need that encourages his carnivorousness and his use of animal products such as eggs and milk.

Excessive Carbohydrates are Invoked by our Fertility Pattern

That these shortages of minerals and proteins vary according to the pattern of soil fertility is demonstrated very clearly by the soils of the United States. The lower rainfalls of the western half of our country (the area of sparse population) have not removed the calcium and the other nutrient cations from the surface soil. These lime-laden, mineral-rich areas have been the prairie soils. It is on these that the legumes as protein-rich, mineral-providing forages flourish widely and profusely. It is these soils that were feeding buffaloes in the early days by their grass

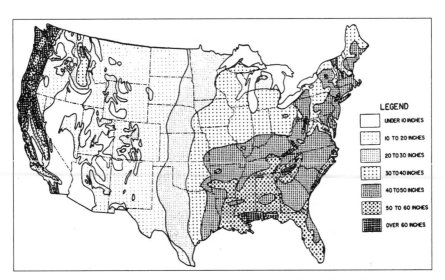

Fig. 1. The higher rainfalls in the eastern United States have leached the minerals from the soils, hence forests in early days and carbohydrate-producing crops today more than protein-rich and mineral-rich products grow there. Distribution of mean annual precipitation in the United States.

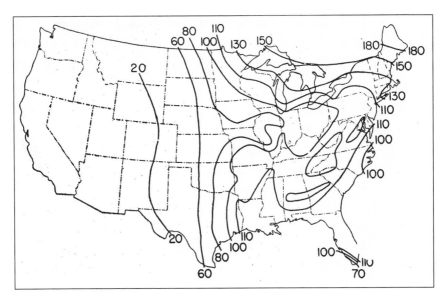

Fig. 2. The lines of constant ratios of rainfall to evaporation (times 100) give pattern to the fertility of the soils. They tell us, for example, that the Cornbelt soils are similar to those farther west under less leaching. They are, therefore, still well supplied with minerals. (According to Professor Transeau, Columbus, Ohio.)

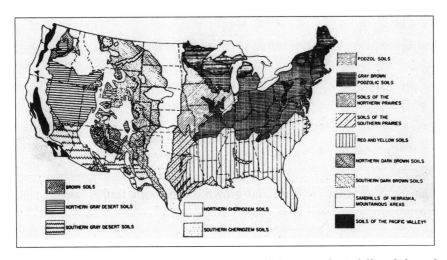

Fig. 3. The soil map shows itself a composite of the map of rainfall and that of rainfall-evaporation ratios. It is the soils that give us an East and a West, and divide the East into a North and a South. Climatic and vegetational soil groups in the United States. (After Marbut, 1935)

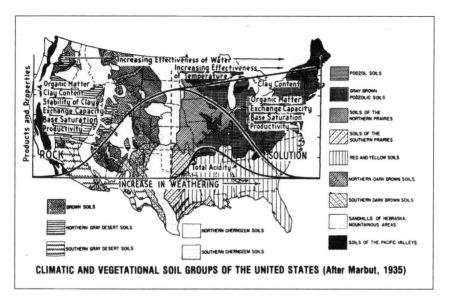

Fig. 4. The pattern of soil development of the United States shows the maximum of soil construction in the mid-continental area. It is on the soils there that maximum of protein and mineral delivery by crops is possible as good feed and food. Climatic and vegetational soil groups of the United States. (After Marbut, 1935).

without purchased protein supplements. It is these soils that are giving us protein products in beef and lamb today.

When one looks at the eastern half of the United States (the area of dense population) this part of our country with its higher rainfalls has soils leached so highly that most of the calcium has gone from these to the sea. In fact, that loss of calcium has made us classify them as "acid soils", as though the acidity rather than the shortage of fertility were responsible for their failure to grow protein-rich legumes. They were originally growing only wood as forests. When cleared of these they have been growing starchy crops. It is on these eastern soils that we fatten the cattle that are born and grown on the soils farther west. These eastern soils can still grow hogs whose carcasses are mainly fat. Such soils if given fertility treatments can produce proteins by reproducing and growing the animals themselves but usually only with much help by attending veterinarians. Eastern United States is the area of increasing troubles with our dairy cattle, such as what is called "brucellosis" when affecting the cows and "undulant fever" when a disease of the human.

Fig. 5. "To be well fed is to be healthy" in the case of plants as well as humans. More clay, though acid, put into the sand (from left to right) made healthier plants.

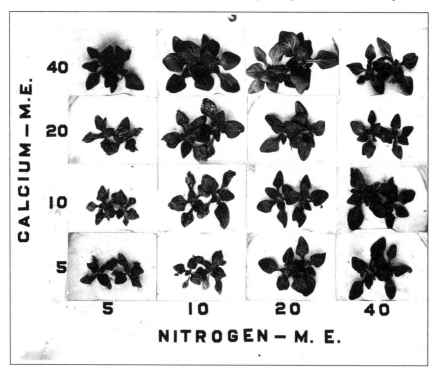

Fig. 6. Spinach fertilized with more nitrogen and calcium, to make it more proteinaceous (right two rows) was protected against the attack by the thrips insects, while that less rich in proteins (left two rows) was not.

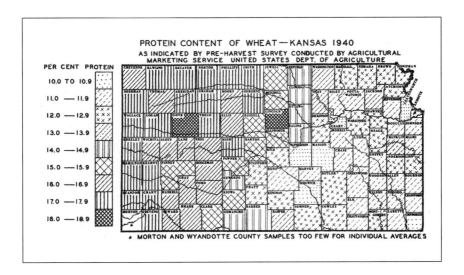

Fig. 7. The protein concentration in wheat of Kansas increased from ten to eighteen percent in going from the Eastern part of the state with 37 inches of rainfall to the Western part with only 17 inches. Plants can manufacture proteins only as the fertility of the soil permits. Protein content of Wheat — Kansas 1940. As indicated by pre-harvest survey conducted by agricultural marketing service, United States Department of Agriculture.

Both of these diseases are still baffling to the diagnostic efforts aiming to locate their fundamental cause. If the Creator himself was making only such carbonaceous products as forests on those soils shall we not believe that such products must represent about the limits of our possibilities when we take over and grow crops on them without adding fertility to the soil?

Soil Exhaustion Spells Deficiencies of Proteins and Minerals but Excess of Carbohydrates

Soils naturally highly weathered are no longer well stocked with nutrient mineral reserves in their sand and silt fractions, nor with mineral fertility adsorbed on the clay. Such soils must of necessity give crops and foods which are mainly carbohydrates and are therefore deficient in proteins and

Fig. 8. Wildlife struggles desperately to get its calcium and phosphorus as shown by this porcupine consuming the antlers in the northern woods.

minerals. But quite the opposite, the less weathered soils under low annual rainfalls are mineral-rich in the silt and sand reserves, and on the clay. Hence they give both proteins and minerals along with the carbohydrates in the plants grown on them.

In these facts we have the suggestion that any soil undergoing exhaustion of its fertility, whether by Nature or by man, is bringing about a change in the chemical composition of any plant species growing on it. This change means that the plant species become more carbonaceous, less proteinaceous, and less mineral-rich. These changes occur within any single plant species, too commonly believed constant in its chemical composition regardless of the soil growing it.

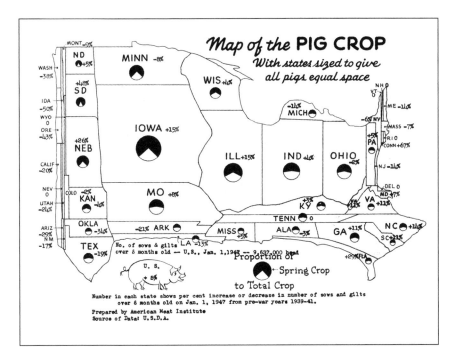

Fig. 9. The eastern states produce carbohydrates more than proteins to make our animals those with more fat rather than protein. Number in each, state shows percent increase or decrease in number of sows and gilts over 6 months old on Jan 1, 1947, from pre-War years 1939-41. Prepared by American Meat Institute. Source of Data: USDA.

Surveys and Experiments Demonstrate the Facts

That we may well take cognizance of this as a principle, has been demonstrated by the study of the chemical composition of the many crops and other plants as they are native to soils that are (a) slightly, (b) moderately, and (c) highly developed under increasing rainfall and temperature. While some thirty plant species, common on the *slightly* developed soils, contained enough calcium, phosphorus and potassium in total to make up almost five percent of their dry weight, this figure dropped to four percent in going to a similar number of plants native to *moderately* developed soils. Then it dropped to less than two percent in going to plants natural to *highly*

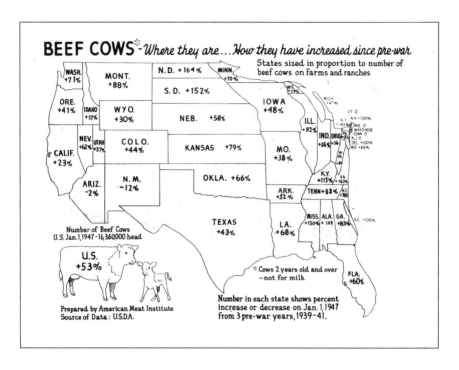

Fig. 10. The western states produce mineral-rich, proteinaceous forages to make our animals those with protein more than fat.

developed soils. As the soils are more highly developed then, or farmed under higher rainfall and temperature, they can provide us, through the plants on them, less and less of these minerals essential for bone growth and less of those associated with synthesis of proteins by the plants.

Experiments by Dr. E. R. Graham at the Missouri Agricultural Experiment Station have demonstrated how less calcareous soils make less of proteins and more of carbohydrates; or that the changing calcium-potassium ratio of higher development of the soil brings corresponding decreases in the protein and mineral contents of the same kind of vegetation. He grew soybeans on soils with (1) a wide, (2) a medium, and (3) a narrow ratio of the calcium to the potassium. He reproduced the conditions of soils under increasing weathering or under increased experience with rainfall and temperature. These three soils represented increasing encouragement for the plants to produce carbohydrates more than to synthesize proteins.

This narrowing ratio of the calcium to the potassium resulted in an increase of vegetative bulk by one-fourth. Such an increased tonnage

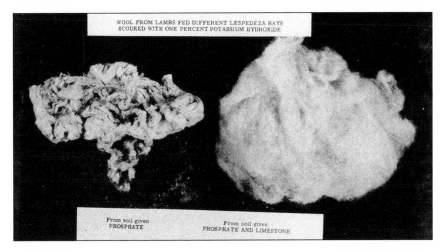

Fig. 11. Animal products, more than the animal body or the plants, reflect soil deficiencies. The wool on the left, which could not be carded, was grown by sheep fed lespedeza fertilized by phosphate only. The wool on the right, which carded nicely, was from sheep fed similar hay grown on soil given both lime and phosphate.

would warrant agronomic applause. But this increase in vegetative mass represented a reduction in the concentration of protein by one-fourth, a reduction in the concentration of phosphorus by one-half and a reduction in the concentration of calcium by two-thirds of that in the smaller tonnage yield.

By modifying the relative amounts of calcium and potassium in the soil much as they are modified under increasing weathering of the soil, the physiology of the plant was shifted to the production of less protein and to the production of more carbohydrates. Higher soil development and more rainfall and temperature, then, bring less protein production by any crop and therefore less proteins and minerals in our feeds and our foods.

Concentration of Protein in Our Food Crops is Being Lowered by Soil Exhaustion

As our soils are being exhausted of their fertility by cropping under the intense economic pressure now being put on them, a single grain crop like wheat is producing itself of less protein and of more starch as time goes on. We say "wheat is becoming soft where once it was hard". In our near-colonial days we produced hard wheat in the valley of the Geneseo River of New York. That wheatbasket, or breadbasket of this country at that time, made Rochester the "Flour City".

Today Rochester is still the "Flower City" with its many parks. But the "hard" wheat has moved westward across the United States, while the "soft," starchy wheat — which we seemingly desire for our pastries — is crowding along in its wake. "Soft" wheat has now gone so far west that even in Kansas the millers and bakers are complaining about its low protein content and their low volume of bread output per unit of flour used. The farmers of Kansas, however, are delighted with their high volumes of output as bushels per acre that are possible when the plants collect only carbohydrates instead of converting these into protein of much less bulk as plant output.

Corn, too, is doing less in its synthesis of proteins. While we have pushed up the volume of its output as bushels per acre by hybrid vigor, we have not realized that the concentration of protein in our corn grain was dropping from a mean figure of about 9.5 percent to only 8.5 percent during the last ten years.

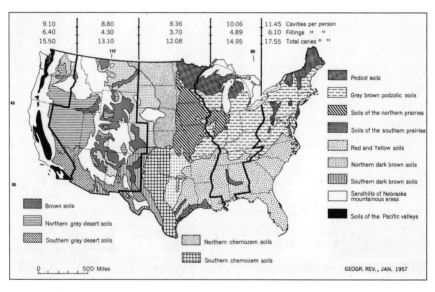

Fig. 12. The concentration of dental caries gives a reciprocal curve of that for soil development under the climatic forces. The minimum of caries are in the midcontinental area of maximum soil construction. They increase in going westward from there to soils less developed, and more so in going eastward to soils more highly developed.

Forage crops, as well as grain crops, have been going to lower concentrations in minerals and proteins. They have been going lower in giving us what may be called the "grow" foods but have been holding up in supplying for us what may be called the "go" foods, namely carbohydrates. But while this is happening there is greater deception by the crop of which only vegetative mass is of concern or is measured, than when the harvest taken is the seed or the plant's efforts for its own reproduction and continuance of the species. As we harvest vegetative bulk we fail to note the low delivery of protein which reports itself as lowered grain yield more noticedly than as less vegetative bulk.

As we mine the soils of their fertility so that the output by one crop as bulk goes down, we search the world and bring in some exotic crop because it can make tons or bushels where the preceding crop failed. If this imported crop makes vegetative tons where the others failed, it must be putting out it products with less of soil fertility in them and therefore they must be more carbonaceous and probably of deceptive nutritional values.

As a consequence of the lowered protein concentration in grains and grasses under soil fertility depletion, we have not only had the westward

Fig. 13. Human health goes with the soil and its fertility. Courtesy F.S.A. Scene from Wadesboro, N. C.

march of "hard" wheat, and the clamor for more "grass" agriculture, but also a westward march of our protein in beef and lamb. Chicago is no longer the major beef cattle market.

That honor now rests on Kansas City. Even the hog market, a trader mainly in fat products, has moved to central United States when it once was farther east. These movements have been under the force of a declining soil fertility and are not merely the result of man's wanderlust or his nomadic nature.

Here, then, in the soil fertility is the pattern of the nutritional values of our foods and feeds pointing out their lowered concentrations of minerals and proteins. Here is the lowered power of growth and lowered capacity for reproduction. Life is not passed from one fat globule to another, nor from one starch grain to another, but only from one protein to another protein molecule. Can a dentist see good permanent teeth being laid down in the jawbone of a foetus when the mother's diet is deficient in minerals and protein? Can he find sound teeth in school children when carbohydrate bulk predominates in their diet because of its lesser cost and easier storage than that of milk and meat? Is it any wonder that we were startled when COLLIERS told us of "The Town Without a Toothache" located in the region of lower rainfall?

Geography of Dental Defects in the United States and the Pattern of Soil Fertility

That Hereford, Texas, is in the part of the United States of highly fertile soils is not so startling when the geography of dental defects on a larger scale is considered. The recent physical examinations of the millions of men taken into the Army and the Navy give a wealth of data in relation to the many possible factors in control of our health and of the condition of our teeth. These data may well be correlated with the fertility of the soil for their suggestive value in listing many of our health troubles as possible deficiencies originating in the soil. In these data and records there is an opportunity to relate the caries of the teeth to the soils of the United States according to their pattern of fertility, or to their degree of development by the climatic forces.

Very recently Comdr. C. A. Schlack and Lt. Birren of the Navy Medical Research[*][1] Institute presented some data by regions of the United States which represented the condition of the teeth of 69,584 men coming on

---

* C. A. Schlack and J. E. Birren. Influences on Dental Defects in Navy Personnel. Science 104:259–262, 1946.

active duty in the Navy in 1941–42. These represented 93 percent of a lot from which 7 percent had already been eliminated for dental reasons. This screening reduced the regional differences, but even in spite of this, those regional differences show a decidedly interesting relation to the development of the soil.

From the report of these naval officers, one is almost astounded at the poor dental condition in this sample of our people. It is especially serious when these naval inductees represented the mean, youthful age of 24 years with 82 percent of them below the age of 30 years. For the group as a whole the report reads as follows: "The mean number of simple and compound cavities was found to be about ten per person ... and five fillings per person." "Few teeth required extraction, despite the large number of carious teeth, the mean number per person being about 0.2. In contrast, the mean number of missing teeth was 4.7 at the time of the examination."

This is a sad commentary on the dental condition of our young men when the statistics list them for an average of 15 carious areas each, in spite of the regular encouragement by the radio to use the tooth brush daily and to "see your dentist twice a year." But when the chemical composition of our teeth tells us that they consist mainly of calcium phosphate, and when the foremost fertilizer treatments needed to grow even carbonaceous vegetation on our soils are lime (calcium) and superphosphate (phosphorus), there is good reason that the poor dental condition of these naval inductees should be connected with the low fertility of these soils. When soils need lime and phosphate to grow agricultural vegetation much more will they need these fertilizer additions of calcium and phosphorus in order to pass these nutrient elements on to the animals and the humans in the chain of decreasing chances to get these soil-borne requisites for good sound teeth.

By recalculating the dental data of these naval inductees so as to make them represent more nearly the soil areas according to increasing degrees of soil development in going from the arid West to the humid East, the correlation is very striking. It is highly significant that the lowest numbers of carious teeth are in the longitudinal belt of dual-state width just west of the Mississippi River. Hereford, Texas, is included in this belt. As one goes either westward or eastward from this belt to other similar belts, the tooth troubles increase. This increase, however, is much larger in going eastward, that is, to the excessively developed soils under higher rainfall and temperatures, than it is in going westward to the underdeveloped soils.

Here is a clear indication that those soils with a high capacity for protein production, because of their high mineral fertility, are the soils that have also grown better teeth. These are the soils of the open prairies.

Quite differently, however, those soils that have a low capacity for producing legumes, beef, and mutton and have been growing starchy grains and fattening the livestock, have a much higher number of carious teeth per person. These are the soils of the forested areas or the potential producers of mainly fuel foods.

The maximum number of caries was exhibited by the men from the New England States where the cavities amounted to 13.5 accompanied by 7.8 fillings per person or a total of 21.3 carious areas per mouth. With such numbers of defects it seems a pity that we can't have more than 32 adult teeth. In the Middle Atlantic States just south of New England, the total figure was 19.6. Still farther south the corresponding value was 13.4 of which 9.7 were cavities and 3.7 were fillings.

In this case of the soil and teeth as one goes south from New England there are three factors that may help explain the decrease in caries. There is first, a decreasing ratio of rainfall to evaporation and therefore less relative leaching of the soil; second, there is less acidity to break down the mineral reserves because of the nature of the clay; and third, in the South there is the more general use of fertilizers consisting mainly of carriers of calcium and phosphorus.

In these regional data there are the suggestions that the curve of the condition of the teeth is the reciprocal curve of the fertility of the soil. We may expect also, from these relations, that the pattern of soil fertility is in control not only of the health of the teeth, but also of health in general. This is strongly suggested by a careful study, reported by Dr. L. M. Hepple of the University of Missouri, of the more than 80 thousand draftee rejections from more than 310 thousand selectees for the Army from Missouri alone. He points out, for example, that Kansas had lower rejection rates than Missouri. This is another way of telling us that the health troubles increase in going from the calcareous soils of Kansas to the lime-deficient soils of Missouri.

Equally as interesting in terms of the increase in draftee rejections as the soils are less fertile, are his data in going across Missouri from the northwest to the southeast, which means going from the legume and cattle area to that of cotton. His series of figures for draftee rejections in making that traverse of the state was 208, 247, 280, 339, and 368 per thousand selectees. Even for an area so limited as Missouri, the health condition in terms of Army standards reflects the pattern of the fertility of the soil.

From all of the data of the inductees into the Army and the Navy there is the suggestion that more of our so-called "diseases" may well be statistically mapped for the United States and compared with the map of the soil fertility. If all other body irregularities as well as those of the teeth were so viewed, it is highly probable that many of our diseases would be interpreted as degenerative troubles originating in nutritional deficiencies going back to insufficient fertility of, the soil. Surely the millions of health records of the inductees into our national defense will not be left lying idle in Federal archives when they can be sorted out as specific diseases, plotted as densities over the soil fertility pattern, and possibly give suggestions for combating the failing health that rests on the great fact that degeneration of the human body goes with the exploitation of the soil.

If the decay of teeth is linked with the declining fertility of the soil, this concept of tooth troubles may well be a pattern to guide our thinking about other health troubles, not as calls for drugs and medicines, but for conservation in terms of a new motive, namely better health via better nutrition from the ground up.

CHAPTER 27

Soils in Relation
to Human Nutrition

NATIONAL CONSCIOUSNESS HAS recently become aware of the great losses from soil erosion. We have also come to give more than passive attention to malnutrition on a national scale. Not yet, however, have we recognized soil fertility as the food-producing source that reveals national and international patterns of weakness or strength. Soil fertility, in the last analysis, must not only be mobilized to win wars, but must also be preserved as the standing army opposing starvation for the maintenance of peace.

What is soil fertility? In simple words, it is some dozen chemical elements in mineral and rock combinations that are slowly broken out of the earth's crust and hustled off to the sea. Enjoying a temporary rest stop enroute, they become part of the soil and serve their essential roles in nourishing all the different life forms. They are the soil's contribution — from a large mass of organic essentials — to the germinating seeds which empower the growing plants to use sunshine energy in the synthesis of atmospheric elements and rainfall into a wide variety of plant food. The atmospheric and rainfall elements are carbon, hydrogen, and nitrogen, so common everywhere.

Soil minerals constitute the 5% that is plant ash. It is this small handful of dust that also makes up the corresponding percentage in the human body. Yet it is the controlling force that determines whether Nature shall construct plant foods of only fuel and fattening values, or of body service in growth and reproduction. Because soil minerals make up only 5% of our bodies, we are not generally aware of the fact that they dictate the fabrication of the other 95% into something more than mere fuel.

We are in the habit of speaking about vegetation by names of crop species and tonnage yields per acre. We do not yet consider plants for their chemical composition and nutritive value according to the fertility in the soil producing them. This failure has left us in confusion about crops and has put plant varieties into competition with, rather than in support of, one another. Now that the subject of nutrition is on most every tongue, we are about ready for the report that vegetation as a creator of essential food products is limited by soil fertility.

Protein rich vegetation, and its synthesis by many unknowns which also help to remove hidden hungers and encourage fecundity of both man and animal, are common in the prairie regions marked by moderate rainfalls. It is the soil fertility, rather than the low rainfall, that gives the midwest, or those areas bordering along approximately the 97th meridian, these distinctions:

(a) Its selection by the bison in thundering herds for the "buffalo grass."
(b) Its wheat which, taken as a whole rather than as refined flour, is truly the "staff of life."
(c) Animals on its range nourish themselves so well that they reproduce regularly.
(d) The greater number of more able-bodied selectees for military service, of whom 7 out of 10 were chosen in Colorado in contrast to 7 rejected out of 10 in one of the southern states.

Carbon rich vegetation abounds in the high temperature, heavy rainfall regions of eastern and southern United States, as the forests, the cotton plants, and the sugarcane testify. These soils have been leached of much fertility, and plants must draw heavily upon air, water and sunlight rather than the soil for their materials. Annual production as tonnage per acre is large in contrast to the lower yields of the western prairies, but the fuel and fattening values are more prominent than the aids to growth and reproduction.

Life behavior is more closely linked with soils as the basis of nutrition than is commonly recognized. The depletion of soil calcium thru leaching and cropping, and the almost universal deficiency of soil phosphorus, directly affect animals, since bones are the chief body depositories for these two elements. In forests, the annual drop of leaves and their decay are a prime necessity for tree mainetnance. Is it any wonder then that animals struggle so desperately to find the necessary calcium and phosphorus to make their bones?

Antlers are quickly consumed by the porcupine, pregnant squirrels, and other animals living on the highly weathered, or rocky, forest soils.

Deer in their browse will select trees that have been given fertilizers in preference to those untreated. Pine tree seedlings along the highway transplanted from fertilized nursery soils are taken by deer when the same tree species in the adjoining forests go untouched. Wild animals truly "know their medicines" when they take plants on particular levels of soil fertility.

The distribution of wild animals, the present distribution of domestic animals, and the concentrations of animal diseases, can be visualized as symptoms of the soil fertility pattern as it furnishes nutrition. It is on the lime-rich, unleached, semi-humid soils that animals reproduce well. It is there that the disease rate is lower and some diseases are rare. There beef cattle are multiplied and grown to be shipped to the humid soils for fattening. Similar cattle shipments from one fertility level to another are common in the Argentine.

The influence of added fertilizers shows itself markedly in the entire physiology of the aniaml. Tests on sheep reveal differences not only in the weight and quality of the wool, but in the bones, and more pronouncedly, in semen production and reproduction in general. Rabbit bones vary widely in breaking strength, density, thickness, hardness and other qualities, as well as mass and volume. Male rabbits used for artificial insemination become sterile after a few weeks when fed on lespedeza hay grown without soil treatment, while those eating hay from limed soil remain fertile. We now have conclusive evidence that the physiology of an animal, seemingly far removed from any slight change in soil conditions, faithfully registers the fertility or sterility of the soil.

The instincts of animals are compelling us to recognize soil differences. Not only do the dumb beasts select herbages according to their carbon or protein content, but they select from the same kind of grain the offerings according to the different fertilizers with which the soil was treated. Hogs select corn grains from separate feeder compartments with disregard of different hybrids, but with particular and consistent choice of soil treatments. Rats indicate their discrimination by cutting into the bags of corn chosen by the hogs, and leave uncut those bags not taken by the hogs. Surely the animal appetite that detects soil fertility so correctly can be of service in guiding animal production more wisely by means of soil treatments.

The pattern of distribution of human beings and their diseases can be evaluated nationally on a statistical basis as readily as crops of wheat or livestock, but these are not yet seen in terms of the soil fertility. Man's nomadic nature has made him too cosmopolitan for his physique, health, facial features, and mental attitudes to be labeled by the particular soil that nourished him. Our collection of foods from far-flung sources also handicaps our ready correlation of our level of nutrition with the fertility of the soil. In addition, we have finally come to believe that food processing and refinement are denying us some essentials. We have not yet, however, come to appreciate the role that soil fertility plays in determining the nutritive quality of foods, and thereby our bodies, and our minds. Quantity rather than hidden quality is still the measure.

Since any civilization rests on its resources rather than on its institutions, changes in the institutions cannot be made in disregard of so basic a resource as the soil. Researchers in soil science, plant physiology, ecology, human nutrition, and other sciences have given but a few years of their efforts to human welfare. It is to be hoped that our national consciousness can be made aware of a dangerously declining soil fertility, and that we will call on our sciences and industries to rebuild and conserve our soils as the surest guarantee of the future health and strength of the nation.

CHAPTER 28

Soil Fertility in Relation to Animal and Human Health

GOOD HEALTH SEEMS to be the one thing all of us desire most. That conclusion follows from the simple observation that when we meet our universal salutation or greeting, is the inquiry, "How do you do?" This expresses our concern first about our health. Perhaps that results from the fact that good health is yet not clearly defined; that the only health we know is, perhaps, a poor one; and that we are all hopefully anticipating the discovery of one that is better, at least in some measure.

Attention has long been going to the lack of health. Professions profiting by that kind of human misery — and the fear of more of it — have built lucrative employment for many. This view of the problem in the negative aspect has too long disregarded the time-worn adage which tells us in the positive that "To be well-fed is to be healthy." Our failure to know how to feed ourselves well — and also our animals — has denied us and them better healths. Perhaps we have been over-fed. Thereby "one third of what we eat supports our bodies, and two thirds of it our doctors." Conversely, perhaps we have been under-fed, when we are told that vitamins are something that will kill us if we don't eat them. More significantly, however, for your consideration under the title listed herewith, is the concept that to be well fed and healthy is a matter of having us consider our foods carefully, not only as to kind or name, but more specifically in their relation to the complete soil fertility by which they, or their contents, were grown. Late research is pointing to the significance of the soil in nutrition.

This is the approach to health from its positive aspect. It is the belief that we need to consider good health as a by-product of good eating under the guidance of knowledge of the physiology of the plants, animals, and humans concerned. It is not a case of calling in pathology, and surgical mechanics, to get names and attempts to explain — or relieve and remove — where physiology is unknown. Instead it is an attempt to undergird the physiology of good health and not a fight with disease.

Foods and Feeds May Fill, but Not Necessarily Nourish

In connection with the production of milk and meat by our farm animals, the economics of the procedure have too often had first consideration. Feeding trials, reported in the many printed volumes, are given to one objective, viz., making cheap gains or cheap gallons. When fats, as fuel foods, either on the carcass or in the pail, are the major objective, it is not unexpectable that calories as measures of heat should have long been the major criterion of nutritional effort. Naturally for a fuel objective, fuel foods, that is, the carbohydrates, would take major concern. Consequently, the carbohydrates have been at the head of the foods list. In that thought pattern the building of the body was taken for granted and only fuel for it was sought. Proteins have been second on the list. Minerals have had attention as the *inorganic* elements. This kept them as a part of the ash rather than of the *organic* compounds which contained them or the synthesis of which they prompted. Proteins and the mineral elements have not been commonly considered together in their close association. The proteins have been considered only as "crude" proteins. They have been classified as those compounds containing nitrogen in total to the extent of about 16 percent. It is in this lack of complete understanding of the protein compounds, of their functions in our bodies, and of the services by the inorganic elements connected with them that much of the irregularity in being well fed arises. Under no fuller knowledge than this, feeding becomes mainly a matter filling with food in general, rather than a matter of nutrition with specificity of function and purpose, of what is consumed.

When animal gains, consisting mainly of more fat and possibly of more water, represent possible sale at higher price — and then usually of a castrated male — we are apt to lose sight of the health involved. Does a fattened, show animal suggest buoyant health? Doesn't it suggest the very absence of it? Feeding operations on such a score and purpose ought not be classified as animal production. Rather, they seem to be a case of mere speculation in a culinary excuse for buying low and selling high. Health would scarcely be an expected associate when the feeding performance suggests its necessity to limit the life span of the animal to that of baby beef and of the barrows in the ton-litters, before the animals breakdown in health disaster under such treatment. One must naturally raise the question whether animal feeding under no more critical criterion than that provided by an ordinary scale is apt to bring good health, or whether it must be bad health. Feeding to encourage the building of muscle, to guarantee fecund reproduction and to protect from the invasion of the microbes calls for a more searching criterion. It calls also for foods and feeds that are more than mere bulk for filling purposes. It demands the appreciation of some physiology, and some comprehension of body functions. It transcends the matters of economics resting on no more than simple arithmetic.

Declining Fertility Goes Unrecognized When Quantity Rather than Quality Rules

That the supplies of essential nutrient elements in the soil supporting all life have been declining has not yet been widely comprehended. The dwindling supply of creative power has encouraged us to search for crop substitutes as soon as a tried and true crop indicated its decrease in yield of bulk or bushels per acre. Rather than rebuild the fertility of the soil to nourish the tried crop, we have searched the corners of the world for another crop to take its place. By this procedure we have introduced more and more of the crops that are making mainly vegetative bulk and are producing less of real nourishment for animals. They have been said to be "hay crops but not seed crops." While juggling the new crops into the farming scheme the nutritional quality as protein, the inorganic essentials, the vitamins, and other necessary compounds of high value as feed for good health, have been juggled out. Carbohydrates, composed mainly of air, water, and sunshine, are amply produced for fattening services, but proteins are becoming scarcer in the feeds to bring about increasing troubles in the health and reproduction of the animals consuming them. Crops that create the proteins are considered "hard to grow." The cost of the extra fertility for the soil to nourish them so they can create the needed helps for better nutrition is sidestepped. A big crop yield but less of protein in it is thereby produced. While failing to see the declining fertility of the soil responsible for less milk, less meat, and poorer reproduction, we are calling for more artificial insemination and other procedures looking more toward improved breeding than toward improved feeding as the possible help.

While one generation of us is a sufficient time period to exhaust the fertility of a farm, it is, in most cases, not long enough to convince the owner of a farm of what has happened. Having never figured the cost of maintaining the fertility of the soil, he is not apt to appreciate the great fact that agricultural products have always been priced under the assumption that what the soil contributed is not a part of the cost of their production.

Depreciation of the soil is not recognized in terms of the income tax question. Only the buildings and the fences are considered as depreciable. Our ignorance of the soil fertility as a mineral delivery source still leaves this basic substance as of no value and of no cost in agricultural production in the minds of those directing internal revenue procedures. Yet oil wells, coal mines, quarries, and similar resources may be depreciated as much as 15-25 percent per year. Minerals are not minerals for all that, apparently, unless the political aspect of lobby pressure rather than common sense so classifies them. Can there be any other result from exploited soils, abandoned farms, and poor quality in our foods than the invitation to bad health in our animals and ourselves when all the qualities determined by fertile soils are so completely forgotten?

Animal Instincts Go Unheeded; the Plow Precedes the Cow

One needs only to look at the beef map or the pork map of the United States to see that the beef cow has gone west to the soils which the buffalo mapped out for his choice in making bone and brawn, but not necessarily in making fat. Beef cows range, and choose their grazing from soils that make the high protein wheat and the nutritious grass. The beef cattle *grow out West. We fatten* them *in the East.* The buffalo that chose that same soil area called for no imported protein supplements, no veterinarian, and no midwifery helps during parturation. He did not populate our East where the dairy cow in close company with the congested human population is expected to serve as foster mother for that crowd.

The buffalo went ahead of the plow to choose the soil under the feed, rather than worry over the particular plant species, or the pedigree of some supposedly choice variety of recently imported forage. The poor dairy cow has no chance to exercise her unique instincts for selecting the forage of higher nutritional values according to the better soils growing it. It was the plow that took her where she is. The fences confine her and so do the stanchions and the feed mixtures until she is little more than a machine for consumption of certain alloted daily amounts of feed according to calculated compulsory delivery of gallons of liquid and pounds of fat. The protein content of the milk, of major value after the reproductive process that gives occasion for it, has been almost completely disregarded and aborted in considering the real values of milk. Seasonal variations in the quantity and the quality of the milk proteins draw little, if any concern. This creative service the cow intends for her calf has not been guarded for the corresponding high value to the cow's foster children.

Isn't this protein problem possibly a part of the picture when the cow breaks through the fence, or when she searches out certain plants in the pasture and eats them shorter while she lets others grow taller? Are not her instincts given to guiding her to produce proteins too and not just fats? When once we think more about milk proteins for healthy boys and girls, as well as calves, rather than just bottles of milk and pounds of fat for sale, we shall be compelled to think of the complete soil fertility required under the cow in making the former rather than just rainfall and sunshine above her giving us the latter. Apparently only some necessity compelling us to think, some threat of disaster, or some disaster itself, will make us appreciate our natural resource, the soil, which we have too long taken for granted.

Soil Fertility Pattern Under Patterns of Animal Distribution Suggests Better Health via More and Better Proteins

With milk proteins, meat proteins, and vegetable proteins now coming into national concern because some few folks are reminding us that our natural resources producing them are dwindling, we may well center our thinking on just this one food requirement, namely our national needs for proteins and the provision of them. When these requisites in our foods are not created, but are assembled, by our animals only as the plants which they eat have synthesized them from the elements of soil fertility, we may well see that the fertility supplies in the soil mark our possible protein supplies of our country.

A look at the soil fertility map of the United States according to the climatic forces that give increasing soil construction on coming out of our arid West to the Midcontinent, and then increasing soil destruction in terms of protein potential on going from there to the East and the Southeast, helps us realize that our soil resources are already so low as to make the shortage of proteins our major national problem. While there are cries for, and hopes in, a grass agriculture which is being propagandized so glibly for cover of the soil against its loss by erosion, a few folks are reminding us that one does not get a grass agriculture by mail order and spread it over the farm. It must be grown on the soil it covers. Even then, it must be more than cover. It must be nutrition for our animals to pay its own costs. For that contribution, it must be a balanced ration for them. It can be that only as the soil fertility is a properly balanced nutrition for the grass, a creation of complete proteins rather than merely bales of bulk.

The rainfall in totals per year, balanced against evaporation in the West and against leaching in the East, gives soils in the West that are under-developed and soils in the East that are overdeveloped for protein produc-tion. In the West, there is excess of the alkalis and alkaline earths, or an excess of soil neutrality in terms of simple chemistry. In reality, it is a defi-ciency both in soil acidity and in soil fertility in terms of plant and animal physiology. In the East there is an excess of soil acidity in terms of simple chemistry, but a deficiency of soil fertility in terms of those physiologies.

The crop pattern superimposed on that of soil fertility tells us that the Creator himself was making only wood on the eastern half of the United States. Even for no more than the growth of the starchy grain of corn, the American Indian in New England was compelled to fertilize the corn plant with some fish protein, as the Pilgrim fathers observed but failed to appreciate fully. Grass, and not forests, prevailed under the Creator's agri-cultural management in the Midcontinent and the West where the Buffalo roamed. High-protein, or "hard," horny, wheat grew recently on those for-mer "grassy" plains. Credit for the high protein in wheat is still given to the pedigree or to the particular wheat variety, because we have not looked deeply enough into plant physiology to see the soil fertility responsible for it. Now that most of the Kansas soils have given us bumper wheat crops to exhaust the fertility, especially the nitrogen, to the point of making "soft" or low-protein grain, we are gradually coming to see that the fertility of the soil was in control of the protein that made quality for nutrition more than quantity for sale. Now that the fertility is gone, we really appreciate what we once had.

Unfortunately it is on to just such soils where denser human popula-tions are now expecting to bring the dairy cow and a diversified agricul-ture. Where intense crop specialization prevails, it is usually the limiting fertility that brings on such prevalence.

From those areas of single crop agriculture there are commonly numerous life lines reaching out to other areas of higher fertility levels, especially to those producing proteins. From the Midcontinent, its soil fertility for protein production, and its livestock markets, numerous life lines run in all directions. From the area of crop specialization known for its cotton farming in the South, one can see the life lines reaching to the Midcontinent when the menus of the hotels down there announce K. C. Steaks, and point back to the beef center of the United States that was once much farther East.

As we mined our virgin soil fertility, we moved on West. The beef cow with her limited output of milk went ahead of the plow. The dairy cow, which is managed under more mechanical operations of herself and her larger milk output, is trailing along behind the plow. Instead of her instincts guiding us to better soils as she assays them for protein production and delivery of high nutrition, or as she would outline for us the soil fertility pattern for that high food value, we have put the plow and other machinery ahead to enslave her physiologically while the significance of that soil fertility pattern in terms of proper soil management for protein production for her and for ourselves has not yet been appreciated.

Gadgets Measured Increasing Soil Acidity but Missed its Reciprocal, the Declining Soil Fertility

Legume plants have long been the cow's choice among forages. Most students of animal nutrition and health have been ready to believe that the higher concentrations of proteins and inorganic elements in these nitrogen-fixing feeds have been responsible. These crops have always been the feed desired by both the cow and her owner. But with the cow on the highly weathered soils, from which virgin forests were cleared, we discovered that the better legume crops failed to grow there except as the soil fertility was given uplift. With the advent of laboratory gadgets measuring the degree of acidity of the soil, it was soon observed that the increasing degree of soil acidity in Nature was associated with more trouble in growing these highly desired forages. Consequently the erroneous conclusion was drawn that acidity of the soil is bad, since it seemingly prohibits many protein-producing crops from growing.

Had we studied the physiology of the plant with emphasis on its biochemistry in place of learning no more soil chemistry than that required to send us out to propagandize laboratory gadgets, we could have seen that soil acidity is not a detriment but an asset. It is the soil acidity that is regularly making mineral nutrients in the rock and soil available to plants. When it accumulates in the soil naturally to a high degree, the resulting injury to our crops is not occurring because the acidity has come into the soil. This results because many of the fertility elements replaced by the advent of that much hydrogen, a non-nutrient, have gone out to leave this infertility take their place.

Instead of seeing lime on the soil beneficial because it provided the nutrient calcium, we saw its benefit in the carbonate it provided to neutralize the acidity, or the hydrogen. Simple gadgets measuring acidity should have been supplemented by means of measuring the plant's better physiology making more and better proteins rather than just more yields.

Now that we have made so many soils about neutral by stocking them heavily with calcium while attempting to drive out all the hydrogen, we find that those soils highly loaded with calcium are no more productive than those loaded to corresponding degree with hydrogen as acidity. What is needed to grow nutritious forage is the balance of all the nutrient elements in the soil rather than only to replace the acidity. Getting rid of the acidity by liming with a carbonate or an alkali is not the equivalent of providing the plant a balanced diet within the soil. Feeding the crop via the soil, not fighting soil acidity, is what is demanded. A little science came in to lead astray the art of agriculture that had long been using lime to grow better feeds but not to wage a fight on soil acidity.

Limited Knowledge is Apt to Propagandize Itself Too Soon

While fighting soil acidity, during the last two decades, unfortunately there was a delay of just that many years in the progress toward better nutrition for better plant and animal health. Fertilizing the soil went into vogue by no more knowledge than that required for one to get bigger crop yields and bigger monetary gains by this practice. The fundamentals of that procedure for better nutrition of all life are not common knowledge. Nitrogen, phosphorus, and potassium became standard fertilizers on their score of bigger yields. Even calcium going on as lime did not — and does not yet in the minds of some — classify as a fertilizer. Sulfur, applied to the soil unwittingly in superphosphate and ammonium sulfate, has not been credited for its values in plant nutrition and better animal nourishment. Nitrogen was not used until recently, because nitrogen fixation by legumes was a hope even if not necessarily a realization. Copper, manganese, zinc, molybdenum, and other trace elements are not yet considered by many minds that are closed to the possible services of these in plant and animal nutrition.

With increased yields of vegetative mass as the major criterion by which to judge the services from soil treatments using fertilizers, much that results therefrom in the physiology of plants, animals, and man is not commonly observed. We therefore have not seen the decrease in plant disease, the less insect attacks, the better seeds for reproduction, the better health of animals, their more fecund reproduction and many higher nutritional values in plant and animal products used as food, all resulting as we discover the nutrient deficiencies in the soil, and adapt the methods of modifying them for better plant and animal health.

Inorganic Criteria are Insufficient. Quality Criteria Point to Organic Differences for Better Health on Better Soils

To date it has been impossible to explain the many plant and animal improvements from soil treatments merely (a) by bigger yields for more consumption, (b) by a higher concentration of ash or the mineral elements in the feeds, or (c) by changes recognizable after the plant has been ashed for chemical study. From recent experimental evidence, there comes the suggestion that the better soils make more and better proteins. Accordingly, then, we may well look to the more nearly complete array of the required amino acids of protein as possibly the nutritional improvement in forages and feeds from fertilized soils. Is it possible that the instinct of the animals is directing them to recognize these better proteins when they break from the fertility exhausted soils of our fields out to graze the grass on the still fertile soil of the highway and railroad right-of-way? Is the imbalance of too much nitrogen, or crude protein, of the grass growing on the urine-soaked spot just as quickly recognized? Cannot the wild animals and the unhampered domestic animals judge the quality of their feeds in terms of health and reproduction more effectively for their survival than we can? Do they not carry their search for quality of feed as far as they can, namely to the fertility of the soil growing it?

Proteins for Better Nutrition and Better Protection Against Disease

It is only when our soils are better in terms of all the essential elements, that they can grow the *complete* proteins. Just when are proteins complete? That is still an unanswered question. They should be complete as regards all the eight or ten different amino acids recognized as required for survival. Some recent research especially with the trace elements, points out that soil treatments may improve the nutritional values of grains and forages by increasing the concentration of some of the amino acids commonly deficient, like tryptophane, and methionine. The use of these trace elements on th soil growing alfalfa and corn, points out by microbial assay that better soils increase the output of these essential amino acids. Rabbits feeding on the corn, balanced with amino acid supplements, suggest that trace elements function apparently through the modification of the amino acid values commonly more deficient in the feeds grown on less fertile soils.

Magnesium and sulfur, not classed as trace elements, come in for similar effects. Magnesium, applied to correct the soil's shortage improved the tryptophane content of forages. Sulfur, applied even in the elemental form, increased the amount of methionine. When these amino acids are produced to higher concentrations in the feed, may we not expect those better proteins in the animal and human bodies by which there is protection against invasion by the microbes? When the common cold and tuberculosis are invasions via the mucous membrane; when both are considered as breakdown of our defense; and when tuberculosis is "cured" by a high protein diet, is it too much, of a stretch of the imagination to theorize that mastitis and brucellosis, may also be microbial invasions through the mucous membrane? Shall we not test that postulate by treating the soil with all possible fertilizers to include the trace elements, and studying the physiology, blood properties, and all other animal manifestations in order to learn whether animal health is not related to the soil fertility?

Studies so far with animals suggest the truth of the old adage and we can say that some dairy cows must be better fed via the soil if they are to reproduce better, to give more milk, and to be healthy with respect to some diseases the cows now have and for which — because of transmissibility to humans — the cows are about to be innocently slaughtered. Surely such a negative approach, by which the cow species would become extinct, ought to be replaced by a positive one looking to better proteins via more fertile soils and better protection against diseases for the animals to keep them living and healthy. Proteins complete for this kind of protection may be a new degree of completeness not yet regularly associated with this organic food substance, much less with the fertility of the soil creating it.

The proteins are slowly being appreciated in terms of the struggles required for their synthesis and their assemblage. Plants are literally struggling for their proteins. They make carbohydrates readily, but fail often in finding in the soil the fertility helps for converting those into complete proteins, and much seed to multiply their species. Animals struggle for their proteins too. They can easily put on fat, but for the proteins needed in their reproduction they go long distances, search over myriads of kinds of vegetation, and are active from dawn to sunset on many of our less fertile soils. But when on good feed on better soils, they fill quickly and soon lie down, in what we call contentment but which is maximum of body physiology in action. Man, too, struggles for his proteins. Unfortunately, he fails to see it as a struggle premised on a similar one by his animal; that premised on the struggle by the plant; and that, in turn, limited because of the insufficient fertility in the soil.

When our best proteins, like those in milk, eggs and lean meat, must be assembled and brought to us through that long creative line connecting back to the soil, surely we shall finally see that the shortage of proteins, which has much to do with our failure to keep well fed and healthy, is not one of economic quarrels between groups of us, but a declinig soil fertility underneath all of us and all lower life forms below us. Soil conservation is not a fad of the 15 percent of our population classed as farmers. It is a necessity to a far greater degree for the 85 percent of us classified as urban and too far removed from the place where the proteins can be created by our own management. When we still have two acres per person in the United States and one acre does well to make only 250 pounds of live beef per year, we may see no reason yet for concern about dwindling soil fertility and our shaky foundation of protein creation. But when we drop to the world level, by taking on world feedership under guise of world leadership, and cut ourselves back to one acre per person, we cannot have our milk and meat proteins provided for us so generously. Then we may be content to call for our daily food allotment of little more than a bowl of rice. Must it take the experience of that situation for us to realize that healthy nations are protein eaters because they have ample acreage, conserve their soils and keep them fertile?

Health in the Positive Via Nutrition, Not in the Negative Via Drugs

Food has long been taken two or three times daily as a pleasant experience looking towards satiation, rather than as a carefully studied effort leading to good nutrition with good health a resulting by-product. Health has become less and less a positive matter resulting from ample quality of food to keep us bouyantly active. It has become more and more a worry about finding drugs under professional guidance to relieve us from the misery of pain and to help us escape the chagrin of insufficient health even to work enough to care for ourselves. We are gradually coming to realize that bad nutrition and poor health can result from deficiencies in quality, or from the hidden hungers, even where ample bulk may be regularly ingested.

Then too, while there are growing numbers of deficiencies expectable with soil exhaustion, the introduction and use of drugs and poisons extensively aggravates the situation still more. Administration of drugs for one service does not prohibit many unknown side reactions by which the ultimate price of the relief may be costlier than the original pain. One does not remove the cause of the headache by taking aspirin. One only blots out the recognition of it, which relief is paid, for in eliminating the aspirin. The advent of sulfa drugs was heralded as a great value in the fight on microbes. But, some of the side reactions of them included inroads on blood corpuscle creation with resulting anemias making the price too big to be paid in many instances for the service they give. Now that we have used DDT to exterminate insects, and hormone sprays to eliminate weeds, the fact is slowly dawning on us that promiscuous scattering of the deadly chemical carbon-ring-structures may be building up consequences of bad health not fully explained by calling them virus X or some other unknown. Such a negative approach toward a better health by working from the worst health, the morgue and grave backward has farther to go to arrive at good health than the effort to reach it by cooperating with the Creator starting at the soil and all that is required from that point of take-off in the assembly procedure.

Surely science and scientists given supposedly to sound reasoning cannot long disregard the great facts of the relation of the soil to good reproduction of any life form when food, in the last analysis, draws its basic essentials from the soil. Can we continue to match one segment of our society against another and survive by one consuming the other? Isn't it about time to realize that the warring human is only a hungry animal, all the more animal and less human with more hunger? When the curve of mounting populations and the curve of dwindling creative capacity — confused with dwindling acreage — are now crossing each other, isn't it about time to face the problem and consider means of holding down the sick and hungry crowd to numbers in relation to the soil rather than permitting one horde to murder another in ignorance of what the great food facts, provoking those quarrels or wars, really are?

Soils are the basic resource not only for feeding cows, but also for feeding humans as well. Perhaps there are still enough humans in close contact with the soil, and perhaps there are still enough thinking folks at some distance from the soil, to carry the responsibility of leading us to undertake the conservation of it and to manage its food potentials wisely. If so, then our population may be balanced against its chance for all to be well fed and thereby healthy. We cannot long survive under growing technologies of exploitation and destruction of both our soils and ourselves without the realization that there is a most significant relation between the fertility stores in our soils and the health and survival of our animals and of us humans.

AFTERWORD

Much of the signal work at the University of Missouri during Dr. William A. Albrecht's tenure as head of the soils department was recorded as student papers. The slow, plodding work that identified correct ratios to complement the usual manuring and liming practices was accomplished in the 1930s. An example: *Relation of the Degree of Base Saturation of a Colloidal Clay by Calcium to the Growth, Nodulation and Composition of Soybeans* by Glenn M. Horner, a graduate student, 1935.

Other papers:

Calcium as a Factor in Soybean Inoculation by Robert W. Scanlan, graduate student, 1927;

Study of the Uniformity of Soil Types and of Fundamental Differences Between the Different Soil Series by Franklin L. Davis, 1936;

The Composition of Soybean Plants at Various Growth Stages as Related to Their Rate of Decomposition and Use as Green Manure by Lloyd Mildon Turk, 1932; *Magnesium as a Factor in Nitrogen Fixation by Soybeans* by Ellis R. Graham, 1938; *Nodulation and Growth of Soybeans Influenced by Calcium and Hydrogen Ion Concentration in Putnam Belt Loam Soil* by George Z. Doolas, 1936;

Effect of Nitrogenous Fertilizer upon the pH and Available Phosphorus of Soils Relation to the Yield of Cotton by Franklin L. Davis, 1939;

Calcium as a Factor in Soybean Inoculation by Robert W. Scanlan, 1928;

Behavior of Legume Bacteria in Relation of Exchangeable Calcium and Hydrogen Ion Concentration of the Colloidal Fraction of the Soil by Thomas M. McCalla, 1937.

Years of work with students served up the bedrock rationale for limestone, the acidic effect of some nitrogen fertilizers, and the effect of decades of fertilizer application on Sanborn Field, and in turn the cumulative effect of industrial farming on human health.

In all the above, it was Albrecht speaking through his students, often sidetracking him from his own publication work because students were more important, and he was godfather of all the above in any case.

BIBLIOGRAPHY

Soils and Men, William A. Albrecht, Yearbook of Agriculture (U.S. Dept. of Agriculture,1938), 347-360.

Annals of Dentistry, William A. Albrecht, "Our Teeth and Our Soil," Vol. 8, No. 4, December, 1947.

Soil Depletion, T.J. Clark www.tjclark.co.nz/jurassic_soil.htm (accessed April, 2011).

Soil Fertility and Animal Health, William A. Albrecht, Chapter XIII, "Impoverished Soils, Poor Animal Health, and Distorted Economics for Agriculture" (Webster City, IA: Fred Hahne Printing Company, 1958).

Albrecht Balanced Soil Fertility — Better Start of Life, William A. Albrecht, in *Let's Live* magazine, December 1966.

Plant, Animal, and Human Health Vary with Soil Nutrition, William A. Albrecht, Modern Nutrition, Vol. 19, February 1966.

Protein deficiencies... Through soil deficiencies, William A. Albrecht, *Let's Live* magazine, Dec. 1952.

The Ideal Soil, A Handbook for New Agriculture, Astera, Michael, Chapter 1, "New Agriculture; What it and what it is not," www.soilminerals.com/TIS_Ch1.htm.

Soil, Grass, and Cancer, Andre Voisin, (London; Crosby Lockwood & Son Ltd., 1959), pp 24-27.

National Center for Health Statistics. "Prevalence of Overweight, Obesity and Extreme Obesity Among Adults: United States, Trends 1960-62 through 2005-2006." NCHS E-Stats, December 2008. www.cdc.gov/nchs/data/hestat/overweight/overweight_adult.htm.

"High Body Mass Index for Age among U.S. Children and Adolescents, 2003-2006," Ogden CL, Carroll MD, and Flegal KM, Journal of the American Medical Association, 299(20): 2401-2405, 2008.

Robert Woods Johnson Foundation, F As In Fat; How Obesity Threatens America's Future, www.pbhfoundation.org/pbh_direct_new/jul09_2010/ Obesity 2010Report.pdf.

Cost Of Treatment For Obesity-Related Medical Problems Growing Dramatically, Rand Corporation, www.Rand.Org/News/Press.04/03.09.html.

Center for Medical and Health Services, NHE Fact Sheet, www.cms.gov/ NationalHealthExpendData/25_NHE_Fact_Sheet.asp.

"Changes in USDA Food Composition Data for 43 Garden Crops, 1950 to 1999," Donald Davis, Melvin Epp, and Hugh Riordan, 2004, Journal of American College of Nutrition, 23:669-682.

"The Dilution Effect in Plant Nutrient Studies," W.M. Jarrell and R.B. Beverly, 1981, Advances in Agronomy, vol. 34:197–224.

Still No Free Lunch: Nutrient Levels in U.S. Food Supply Eroded by High Yields, Brian Haweil, The Organic Center, September 2007, www.organic-center.org/reportfiles/Yield_Nutrient_Density_Final.pdf.

State of Science Review: Nutritional Superiority of Organic Foods, Charles Benbrook, Xin Zhao, Jaime Yáñez, Neal Davies and Preston Andrews, The Organic Center, March 2008, www.organic-center.org/ reportfiles/5367_Nutrient_Content_SSR_FINAL_V2.pdf

USDA Major Trends in U.S. Food, www.ers.usda.gov/publications/foodreview/ jan2000/frjan2000b.pdf

The Encyclopedia of Farm Animal Nutrition, M.F. Fuller, CABI Publishing, Cambridge, MA., 100.

Home Box Office Network, *Weight of the Nation, Confronting America's Obesity Epidemic*, 2012, theweightofthenation.hbo.com.

"Healthy Soils, Healthy People; The Legacy of William Albrecht," John Ikerd, Acres U.S.A., vol. 42, no. 5: 46-52, May 2012.

Plant, Animal and Human Health Vary with Soil Fertility, *Modern Nutrition*, volume 19, 1966.

Soil and Livestock, *Your Farm*, pp. 97-105, 1945.

Soils — Their Effects on the Nutritional Values of Foods, Consumer Bulletin, volume 44, number 1, pp. 20-23, 1961.

Soil Builders Build Better Cattle, *The American Hereford Journal*, 1947.

Our Livestock — Cooperative Chemists, *Brangus Journal*, volume 12, number 5, pp. 4-10, 1964.

A Late Announcement Cites Hemophilia (Bleeding Disease) of Hogs as a New Disease, Missouri Farm News Services, 53: No. 27, March 4, 1964.

Wm. A. Albrecht, "Our Teeth and Our Soils," *Annual of Dentistry*, 6:199-213, 1942. Also Missouri Agriculture Experimental Station Cir. 333, 1946.

George Gamow, "The Creating of the Universe," The American Library, Madison Avenue, New York.

Runar Collander, "Selective Absorption of Cations by Higher Plants", *Plant Physiology,* 16:691-780.1941.

B. Sjollema et al. "Investigations into Hypomagnesemia in Bovines," Tydschr, Diergeness 80:579-604, 1111-1134, 1955.

André Voisin, "Grass Tetany, Part II," *Mineral Balance of Soil and Mineral Balance of Grass*, Crosby Lockwood and Son Ltd., London,1963.

Blake F. Donaldson, Strong Medicine, Doubleday; New York.

Livestock Can Teach Us a Lesson on Nutrition from the Ground Up, *Breeder's Gazette*, volume 129, number 4, pp. 13-15, 1964; pp. 11-15, number 5, 1964. Also, Let's Look at Nutrition from the Ground Up, *Polled Hereford World Magazine*, volume 18, p. 440 ff., 1964.

E. Douglas Hume, *Bechamp or Pasteur: A Lost Chapter in the History of Biology*, C.W. Daniel Co., Ashingdon, Rockford, Essex. 1923, 1932, 1947.

Paul O. Sapp, Ashland, Missouri, Reported in person.

W.H. Pfander, Rumenology, Missouri Agricultural Experiment Station Bulletin 619. 1954.

Soil Fertility and Animal Production, *58th Annual Report of the Indiana State Dairy Association*, Purdue University, pp. 35-52, 1947.

Soils and Livestock Work Together, I: The Protein Problem and the Pattern of Soil Fertility, *Meat*, pp. 192-1194, 1947.

As Animals Judge Your Crops, *The Furrow*, 1946.

Feed Values are Soil Values, *The Nation's Agriculture*, probably 1947.

In Defense of the Cow, *Livestock Weekly*, March, 1953.

Feed Efficiency in Terms of Biological Assays of Soil Treatments, *Farm for Victory*, 1944.

Are We Poisoning our Sheep?, *Organic Gardening and Farming*, volume 1, number 4, pp. 30-33, 1954.

Better Soils Make Better Hogs, *Hampshire Herdsman*, 1947. Also in the *Practical Farmer*, 1948.

Hogs Benefit from Crops Grown on Fertile Soils, *Weekly Kansas City Star*, 1943.

Healthy Soils Means Healthy Humans, *Here's Health*, volume 11, number 128, pp. 115-120, 1967.

Soil Fertility and Food Quality, *Proceedings of the Soil Science Society of Florida*, volume 6, pp. 108-122, 1944.

Soil Fertility, Food Source, *Technical Review* (Massachusetts Institute of Technology), volume 46, pp. 3-7, 1944.

Soil Fertility and Nutritive Value of Foods, *Agricultural Leaders Digest*, 1948. Also in *The Land*, volume 7, number 3, 1948.

Our Soils, Our Food and Ourselves, *Farmer's Digest*, 1948. Also *Organic Farming*, pp. 9-13, 1950.

Soils in Relation to Human Nutrition, *The Challenge*, Issue 5 pages 9-11, 1948.

Soil Fertility and its Health Implications, *American Journal of Orthodontics and Oral Surgery*, volume 31, pp. 279-286, 1945.

Soil Areas, Medical Rejectees Give Similar Maps, *Missouri Farm News Service*, 1955.

Human Health Closely Related to Soil Fertility, *School and Community*, volume 46, pp. 20-21, Missouri State Teachers Association, Columbia, Missouri, 1959.

The Fertility Pattern, *The Land*, volume 12, pp. 217-220, 1953.

Proteins and Reproduction, *The Land*, volume 11, number 2, 1952.

Our Teeth and Our Soils, *Annuals of Dentistry*, Vol. 6, No. 4, December 1947.

Soil Fertility in Relation to Animal and Human Health, *Milk Industry Foundation 44ᵗʰ Annual Convention Proceedings*, Vol. 5, Milk Supplies Section, Detroit, Michigan, 1951.

Publisher's Note

This bibliography contains reference works that Dr. William A. Albrecht used for research when working on many papers contained in this book. Some selections are not available from works that have been obtained from Dr. Albrecht's personal papers.

INDEX

Acres U.S.A. — books are just the beginning!

Farmers and gardeners around the world are learning to grow bountiful crops profitably — without risking their own health and destroying the fertility of the soil. *Acres U.S.A.* can show you how. If you want to be on the cutting edge of organic and sustainable growing technologies, techniques, markets, news, analysis and trends, look to *Acres U.S.A.* For over 40 years, we've been the independent voice for eco-agriculture. Each monthly issue is packed with practical, hands-on information you can put to work on your farm, bringing solutions to your most pressing problems. Get the advice consultants charge thousands for . . .

- Fertility management
- Non-chemical weed & insect control
- Specialty crops & marketing
- Grazing, composting & natural veterinary care
- Soil's link to human & animal health

For a free sample copy or to subscribe, visit us online at

www.acresusa.com

or call toll-free in the U.S. and Canada

1-800-355-5313

Outside U.S. & Canada call 512-892-4400
fax 512-892-4448 • info@acresusa.com